PATTERSON SMITH REPRINT SERIES IN
CRIMINOLOGY, LAW ENFORCEMENT, AND SOCIAL PROBLEMS

A listing of publications in the SERIES *will be found at rear of volume*

AUGUST DRÄHMS

PUBLICATION No. 114: PATTERSON SMITH REPRINT SERIES IN CRIMINOLOGY, LAW ENFORCEMENT, AND SOCIAL PROBLEMS

THE CRIMINAL

HIS PERSONNEL AND ENVIRONMENT

A SCIENTIFIC STUDY

BY

AUGUST DRÄHMS

RESIDENT CHAPLAIN STATE PRISON, SAN QUENTIN PRISON, SAN QUENTIN, CALIFORNIA, U.S.A.

WITH AN INTRODUCTION BY

CESARE LOMBROSO

PROFESSOR OF PSYCHIATRY, UNIVERSITY DE TORINO, ITALY

Reprinted with a New Introduction by
STANLEY GRUPP

MONTCLAIR, N. J.
PATTERSON SMITH
1971

97688

First edition published 1900 by The Macmillan Company
Reprinted 1971 by special arrangement with The Macmillan Company
Patterson Smith Publishing Corporation
Montclair, New Jersey 07042
New material copyright ©1971 by
Patterson Smith Publishing Corporation

SBN 87585–114–2

Library of Congress Catalog Card Number: 72–108231

This book is printed on three-hundred-year acid-free paper.

TO MY OLD COMMANDER

Major General Grenville M. Dodge

COMMANDER 16TH ARMY CORPS, U. S. VOLUNTEERS

AND LATTERLY

COMMANDER OF THE DEPARTMENT AND ARMY OF THE MISSOURI

This Volume

IS AFFECTIONATELY INSCRIBED

INTRODUCTION TO THE REPRINT EDITION

AUGUST DRÄHMS, 1849–1927, belongs to an era of American criminology that is largely neglected today. His work is not particularly well known even among criminologists. One sees only occasional reference to him in the literature. This neglect and lack of acquaintance is chiefly due to the fact that twentieth-century writers of criminology textbooks and to some extent of other criminological works have been primarily social determinists. The work of Drähms's period, the age of criminal anthropology, is known only slightly in the United States and is often regarded as unimportant—perhaps a period better forgotten than studied. Not uncommonly the work of that time is dispensed with by cursory reference to the assumed biological determinism of Lombroso, whose work is often used as a scapegoat for an attack on the biological school. Yet the record will demonstrate that Lombroso's theories played an important role in early American criminology, that a considerable amount of writing and some research was undertaken in this country under the Lombrosian banner,[1] and that the biologi-

[1] Work undertaken at the Elmira Reformatory under the tutelage of Zebulon Reed Brockway and to which Drähms makes several references is a case in point. Brockway is commonly acclaimed as a great prison reformer, ostensibly with a commitment to the rehabilitative ideal. His belief in a biologically determined criminal is less known and is not often referred

cal theme remained very strong at the turn of the century. The little-known work of August Drähms, *The Criminal: His Personnel and Environment,* is an excellent example of the anthropological school and of the type of criminological investigation that took place in the United States during the late nineteenth and early twentieth centuries.

At the time of publication of his book in 1900, Drähms was Chaplain at San Quentin Prison in California, a position he held from 1891 to 1909. Born in Pomerania, Prussia, on March 4, 1849, he had migrated to the United States with his parents, settling in Geneva, Illinois, when he was six years old. At fifteen years of age he joined the Union Army, serving from early 1864 to 1865, part of which time was spent as a headquarters clerk under General Grenville Dodge, to whom he later dedicated his book.

Drähms seems to have cherished his Army experience throughout his life. His scrapbooks contain several Civil War memorabilia.[2] He was a long-time and apparently active member of the Grand Army of the Republic and served as its national Chaplain-in-Chief in 1900–1901.[3]

---

to in present-day writing. For a discussion of this orientation as it existed at the Elmira Reformatory see Stanley E. Grupp, "Criminal Anthropological Overtones: New York State Reformatory at Elmira, 1876–1907," *Correction* 24, nos. 5–6 (May-June 1959): 9–17. For a detailed discussion of the consideration given the biological dimension of criminality in the United States see Arthur E. Fink, *The Causes of Crime: Biological Theories in the United States 1800–1915* (Philadelphia: University of Pennsylvania Press, 1938).

[2] I am especially indebted to Mrs. Margaret Plummer, granddaughter of August Drähms who so graciously lent me his personal papers.

[3] Obituary, *Wilmar Chronicle,* Wilmar, California, January 13, 1927.

Always a proud American, Drähms at an advanced age volunteered his services in World War I in the following letter, which bespeaks the antipathy toward German-born citizens which was then common:

> I beg to offer my services to the army of the United States in any capacity I may be called upon. . . . I am a true, loyal and sincere American: I AM NOT A GERMAN,—I AM AN AMERICAN. . . . I am sixty-eight years of age, and in superb health and spirits.[4]

At the close of the Civil War General Dodge recommended Drähms for a West Point appointment, but it is not known if it materialized. Following his discharge from the Army, Drähms entered the office of the Circuit Clerk and Recorder in Geneva, Illinois, where he remained a number of years. During this period Drähms also attended Wheaton College and Garrett Theological Seminary in Evanston. His professional career was to be spent as a Congregational minister. In addition to the years as prison chaplain at San Quentin, he served at least seven congregations, six in the Western United States (chiefly California) and one in Hawaii.

In 1891 Drähms took up the chaplaincy of San Quentin Prison. Although he remained at his post for nearly two decades, there is evidence that he was not entirely satisfied and that his departure in 1909 resulted from conflicts with the warden, who secured his removal by abolishing the office of Chaplain.[5] For example, in a let-

---

[4] Letter, Drähms to Secretary of War, April 6, 1917. Photocopy provided by National Archives and Records Services, General Services Administration.

[5] These events are reported by Kenneth Lamott, *Chronicles of San Quentin: The Biography of a Prison* (New York: David McKay Co., 1961), pp. 179–180.

ter to General Dodge enlisting his support in securing a Chaplaincy in the United States Army, Drähms wrote, "I have been for the past six years engaged in the line of my profession as Chaplain of this institution, a very trying and self sacrificing field of labor."[6] Again, when he had left his prison position, Drähms was quoted as saying:

> I was greatly interested in my work among the criminals. . . . And I was afforded an excellent opportunity for study of these people, learning many things at the same time, such as tact and self-control. I was certainly always sure of having a large congregation, and they were attentive hearers. Some one said that they were all under conviction, and that was surely true. However, I have now finished my work in that line, and shall not take it up again. I consider that I have done my duty to those people, and that I may lay it down now.[7]

After leaving San Quentin, Drähms took up a ministry in Hawaii and five years later returned to the mainland to serve two more parishes. In 1919 he retired to spend his remaining years in Wilmar, California, pursuing his horticultural interests. He died on January 7, 1927, of carcinoma of the liver.

Drähms's interest and work in criminology appears to have been entirely concentrated within his tenure at San Quentin. The publication of his book, by The Macmillan Company, was an event in which he took considerable pride. He collected reviews from many newspapers and

---

[6] Letter, Drähms to Dodge, March 29, 1897. Original document held by the Iowa State Historical Society. Copy provided by the Society.

[7] *Hilo Tribune,* Hilo, Hawaii, July 27, 1909.

professional journals, meticulously pasted them in a scrapbook, and worked aggressively at promoting the book. His personal papers include many letters from grateful recipients of copies. Among the important sociologists and criminologists of this period with whom Drähms is known to have had some correspondence are E. A. Ross, Zebulon Reed Brockway, Charles R. Henderson, Arthur MacDonald, Charles H. Cooley, Franklin H. Giddings, Charles A. Ellwood, Frederick H. Wines, and, of course, Cesare Lombroso, who provided the introduction to his book. Evidences of Drähms's writing in the field of criminology other than the present volume are not extensive, only five articles having been located.[8] (Drähms also had an interest in writing poetry, some of which he published.) In 1909, the year Drähms left San Quentin, the last two of his magazine articles appeared and Macmillan declared his book out of print. Beyond this year there is no evidence of an active interest in criminology on the part of August Drähms.

Drähms has been assessed both negatively and positively in the literature. Havelock Ellis was scathing in his review of Drähms's book and in his reply to Drähms's rejoinder. Ellis notes, for example, omissions of recent contributions to the literature and gross errors in the spelling of innumerable proper names, and he accuses

[8] "Reformatory Movement in California," *Overland Monthly,* 2d ser. 22 (October 1893): 424–430; "The Increase and Decrease of Crime in Civilized Countries," *Proceedings of the Annual Congress of the National Prison Association,* 1900, pp. 272–288; "The Law of Criminal Fluctuation," *ibid.,* 1903, pp. 355–364; "Modern Penological Movement," *Overland Monthly,* 2d ser. 54 (July 1909): 114–115; "Last Census and Its Bearing on Crime," *Popular Science Monthly* 75 (October 1909): 398–403.

Drähms of a general lack of depth in his presentation.[9] In contrast, Charles A. Ellwood, in an article some years later, was complimentary.[10] More recently, Arthur Fink has observed that Drähms's work "may be regarded with fairness as the first book on the American criminal that attempted an anthropological, biological, and psychological approach."[11]

However anomalous it may appear today, it was not uncommon during Drähms's time for a clergyman to engage in non-theological writing.[12] Yet Drähms's "scientific" investigation in criminology did provoke the following comment from his distinguished contemporary Zebulon Reed Brockway, who wrote to the author, "I am somewhat confused, Dear Mr. Drachms, [sic] to decipher how it is that a clergyman, a chaplain, in good standing in orthodox religious organizations could conceive and have the boldness to publish such a book, so much of rational truth on the subject it treats of."[13]

Lombroso's willingness to write an introduction to Drähms's book and his glowing praise was surely consid-

---

[9] See Havelock Ellis, Review of August Drähms, *The Criminal: His Personnel and Environment, Science* 12 (October 19, 1900): 610–611 and reply by Drähms with rejoinder by Ellis. *Science* 12 (December 14, 1900): 930–931.

[10] "The Classification of Criminals," *Journal of Criminal Law* 1, no. 4 (November 1910): 536–548.

[11] Fink, *op. cit.* (note 1), p. 119.

[12] The work of the Englishman, William Douglas Morrison, whose work Drähms refers to is a case in point. See Gerald D. Robins, "William Douglas Morrison," in Hermann Mannheim, *Pioneers of Criminology*, 2d ed. (Publication No. 121, Patterson Smith Reprint Series in Criminology, Law Enforcement, and Social Problems [Montclair, N. J., 1971]).

[13] Letter, Brockway to Drähms, June 13, 1900. The record indicates that Brockway did not hold in very high regard the contribution or potential contribution of religion in dealing with

ered a coup by Drähms and was widely referred to in reviews. In view of Lombroso's stature his preparation of the introduction is alone of sufficient significance to warrant a place of importance for Drähms's work in the annals of criminology. Ellis observes, however, "It is possible that even the author himself may have been surprised at the excess of this [Lombroso's] appreciation; for Mr. Drähms is by no means so much in sympathy with Lombroso, as Lombroso is with Mr. Drähms." [14] Just how carefully Lombroso actually read Drähms is not known. They do appear to differ on a number of points. For example, although Drähms accepts the idea of an instinctive criminal, he questions some of the findings of Lombroso and other investigators regarding the existence, the nature, and the universality of the criminal type. Noting the disagreement among writers and calling attention to the lack of adequate data as well as the absence of truly scientific reasoning with respect to the criminal type, Drähms at times seems prepared to reject the notion entirely. He does, none the less, recognize the existence of a congenital criminal type. Drähms states:

> To the depths of the bio-psychological, then, with its co-related physiological and neurotic phenomena, we must go to know him as he is, and to trace the causes and origin of his distinctively anti-social and degen-

---

the criminal problem. For example, at one point in his autobiography he refers to himself as having "emerged from the traditional theological or fictional stage of mental attitude." See Zebulon Reed Brockway, *Fifty Years of Prison Service* (1912; reprinted as Publication No. 61, Patterson Smith Reprint Series in Criminology, Law Enforcement, and Social Problems [Montclair, N. J., 1969]), p. 174.

[14] Ellis, Review, *loc. cit.* (note 9).

erative functions to their ultimate sources.

> The burden with which the congenital offender comes already laden, and from which he draws his inspirational forces, is purely congenital. [P. 142]

Still other evidence indicates that Drähms may have liked to disassociate himself from the Lombroso label that had been attached to him by many of his contemporaries. In response to a letter from Drähms and in conjunction with the reading of proofs apparently in preparation for a second edition of Drähms's book, one correspondent observed:

> I am truly obliged to you for the proofs, which I have read with care, glad to find that they show you, in intention at least, quite dissenting from the naturalistic empiricism of Lombroso and his school. But you cannot avoid the public's taking the impression that you are with him and them, when you go before it under his special *Imprimatur* and his introduction.[15]

It is of interest to note that for all the attention given the instinctive criminal, Drähms feels that they account for only "about ten per cent" of the criminal population (p. 194).

Drähms reports anthropometric data for two thousand San Quentin inmates, presumably recorded as part of the Bertillon system of identifying criminals by body measurements which was in common use in prisons in the late nineteenth century. These anthropometric statistics seem to represent the extent of Drähms's efforts to collect or report original data. Viewed by contemporary standards

---

[15] Letter, G. H. Howison to Drähms, February 26, 1907. Howison was a member of the Department of Philosophy at the University of California.

his failure to obtain data from control groups is inexcusable. By the prevailing standards of his day, however, he can hardly be condemned. His presentation of comparative anthropometric data from Amherst College and the Elmira Reformatory does suggest an awareness of the value of and need for control data. In this regard it is instructive to contrast the work of August Drähms with that of Charles Goring, a figure who is better known today. It can be argued that it was Goring's use of controls and statistical techniques, both neglected by Drähms, that has established Goring's work as noteworthy by contemporary criminologists and not Goring's rejection of the hereditary inferiority of criminals which is sometimes erroneously attributed to him.[16]

The chief merits of Drähms's contribution lie in his critical assessment of the concept of the criminal type, in his attention to social and psychological perspectives, and in his effort to incorporate these latter dimensions within the biological frame of reference. In these respects his work deserves the recognition of contemporary criminologists, particularly those interested in the antecedents and evolution of the discipline. Drähms's integrative point of view marks him as a transitional figure in the development of modern criminology in the United States from its earlier biological viewpoint to its present heavy emphasis on social and psychological factors.

Throughout Drähms's work the jargon and flavor of

[16] Charles Goring, *The English Convict: A Statistical Study* (London: H.M.S.O., 1913). See Edwin D. Driver, "Charles Buckman Goring," in Hermann Mannheim, *Pioneers of Criminology*, 2d ed. (Publication No. 121, Patterson Smith Reprint Series in Criminology, Law Enforcement, and Social Problems [Montclair, N. J., 1971]).

the argument reflect the heavy hand of a criminal anthropological orientation much as we find in the late nineteenth-century writing of the Italian School. Drähms's interest in the biological criminal was indeed consonant with the time. The neglect of this period in our criminological history is regrettable. Not only does the record need to be clarified but also an examination of the ways in which Drähms agreed or disagreed with other writers of his day who were interested in the biological criminal could provide benchmarks for investigating the role of biology as an influencing factor in criminal behavior. Recently there has been some concern about the need for integration of biological and sociological principles and the need for exchange between these disciplines.[17] In view of our ignorance about the wellsprings of human behavior, who is to say that past minimization of the part played by biology may in time prove to have been premature?

Another aspect of Drähms's work worthy of note is his threefold classification of criminals: the instinctive type already mentioned, the habitual criminal, and the single offender. While these concepts were not original with Drähms, his recognition of the usefulness of distinguishing between the second and third types continues into modern practice.

An indication of the stature Drähms was accorded by some is suggested by the correspondence between Drähms and Frederick H. Wines, an avowed critic of the heredi-

---

[17] See Bruce K. Eckland, "Genetics and Sociology: A Reconsideration," *American Sociological Review* 32 (April 1967): 173–194. The Committee on Biological Bases of Social Behavior of the Social Science Research Council is another example.

tary criminal concept. Regarding Drähms's book Wines wrote:

> With most of the positions which you take I am in sympathetic accord. The least satisfactory portion of the book to my mind is that in which you labor to establish a generic difference between the instinctive criminal and the single offender. The difference seems to me to be almost wholly one of degree like that between a recent and curable case of insanity and a confirmed lunatic.[18]

Later in the same letter Wines invited Drähms to appear as a discussant at "The Criminal Group" section of the International Congress of Arts and Sciences to be held in St. Louis in September, 1904. At the time of writing Wines anticipated that both he and Lombroso himself would be addressing the section. It is not known whether Drähms attended this meeting. Lombroso, although invited to the United States many times, never made the journey.

Persons not familiar with the status of criminology in the United States at the turn of the century will find Drähms's book invaluable. In the opinion of this observer he is an important transitional figure, one who anticipated the increasing social and psychological emphasis which developed during the twentieth century. August Drähms deserves our attention and a place among the pioneers in American criminology.

—STANLEY GRUPP

Illinois State University
April, 1970

[18] Letter, Wines to Drähms, August 16, 1904.

PREFACE

THESE pages present in modest pretension the summary of several years' study and practical contact with a subject hitherto lightly esteemed, and less understood (save by the few), and yet of more than passing importance.

I have sought to examine the same in its twofold phases: in its purely personal aspect, and as a social phenomenon.

Since the proper study of mankind is man, it follows that equal importance attaches to that morbid or variational form in respect of which he differs morally and sociologically from his fellows. This circumscribes the scope and limit of practical criminology.

Physical and moral soundness excites no criticism and creates little interest, it being the normal condition of man. Departure therefrom arouses attention in proportion to its seriousness, and lays open a wide field of speculative inquiry in the direction of cause and cure, as exploited by theorist and experimentalist. This constitutes the ground of criminological science, if such it may be termed.

Crime is largely a social disease. Its personnel is the bacilli that infect the collective organism. As such, it is clearly not an accident, nor a misfortune, nor yet an

incident that clings to the skirts of advancing civilization, but is the result of distinct causes, whose genesis
and amelioration through prevenient methods and the
application of proper remedial agencies, it is becoming
more and more the fashion of cotemporary thought
to explore. As every physical ill has somewhere its
disturbing causes, so in the sociological and psychological spheres, each moral functional derangement and
distinctively social morbidity points backward to causation, and forward to the remedy. "They [criminals]
are neither accidents nor anomalies in the universe,"
says Maudsley, "but come by law and testify to causality ; and it is the business of science to find out what
the causes are and by what laws they work." Criminology, therefore, as the patron of patho-sociology,
reaches the dignity of a science by the same right of
necessity that gives to the medical profession its place ;
the therapeutics of the one dealing with the physiological (neurosis), and the other with the psychological
(psychosis), side of the subject. That there is a debata-
ble territory between the mental and moral phases of
the problem as it hedges upon the material, is undeniable.
Its challenges remain unanswered in these pages, as
they do to the inquiry of the ages. I have endeavored
to remain as near shore as the exigencies of the case
will permit, keeping distinctly in view certain well-
defined landmarks by which I have cautiously sought
to guide my frail bark in a dubious sea. The strictly
anthropological features here brought out have been
accepted mainly as the properly accredited data of
trained writers, the latchets of whose shoes I am not

worthy to unloose, but whose conclusions nevertheless are taken under a general demurrer ; in which
respect, however, I have the consolation of knowing
that I am in excellent company.

As to the general sociological character of the work,
be it said in extenuation, crime is an eventuality essentially human. It is inexplicably bound up with the
social unity. The special value of criminological investigation lies in this : that what tends to affect the
individual factor invades the social mass, and whatever
influences society affects the personality. Touch one
and you disturb the whole. This is at once the despair
and the hope of the social problem. Each step toward
a clearer apprehension of this law, every attempted application of its tentative precepts to the social anomaly,
is a step in advance, and promises by so much a final
remedial dispensation. *The same root principles that
underlie the transformation of the criminal activity also
bespeak the social regeneration.* To elevate the foundation is to carry the superstructure with it.

In the hope that this contribution may aid, in a feeble
way, to the better understanding of the subject in its
varied moral, social, political, and economic bearings,
these pages are contributed to the general bibliography.

I desire to express my thanks to friends and critics,
and to acknowledge my obligations to the labors of
those who have passed this way before me, from whose
pages I have quoted, and to whom I have sought to
give due credit. I especially express my thanks for the
generous appreciation as well as kindly personal sug-

gestions of Rev. William Rader; Professor Frank A. Fetter, of Leland Stanford Jr. University, California; Hon. Z. R. Brockway, Elmira Institute, New York; Frederick H. Wines, late Special Agent U.S. Census; Dr. Arthur MacDonald, Specialist of the Bureau of Education, Washington, D.C.; and Professor Cesare Lombroso, the eminent Criminologist and Professor of the University of Turin, Italy, whose commendation lends value to this work.

AUGUST DRÄHMS.

SEPTEMBER 10, 1899.

CONTENTS

CHAPTER I

XXV

97688

CHAPTER IX

CHAPTER X

CHAPTER XI

CHAPTER XII

CHAPTER XIII

INTRODUCTORY

I HAVE not had the good fortune for some time to find an author who so thoroughly understands my ideas, and is able to express them with so much clearness, as the author of this book.

In this treatise, I found nothing contrary to my own observations and convictions, excepting where the author holds that "the American criminal differs in physiognomical type from his European cotemporary."

Now, while it is true that the majority of criminals retain the type of their native country, nevertheless, this is so only of the "criminal by occasion"; that is, criminals made so by environment or circumstances, and in whom degeneration is not so universal and pronounced as in the congenital criminal.

These latter agree with all other degenerated species — microcephalics, epileptics, and cretins — mental, moral, or physical, in possessing a marked resemblance one to another, even though born in countries most widely separated. These anthropological conditions are the manifest result of an arrested embryological development.

Returning to the primitive state of humanity, and evading the barriers formed in one way or another by a few centuries, man approaches nearer the savage than to the civilized state, and there the distinctions between nationalities are obliterated.

This slight difference of opinion existing between myself and the author, however, is insignificant as compared with the lucid exposition, the profound and original thought, with which the work is embellished.

This treatise, written by the chaplain of a penitentiary over his own signature, is an evidence of the advancement of the American over the ultramontane countries of Europe, where, if a clerical could be induced to touch upon such a theme at all, it would be only to combat one's theories to the bitter end, even to the extent of employing the weapons of calumny and malice.

"Ad Deum majorem gloria."

C. LOMBROSO.

TURIN, ITALY.

THE CRIMINAL

HIS PERSONNEL AND ENVIRONMENT

THE CRIMINAL

CHAPTER I

THE PHILOSOPHY OF CRIME

Its Genetical and Historical Outline

CRIMINOLOGY is that department of social science that relates to the causes, nature, and treatment of crime with special reference to its individual exponents regarded from a psychological, physiological, and socialistic standpoint.

Criminology may be divided into three departments: General, Special, and Practical. The first embraces the ordinary scope and outline of the subject, including its statistical and dynamical features and general detail; the second relates to the personal factor, the criminal offender, his general identity, bio-genesis, and classification, with such correlated phenomena as the subject may warrant; and the last treats of the judicial, incarceral, and practical methods involved, with special reference to prevention and cure.

Special Criminology, in its broadest acceptation, includes both the individual and social concept. Crime has been generically described as an anti-social act. It is anti-social because it is first anti-individualistic, as the part is before the whole. The attack is made upon the organism through the individual member.

Crime is a psychological manifestation. All responsible action is primarily postulated along the line of free will functioned upon the moral intuitions. Where freedom ceases, automatism begins. Beyond that point conduct may be a menace, but it can never be a crime ; it may be an event, but in no sense an act. All legal as well as ethical distinctions draw the line between determinism and free will, relegating the moral delinquent and the defective to their relative spheres under judicial and alienistic jurisdiction, respectively.

The germinal idea of the ethical notion is self-love. It lies at the basis of all rational individualization and finds its concrete expression in the self-preservative instinct, the primal impulse and guarantee of integrity. In the individual it is egoism ; in the state, patriotism ; and in the highest Christian thought it stands for the universal altruistic sentiment of mankind, the well-being of the race. The essential polarities of the ethical ideal are embodied in the dual concept of right and wrong, the pillar and foundation of the moral constitution. One is the antithesis and logical corollary of the other, coördinate in thought but subordinate in fact. Right is the anterior to wrong, and either is inconceivable as moral entities save in their duality. Dr. Wines, in his admirable treatise on " Punishment and Reformation," has, indeed, ventured the assertion that "the sense of wrong must have preceded the sense of right in the individual and common consciousness." The misconception, if such it be, must be due to confusion of the abstract idea with the concrete term, in which interpretation it may be true, as he afterward adds, "The notion of right was slowly evolved through the instinctive opposition felt to successive and repeated injuries." That wrong, as an abstract principle, should antedate right, is unthinkable. Right is an original moral concept of the soul. The sense of wrong is its simple negation; but there can be no negation without first an affirmation; and how can a notion of wrong be predicated without first such preëxistent right? The very nature of wrong presupposes an attack upon moral principle. The notion is coexistent with the moral ego whose primal principle is expressed in the right *to be*, and a trespass thereupon is the origin of the first wrong. In its purely concrete sense as an interpretation of juridical principle, it is true, wrong-doing derives its chief force from the sanction of positive law, and in which sense Lubbock has well said, "Law is anterior to justice." This, however, is an expression of the ethical faculty in its lowest term, wherein law and morality become largely matters of relativity, their quantities variable. Essential right is unchangeable.

Whatever may be its perturbation, the great cardinal principles of morality that control human action and underlie conduct are primarily everywhere and at all times essentially the same. This is what Aristotle meant when he wrote: "Of the political just, one part is natural and the other legal. The natural is that which everywhere is equally valid, and depends not upon being or not being received. But the legal is that which originally was a matter of indifference, but which, when enacted, is so no longer."[1]   There has never been a period in human history that the moral potentialities, however obscure, did not outline themselves dimly in human consciousness.   "Life," says Taylor, "even in the uncivilized world, is fettered at every turn by chains of custom.   Society even among wild men is far from being under the sway of brute force.   They all have their rules of right and wrong."

Custom is the precursor of law.   Custom must have had its prepotency in choice, and choice environed in conscience, or convoked by necessity, must have been swayed by that self-preservative instinct which, as we have already seen, is the essence of morality, and in its last analysis conserves society in the individual.   It moved like a brooding spirit upon the face of all past history, assuaging its primitive storms, and acting as the modifier of its savage intuitions.   "It is hazardous," says Sir Henry Maine, referring to these facts, "to suppose that the childhood of nations is always a period of ungoverned violence."   Doubtless the pages of the past were blotted by ensanguined wrongs, perhaps winked at then as now, nevertheless ever under the sway of an unwritten law oftentimes administered *vox populi*, as recorded of the ancient Teutons.   Law is variable, but it is its provincial interpretation that gives it its mutability; at bottom its cardinal principles are ever the same.

The criminalistic concept, based on law and rooted in the ethical notion, thus shares in the general perturbation that characterizes all moral and social fluctuation. Law regulates the criminalistic expression.

[1] "Ethics," p. 135.

Crime is a violation of the law. This simple definition is sufficient from the standpoint of cotemporaneous civilization safeguarded by custom and brought to
its highest ethical and civil perfection. The criminal
anthropologist must go hand in hand with his collaborators, the metaphysician and the scientist, to penetrate
the moral genetics of crime. They are founded upon
the primal intuitions of right and wrong, differing only
in the degree of accredited injury inflicted as the outcome of such immoral conduct. The distinctiveness
between sin and crime is one of modality rather than
essence — generically alike, objectively distinct, under
the challenge of the juridical attribute. Sin is personal;
crime is civil. Sin is a violation of the individual conscience; crime is a challenge to the social order. One
is an enlarged expression of the other. The first sin
was against Deity; the first crime was against man's
brother. Dimitri Drill has somewhat metaphorically
represented crime as the "sensible measure of the degree of health, strength, and prosperity of a given society
in a given moment of existence." Mr. Ellis more
severely defines it as, "the complex relation which the
law creates between itself and the lawbreaker. The
law creates the crime." The former clause is clear;
the latter is paradoxical, for it may be equally well
shown that *crime creates the law*, since it is the repeated
act of violence that constitutes the *necessity that enacts
the law.* At any event, it is clearly seen from these
definitions that crime is primarily focussed upon the
moral perceptivities as mediately or immediately associated with the ego. Crime, technically, is an attack upon

social organism through the individual factors, with a corresponding reaction back upon self. Every wrongful act in defiance of mandate is both an individual and a social menace.

The study of Special Criminology may be said to group itself into three general divisions, under which its investigation may be scientifically pursued; viz.: —

(*a*) The *Individualistic* phase, having its genesis in the personal characteristics, psychological and physiological, with predisposing causes, inherited or acquired. This is largely subjective in its nature, and inductive as to process.

(*b*) Non-individualistic, or external, receiving its impressions directly from without, incited and developed through the media of environment. Training, education, civil and cosmic conditions, social and economic relations, one and all are laid open to its incursion. This is objective in character, and largely deductive as to form.

(*c*) Historical. This is bio-zoölogical in inception and detail, and historical as to data and outline, allying itself with predisposing causes inherent in the race, and linking itself with primal conditions through a long chain of antecedent biological and anthropological sequences, following the well-known law of homogeneous to heterogeneous, but with ever increasing distinctness. It is evolutional in form, and follows the scientific method.

The consideration of criminal man as he comes under the two former general divisions will be more particularly the subject of these pages, with special stress upon the individualistic features which constitute the essence of the subject, as the non-individualistic and the historical setting conform to the more indirect and incidental features of the same.

It will be unnecessary to refer more than briefly to the bio-zoölogical conception as to the origin of crime, so frequently dwelt upon by the modern investigators of the advanced school of criminal anthropologists. The natural origin of crime, according to them, must be sought in the analogies of the zoö-psychological and embryological, commencing in its natural order with the lower animal creation, in which light its advocates affect to trace the movements of the incipient criminalistic propensity, even going to plant life, such as the insectivorous, and some other species, for its primary explanation. They have not hesitated to ascribe to animals the rudimentary sense of responsibility, and the idea of punishment as subservient to the higher preventive aims in deterrence from wrong-doing. The validity of the assumption, of course, lies in the degree of demonstrable proof to substantiate the fact. This lacking, the argument falls to the ground. Nevertheless, its advocates hold thus far, and it must be said with some show of reason for their deduction, that criminal activity in man is but the reproduction and prepotency of similar instincts in the lower animal creation, plus the mental and moral endowments of the former, in modification. In its rudimentary sense it can be traced in its varied manifestations throughout the animal kingdom. As in man, so in beasts, there are apparently some more prone to criminalistic tendencies and to certain forms of purposive wrong-doing than others, as, for instance, theft in the monkey and the dog, homicide, infanticide, cannibalism, and even suicide in animals ; while with the higher grade of mental activities, as in the industrial and commercial instincts of the bee and the ant, strongly prophetical indications of criminal propension are shown in their inclinations to go to war, their tendency toward pillage and enslavement of their prisoners, the revengefulness of the elephant when ostracized from the herd, and its well-known retaliatory vindictiveness for wrongs offered it, even after many years have elapsed. Maintaining this ground with strong reasons and show of probability, the conclusions are not by any means far-fetched nor unreasonable. A closer study of the lower animal kingdom may result in cumulative proof of the position.

Without going extensively into the theory of criminal embryonics as exemplified in the phenomena of child life, it is sufficient to say it presents features equally plausible. The innate cruelty of children, their tendency to lying, together with that proclivity to impulsive wrong-doing so peculiar to youth, all point strongly to original rudimentary criminalistic propensities, the remnants of past racial proclivities. Indeed, some of the advanced school have maintained that the germs of moral insanity and crime are both equally normal in the first years of man.

From these vague and undefined fields of the speculative, the subject takes wide range as we advance to firmer foothold within the domain of appreciable facts. As we emerge from the uncertain twilight, the main factors become more distinct.

Man in his social relation circumscribes the whole arc of empirical criminality. The earliest form of the collective expression was the family relation. It is the unit of the social equation. The nuclei around which it rallied as its unifying centre and primitive authoritative fountain was patriarchal. The early hereditary dignitary clothed himself with administrative functions and became at once priest, king, and legislator of a miniature kingdom. The Hebraic records preserve to us in striking simplicity this early picture of the authoritative family relation, fresh with dew of morning, set in primal colors and musical with bleating herds, himself the presiding genius and tutelary divinity of the primitive quasi-political commonwealth. With the natural paucity of the social content incident upon the few and simple wants of these early times, we have the anti-social factors of the criminal content reduced to a minimum. Possessing all the power of the *patria potestas* of the latter Roman period, one perceives here the authority of the civil and judicial arm conjoined with supreme autocracy amounting at times to life and death. It is easy to infer that the movement of such simple judicial machinery, if such it might be called, must have been noiselessly effective, leaving but slight opportunity for aggressive wrong, or for the play of corrective forces. Judicially considered, it reduced the criminal problem to its lowest terms. Where there is no law, there can be, legally speaking, no crime.

The enlargement of the family relation, or, more correctly speaking, the subsequent development of the

family into the tribal state, must of necessity have
tended to alter materially the face of the primitive
social problem in the direction of greater complexity
and detail.   Cosmic, economic, and local conditions,
together with other and subtler personal causes, contributed to crystallize these transformations into more
permanent ethnic and race differentiations, each clan
or *gens* preserving its own distinctive peculiarities to be
assiduously guarded, thus commensurately broadening
and deepening the scope of the mora land civil concept,
and with it, of necessity, the anti-social proclivities incident to growing class jealousies and tribal innovations.
These tribal distinctions, born of the enlarged social
concept, brought with them corresponding incentives to
repeated criminalistic outbreak, and helped swell materially the first rude tendencies toward homicide and plunder within and without the tribal limitations, together
with all those attendant trains of horrors and lawlessness
that ever characterize primitive man, and that here
formed the prolific germ of the earliest anti-social instincts of the race and the individual.   We find now
stirring the rudimentary movement of the first crude
repressive measure couched in the "law of private vengeance," which gave to the individual member of a
clan the privilege to take into his own hands the right
of visiting summary punishment for wrongs inflicted
upon him by a tribesman.   It judicially safeguarded
not only the rights of the individual, but indirectly con-
served the inviolability of the tribal relation, and was
thus the forerunner of the subsequently perfected civil
and legal ideal.   Its rougher edges verge closely upon

criminalism, and doubtless gave loose rein to the play of the latent homicidal instinct.

The first tribal laws, while not based upon nice distinctions of abstract justice, were thus, nevertheless, suited to primitive times. Gradually the narrow conception of private vengeance merged into the more equitable notion of retaliatory justice, afterward the "*lex talionis*" of the Roman Pandects, and the essence of the still earlier Mosaic laws. Reciprocity is the basis of all equity. It stands for strict mathematical justice. The commutation of the penalty into a material indemnity, together with the right of sanctuary, followed, and early laid the foundation of compensatory damages, thus tempering justice with mercy. Equity now began to be ministered by representative tribunals, as subsequently described by Tacitus, and followed by the legal period of Roman jurisprudence. Thus we see, everywhere, as Taylor has pointed out: "The controlling forces of society are at work even among savages, only in more rudimentary ways than among ourselves. Private motives fall away when minds come together, and public good encourages the individual to set aside his private wishes and give up his property, or even his life, for the commonwealth." [1] All was not unalloyed savagery, as might be inferred from the apparent barrenness of the legal ideal viewed from our distant standpoint.

Trespass against the person circumscribed the arc of aggressive conduct of the primitive peoples. The right to life, locomotion, and enjoyment of natural physical privileges received the shock attending the first viola-

[1] "Anthropology," p. 408.

tion of concrete rights. The fewer those rights the more jealously protected were they, and hence commensurately the more aggravated the assault. Retaliatory reaction was summary and severe. There was no intermediary deliberative body to weigh alternatives or parcel out nice distinctions between the judicial and the executive arm. The earliest forms of legal justice, under the Twelve Tables, were administered by committees rather than by tribunals, and what we now term crimes were then considered rather in the nature of torts, or *sins* against the individual, of which the state took no cognizance. The first formal criminal law was promulgated B.C. 149. ("Ancient Law," Maine, p. 358, etc.) Justice was clothed in thunder, and her bolts, let us believe, were quick and sharp as handled by the aggrieved party.

Homicide was the typical crime of the early ages down to times of Christian ascendency ; though women, it may be said, were rarely homicides, their offences being chiefly of a negative character, as sins of impurity and covert crimes, mutilation of the dead and wounded in battle, etc.

Many of these primitive offences group themselves around the central figure with startling distinctness, frequently under the guise of social custom, and at the instigation of economic alternatives; as infanticide and abortion, in order to hold in check the increase of tribal population. The destruction of the aged and decrepit (which has survived even into historic times, as witness the customs of the Scandinavian nations) was almost universal, and was defended on humanitarian grounds.

Homicides, associated with the religious theories or arising out of motives of personal prowess, sheer brutality, or cannibalism (held by some writers to have been common to all peoples of antiquity), characterized the period of unwritten history in the ancient world. The savage proclivity to go to war upon the slightest provocation, such as vengeance, conquest, or pure wantonness, has ever been the prolific source of destructive tendencies and unparalleled atrocities from the earliest period to the present time. War has ever been the trade of the human race, and all other crimes have been legitimatized under its cruel sway. The inclination to destroy life under the glamour of the warlike propensity constitutes the dregs of the savage nature, continually pushing up through the cumuli of past ages, mitigated, but not destroyed, by the superincumbent civilization. It is the vent of criminalistic propensity, not wholly unstigmatized, for even the lowest races have ever decried the wanton taking of human life within their own tribal limitations. Thus Cæsar, in his history, notes that "robberies beyond the bounds of each community have no infamy;" though the same offences were punished severely within their own jurisdiction, even to the extirpation of the families of such offenders, ostensibly to safeguard the community at the expense of a part.

Criminality is modified by external conditions. In the history of progress it may safely be assumed that an increasing regard for the sacredness of human life began with the multiplication of the *acquisitions that make life desirable*. The growth of the social environment has an undeniable effect upon character and temperament, widening the field of active operations and proportionately broadening the scope of the criminalistic propensity at the expense of intensity; that is, crime against person perceptibly disappears before the advent of the property instinct which now shares in the general criminal aggression. The compounding with the blood avenger, already referred to, as "Bot," for trifling offences, and "Wehrgeld," for blood money, among the early Anglo-Saxon tribes, now opens the door for the interjection of two new principles into the problem, hitherto unrecognized; viz., the individual who received part of the indemnity, and the community that took the balance in compensation for the loss of a tribesman. It foreshadowed the politico-legal relation between the individual and the State. Henceforth, the latter assumes the rôle of arbitrator in private compromises, and finally evolves the full legal function of plaintiff and defendant, in matters derelict. Now we enter, for the first time, upon the *legal period*, where crime and the criminal action are no longer unknown quantities, but are moulded into set form, and become a politico-social entity of which the solidarity takes due cognizance. Now crime is parcelled out into choses, and the social aggression is distinctly marked out with penalties affixed; and he who openly defies its mandates and violates its principles is designated as a social outlaw and an enemy of his kind. With the poverty of the social content, we now see these retrogressive activities centre, in the main, about the personality, and manifest themselves, if at all, in acts of aggressive violence. Enriched with the sense of ownership, and his horizon expanded, the property instinct becomes a factor in the problem that must hereafter be taken into account in making up the criminal consensus.

Originally, there was no property in the soil, as we understand the term. Even down to the Roman period, land was termed "res nullius" — a thing without an owner. Occupation constituted the sole right of ownership, with necessity for its moving cause. The first land privileges were confined to tribal limitations for use in chase, the game captured alone being property. Latterly, the plot immediately surrounding the hut was cultivated for family use, and the property instinct began to take root in the soil. We trace the first step out of barbarism in the subsequent right of domicile. True, the original fief was carved out by the sword of feudalism in reward for service rendered, but that was only incidental; the main fact of ownership already existed, at least as early as the days of the patriarchs. By a series of steps it advanced from simple tenure for personal service into rental in crops, and then was commuted to money value,—the foundation of the tax system, and the beginning of modern land tenure. Tracing thus gradually the transference of the seat of administrative authority from patriarchal to tribal, and from tribal to feudal relations, we see the latter suddenly emerge from numerous petty land baronies, and expand into larger proprietorships with an increasing clientage and dominion, until lordly authority centres in one of exceptional prowess who becomes "*king*," holding the realm by reason of sovereign right, which, by a fiction of transference, gives us the right of "eminent domain." In process of time the commoner, no longer a "thing," becomes a "*villain*," with the right of property by service and purchase in fee. With these portentous changes from a nebulous and imperfect individualism into more distinctively socialistic and political existence, the index of moral and legal accountability now veers to the collective side of the arc — the social phenomena, with its complexities and inevitable tendency toward methodical and institutional life. With the increase of temptations, and the incentives to transgression through growing cupidity, that ever keeps pace with temporal prosperity, the jealousies engendered through the competitive spirit, and the tendencies toward unrest that always wait upon civilization, all go to help swell materially the anti-social proclivities that originally gravitated about the bare personality. We have little to show as to the direct effect upon the bulk of wrong-doing of the expansion of the criminalistic proclivities thus traceable through these new conventionalities. If, as has been pointed out, the results of social and material progress are to render the struggle of life less severe, in the sense of being less direct, the natural tendency must also have been to crowd down the criminalistic propensity to its zero. Doubtless, on the whole, the increase of crime in the past has more than kept pace with the march of civilization and the numerical increase of population; and this is due to several causes, among them, the expansion of the field of criminal operation through multiplication of environment, and the increasing moral virility of the race, which (as in the physiological sense) with increasing vitality also manifests a greater ability to precipitate its deleterious germ to the surface. So far as observable, what has now been subtracted from the grosser has simply been transposed to the less gross side of the criminal equation. Homicide, torture, rapine, all typical crimes of the primitive world, have now given place to those milder forms of wrong-doing against property — the prevailing offence of civilization. The refining influences belonging thereto must have tended to modify materially the more brutalizing propensities, thus transferring the storm centre from the personal to the non-personal area.

Thus far in our research, we have been wholly unable to trace in the past anything like a distinctively criminal *temperamentia*. History nowhere, at any given moment of its evolutional process, affords sufficient data to enable the student to formulate definite conclusions with reference to that patho-psychological phenomenon we call "criminality." At no time does it present itself as either a distinctively recognized dynamical, historical, ethical, or social entity, save as it stands revealed in those numerous spasmodic outbursts that characterize semi-political and racial agitations. Up to the common law period, we have little reliable social, or even legal, material to build with. Stephen describes the incipient legal expression as at first crude, until the semblance of a criminal judiciary machinery is traceable, when crime becomes for the first time a matter of civil concern. Up to that time the civil and socio-criminal affection was merely symptomatic, and none stood by to register the pulse or diagnose the disease. *History thus far precipitated no criminal problem, as such.* The whole subject was nebulous, and merited no passing consideration. Its personnel was but the detritus thrown off in the friction between society and the individual, accounted but as the impalpable dust beneath the feet. Extirpation was the sole remedy and solution of the criminal problem. " Our criminal procedure appears in many instances to point only at the destruction of the accused," wrote Beccaria, the pioneer penologist, even as late as 1764.[1] Like a chemical ferment, the social mass was left to clarify itself by destroying all deleterious germs through its own impromptu processes.

The details of past criminal amelioration have been simply the recital of unnumbered wrongs, intimidation and torture, trial by ordeal and compurgation, rationalized latterly by ameliorating customs, as, for instance, the oath of friends (usually twelve) swearing to the innocency of the accused, succeeded by the wager of battle ; and finally followed by the inauguration of the jury system, composed of peers of the accused, who were originally at once accuser, witnesses, and judges, the severities of whose sentences were modified by a foolish custom known as the " Benefit of Clergy," which was not abolished until 1706. The barbarities of these early criminal procedures are amply evidenced by the animus of English law that continued to visit with death numerous minor offenders, such as poachers upon preserves, thieves (to the extent of a shilling), etc., in vogue from the thirteenth century to as late as the year 1827.

Legal and judicial procedures, in the absence of more direct testimony, may thus be said to reflect but imper-

[1] " Crimes and Punishment," p. 224.

fectly about all we can learn of the eruptive phase of the social disease that manifests itself in overt outbreak, and of which the judicial processes may therefore fairly be termed its sole historical setting. The legal phenomenon was as the shadow cast by the body of crime, and as substance to shadow it affords but a faint glimpse of the distorted features beneath the legal mask. A detailed history of crime as a concrete phenomenon is therefore impossible, and would be but the discordant recital of a series of harsh and spasmodic moral upheavals, of social and political convulsions, of the fierce struggle of contending factions and classes, the dread perturbation of a perverted religious enthusiasm that for ages shared with the judicial arm in the task of parcelling out individual metes and bounds, and, lastly, the bloody annals of war, the apotheosis of lust and murder, all these without any individualism to particularize or lend distinctiveness to the unhindered march of the disease.

A schema of crime from a purely historical standpoint, were that possible, would thus involve more space with fewer compensatory results than these pages will warrant. The civilization of the ancients, in a great measure obscure in matters that pertain to the level of ordinary life and common affairs, presents but a fragmentary indicium of its socio-moral aspect. Sin and crime are the joint inheritance of the race, one being but the intensified expression of the other. A history of crime is the history of its socio-pathological morbidity, whose course no pen has recorded, and whose cotemporaneous details elude the comprehension, so closely is it interwoven with the common personality.

CHAPTER II

CRIMINAL IDENTIFICATION AND TYPE

IT speaks hopefully for the future of both the science of criminology, and the welfare of society, that the individualistic and socialistic features of the criminal phenomena have been of late so prominently pushed to the front as legitimate subjects of inquiry, and that the interest manifested on the side of institutional and corrective agencies as well, has taken so prominent a hold upon the public mind.

To properly understand the subject of special criminology, we must first know the personal factors involved therein. Their proper conception advances the subject one step nearer the sources of criminal causation, and by so much approaches a better understanding and proper solution of the problem.

Before a systematic investigation of the subject of criminal man can be scientifically pursued and understood, a preliminary inquiry into the accepted standards of personal and physical identity is necessary. Who and what is he? In what do his physical and moral characteristics inhere? Is he differentiated from the rest of mankind? and if so, how, and in what respect? Is he as one set apart from the normal by reason of peculiar physiological or anatomical idiosyncrasies, or functional derangement? Does he bear the mark of

Cain — the accepted stigmata of moral and physical degeneration — upon his forehead? These are important and interesting inquiries that may very properly preface a tentative study of the subject of recalcitrant man.

The positivist school of modern criminal anthropologists have sought to answer these questions in the affirmative, basing their deductions broadly upon the fact of physiological and anatomical asymmetry in confirmation of well-defined type in identification of criminal man. The theory, in its philosophical inception, is apparently founded upon the materialistic notion of the subject, not only in solution of the phenomenon of moral degeneration, but also as implicating the whole range of psychological attributes.

Crime is symptomatic, in the concrete sense; that is, it is indicative of the existence of a serious disturbing element existing apart from all mere external conditions. Generically, in its larger sense, the social unity may be said to be the seat of the disease; individually, it stands associated with organic phenomena; and genetically, the vitiated moral centres are the absolute sources of the disorder.

All moral phenomena are essentially psychical in origin and manifestation. That they sustain an indirect relation and certain sympathetic correspondence with their physical cortex, is undeniable, but that relation is only retroactive and reflexive, with a certain directness, physiologically speaking, up to a given point. That it is absolute, involves an irreconcilable hypothesis that surrenders the whole subject over into the grasp of a determinism utterly at variance with any rational theory of consciousness consistent with the subject under consideration. Without entering into a refinement of controversy which yields so little profit, let it be said at the outset that the materialistic hypothesis is wholly inadequate to solve the problem of criminal causation as here presented, but leaves it rather involved in still greater obscurity, all attempted explanation of the fact of consciousness by way of nerve incitation or cerebral activity in the sense of causation, being manifestly useless. In short, both purely materialistic or idealistic theories, starting as they do from opposite polarities of thought, are certain to meet in common contradiction, either failing to bridge the gulf or harmonize the distinction between the physical and the spiritual. The sole satisfactory explanation in connection with the twofold phenomena here presented lies in the classical hypothesis of the dual conception of mind and matter—the organic and the inorganic as distinct though coördinate entities, not absolute but incidental and mutually reflexive, whose chief difficulties of explanation lie not so much in the *fact* as in the *modality* of such co-relation.

The science of modern criminal anthropology following along this commonly accepted fundamental assumption, two distinct schools of criminological investigation have sprung up which have each pursued their respective studies in somewhat diverging lines : the Positivist, or materialistic ; and the Spiritualistic, or classical. The origin of systematic criminological pursuit extends back to the times of Galt, Beccaria, Spurzheim, and Lavater (the first of whom may be called the father of empirical anthropology); and these, taking their cue from the newly aroused scientific spirit, about the latter part of the seventeenth and the dawn of the eighteenth centuries, have pressed their inquiries into this promising field with varying degrees of success. Latterly, it has been reduced to more scientific methods by Italian, French, and German savants, the first of whom, especially, has rallied to its standard many eminent followers, and given its own name to the comparatively new science, under the leadership of such men as Professor Lombroso, Messieurs Ferri, Garofalo, Ferreri, Ottolenghi, Salsotto, Despine, Rossi, Lacassagne, Manouvrier, Laurent, Benedikt, Von Homel, Von Hölder, Von Röder, Von Liszt, Holtzendorff, Ekert, Dr. Baer, Dr. Wichern, Forel, Corre, Topinard, and others. Perhaps the first distinctive stamp as an independent science dates from the publication of Lombroso's "The Criminal" (1876), though Broca, who originated the anthropological society of Paris, in 1859, has been known as among the first of modern penologists, in name, if not in rank. These investigators have studied the subject, usually on the side of its morphological and organic changes, in support of the theory of type as the true explanation of criminal degeneration. To what extent is he normal or abnormal? Whence these deviations? Are they prenatal, or postnatal? congenital or acquired? Are their causes immediate or remote? Are they due to inherent defective changes, or to acquired tendencies and characteristics, either through defective will power or by way of superinduced organic or functional derangements? Cranial and facial asymmetries, brain

defection and neurosis, anthropometric measurements
in deviation from the standard, and many other known
variations from the normal, comprise the data from
which these schools draw their conclusions and formulate their creeds.   The patience and minuteness of investigation, as well as the vast accumulation of data
that has rewarded their researches, have been undoubtedly great.   Thus, Professor Lombroso, in his résumé (1890), gives details from the personal study of
177 craniums of criminals, in addition to measurements
made on 25,447 normal persons.   The same author, in
his work, "The Female Offender" (in conjunction
with Ferreri), records the total observations made on
1033 female delinquents ; 176 observations on the
skulls of such subjects; 685 on the skulls of prostitutes ; 225 on normal women in hospitals ; and on 30
others also normal.   The results of such examinations
at the hands of competent specialists may be grouped
under several heads, not however always with uniform
success on the whole.

The authorities above quoted gather up the anomalies
thus presented in varying degrees of scientific accuracy,
and, grouping them in regular order upon the basis of
biological anthropometry, assume to construct upon
their foundation a stereotyped anthropological order
that may be readily recognized as unfailing criteria
for all future criminal identification.   Anatomical and
physiognomical characterizations — peculiarities, for instance, of the frontal sinuses, voluminous orbital capacity, the zygomatic process, large and prognathic jaw,
facial and cranial asymmetries, thickening of the media

occipital fossa, pteleiform type of the nasal opening, the lemurian appendix of the jaw, etc., etc. — are all called into requisition and advanced as the accredited insignia of so-called type. These physical and anatomical peculiarities, gathered up in varying degrees of impressionability, are briefly summarized by the master hand, and fashioned into the central personality that gives us the conventional criminal as one possessing a feeble cranial capacity, an abnormal and a symmetrical cranium, with large orbital capacity, heavy jaw, projecting superciliary ridges, with flat and usually crooked nose, projecting asymmetrical ears, and scanty beard, and weak muscular force. To fill up these bold outlines, and to substantiate their position by empirical data, are the chief purposes of the physiological school.

In his recent work on homicides, the eminent authority above named passes in review 1711 individuals, of whom 711 were soldiers; 699, criminals; and 301, madmen. In his anthropometric research (according to his reviewer), he reaffirms his views with reference to the inferiority of criminals as compared with normal men, and from certain defective characteristics present deduces criminal degeneracy. The homicide, according to his diagnosis, presents less cranial capacity and minor frontal diameter than the normal, while his upper jaws are more developed. Numerous other qualifications are brought forward by way of comparison to reënforce particular cases, frequently descending into minor details that illustrate the refinements of special pleadings rather than the requirements of logic or the demands of science. The method thus employed is manifestly the precursor of criminal classification on the basis of organic degeneration ; or, as their apologists put it, "where their moral degeneration corresponds with their physical." This comes very near defining crime as a physiological manifestation with a corresponding and secondary relation back to psychological conditions, thus relegating the whole subject fundamentally and organically to the domain of pure physics.

The positivist school has succeeded, upon these bare premises, and to their apparent satisfaction, not only in establishing a generally well-defined theory of anthropological criminal conformation, but has arbitrarily attached to it all that special significance and those enduring qualities that are necessary to a universally accepted standard of comparison. According to Garofalo, a criminal type is apparently as well established as an Italian type ; not a single characteristic constantly distinguishing it ; but the proportion of congenital anomalies, according to such authorities, is larger in any given number of criminals than in an equal number of non-criminals. Indeed, so far have its advocates carried their assumptions, that they have not hesitated to press it to its farthest logical conclusion, insisting not only upon the existence of criminal type in general, but also upon a *special* type, applying tentative principles in such an arbitrary manner as to meet the ever varying forms of the criminal category, and finding a corresponding physical type for each. Conforming to this position, Lombroso, in his formal reply to his critics, asserts his belief in " not a single, but in many particular types, as the thief, the swindler, the murderer," etc. Reasoning along these parallels, we have the whole schema of criminal identification revealed upon purely materialistic grounds, subject to pathological conditions clearly predetermined by physical law, and carrying with it its own *ipse dixit*. In brief, *organism* is made the sole absolute explanation of all criminal phenomena, as it is of all sentient life, of which the former is but a different mode of expression falling back upon persistent pathological deviation. According to their dictum, crime is but a neurosis based upon cerebration; all forms of wrong-doing are a kind of physical degeneration dependent upon molecular changes, or upon anatomical or functional modification and derangement, to be cured, if at all, by a "prescription," or by elimination.

While the advocates of this hypothesis have been thus far unable to verify their theories of special type to any appreciable extent, or with any degree of unanimity, they are substantially agreed upon the central position with reference to a general type to cover all classes of delinquents who, by reason of profound moral diathesis, have departed from the normal and become permanently affixed in the canon of moral degenerates.

Type may be briefly defined as the permanent grouping of characteristics under similarities. Its process is synthetic. In essence, it may be said to depend upon two general principles that go to determine its value as a special unifying centre, viz.: (1) the emphasis or weight of the individual characteristics involved when minimized as to numbers; and (2) their numerical value, when such individual characteristics are in themselves insignificant. The fulfilment of either of these conditions may be considered as reasonably sufficient to establish type. Falling back upon these criteria, the advance school would seem to have much in its favor; as one has well said, "in practice two or three reunited physical characteristics are sufficient" to realize type. This, however, is not reckoning with all the factors. The weakness of the position (if such it be) reaches farther back. It lies at the centre of the assumption as a seemingly insuperable bar toward attaining the goal. The difficulty of realizing type as the outcome of their method is in the insufficiency of the data presented and upon which they purpose to erect their anthropological superstructure. That insufficiency consists, not so much numerically in the data which it has gathered with so much painstaking labor, as it does in the error of the assumption as to the groundwork of the comparison, and the faulty synthesis employed therein. Simple statistics, numerically used for comparison, are by no means to be considered conclusive. The force of such comparison, it must be observable, lies not so much in the number of anomalies presented in delinquents as compared with normals ad libitum, as in the preëstablishment of a fixed basis for the comparison in the normals themselves. Before we can intelligently classify delinquents on the basis of anomalous characteristics, it is necessary to first determine what normality itself consists in, and to what extent abnormalities are present in the normals; to find out their proportions; to ascertain if possible the exact line of departure, as well as the superinducing causes; and after careful analysis and investigation, to separate accidental and incidental from the absolute, and to assign each its proper place in the anthropological chain. We must first know precisely in what physiological and anatomical normality consists, before we can definitely affirm in what it does *not* consist. It is not sufficient to institute comparison from chance material, and upon uncertain premises. It calls for a vast aggregation of facts scientifically deduced, and properly classified and arranged, with due reference to all the facts of racial, social, and class distinctions, as well as personal and intellectual considerations, upon a scale commensurate with the problem, comprehending data of which the present are but as the droppings before the shower. Dr. Wines has well pointed out the difficulties here briefly touched upon. "If all criminals in the world were examined and accurately tabulated, it would nevertheless require an equal number of persons never convicted of crime as a background for comparison, before the assertions that any particular grouping is even *prima facie* evidence that its subjects belong to a separate anthropological type." [1]

The exact extent to which certain anomalies invade the realms of the normal is vital to the issue, and is as yet unknown. For example, the excess of Wormian bones said to characterize the criminal skull has also been shown to be not peculiar to them alone, but to distinguish all the lower races, criminal or non-criminal, indicating that it is a transmitted mark not of individ-

[1] "Reformation and Punishment," p. 256.

ual, but rather of racial, inheritance. The same holds true with reference to the premature closing of the cranial sutures, and perhaps other peculiarities noted in these classes, and frequently brought forward to substantiate the criminal type theory. Here the statistical method so persistently evoked falls short of attaining its object in that it fails to properly emphasize this vital fact of social and class distinction, as well as the modifying influence of the particular intellectual and moral plane from which their normal subjects are usually drawn for comparison. This is of far greater importance in reaching satisfactory conclusions than any mere array of data and bare averages. It is absolutely necessary to the establishment of just anthropological standards that the subjects of such comparative tables, both criminal and non-criminal, be taken from uniform racial, class, and social conditions, as an absolute prerequisite to fair and impartial investigation and conclusion. Of what avail is it if the material for the comparison be selected from widely diverging intellectual, social, and civil conditions, varying in economic and industrial relations and walks in life? For example, if the subject transfixed with the criminal stigmata, and belonging apparently to a lower social level, be placed in contradistinction with those in the higher walks of life, what does such comparison tend to show but that one class less favorably surrounded, and of a lower social or mental stratum, is more prone to criminality than more fortunately circumstanced ones? In brief, it has simply demonstrated that one given class or rank produces more delinquents than another.

It is, therefore, safe to conclude, from this line of reasoning, that what experts claim as an indication of criminal degeneracy can hardly be construed as anything more than simple class characterization based upon racial differentiation, and of which the recalcitrant is merely a refractory offshoot. As pertaining to certain special features in this respect, some of its apologists readily admit as much, as, for example, Professor Lombroso, when he affirms that "Certain shapes of heads popularly accredited to criminals are nothing more than marks of ethnic distinctions."

It is worthy of note, in this connection, that the leading criminal experts are not agreed with reference to the subject under consideration. Some of those best qualified to speak are at variance upon the theory of type, and not a few opposed to its cardinal assumption; while doubtless none would be willing to apply it *ad hominum*. Dr. Emile Laurent, the eminent criminologist of Paris, claims that "The same anomalies that characterize criminals are also found among good men, and that these signs are not sufficient to indicate criminality." Manouvrier is quoted as advancing the opinion that he "did not find any distinctive differences in his comparative studies between criminals and normal men, except in surrounding conditions which modify the associations or combinations of habitudes and correlatively the anatomical conformation."[1] Dr. Corre did not find anything strictly peculiar to criminals, and rejects the criminal type in the sense of anthropological unification; and believes that the cerebral inferiority

[1] See A. MacDonald's "Abnormal Man," p. 107.

of the criminal has its origin in a sort of arrest of development in childhood.[1]   Dr. Von Hölder affirms: "It is impossible from cranial asymmetries to conclude as to psychical characteristics, and that physical signs of degeneration indicate nothing further than the presence of a tendency to psychical degeneration." It is scarcely a pardonable error, he declares, to consider every man with these characteristics as a predestined criminal, as some of the Italian school would do.[2]   Dr. Wines thinks that "In a strictly scientific sense the existence of an anthropological criminal type has not been proved, and it is doubtful whether it can be proved."[3]   "Cranial and facial anomalies characterize hardly ten per cent of them," says Dr. Seifers.   "I cannot go so far as to believe in a special type of criminal brain," writes Dr. Jacobi, of New York.   Dr. Arthur MacDonald, the eminent specialist of the Bureau of Education, at Washington, says: "The study of the criminal can also be the study of a normal man; for most criminals are also so by occasion or accident and differ in no essential respect from other men. Most human beings who are abnormal or defective in any way are much more alike than unlike normal individuals."

Mr. Ellis is equally conservative upon this subject; together with many leading criminologists in the United States, such as Mr. Brockway, of Elmira Institute, New York, Dr. H. D. Wey, Dr. Baer, Dr. Flint, and others.

[1] "Les Criminelles," Paris, 1889.
[2] "Ueber die körperlichen und geistigen Eigenthümlichkeiten der Verbrecher," 1889.   [3] "Punishment and Reformation," p. 258.

Mr. Z. R. Brockway, in commenting upon my published opinion in the "Summary," gives as his view that, "although not yet able to discover the anthropological type of criminals, I hold that appreciable subjective cause of criminal conduct by any individual is in the organism of the nerve tissue; this revealed in registered stigmata of degeneration or in the defective quality of tissue, not so manifest in asymmetries." Dr. Austin Flint, though believing that the born criminal almost always presents physical signs of degeneration, nevertheless concludes that all of the purely physical characteristics observed in the born criminal exist in normal individuals very frequently; and that such abnormalities, "even with criminal ancestry, are never in themselves absolute evidence of criminality, but that we must first resort to the courts for our incriminating proofs." Dr. Wey, who passed in critical review several thousand delinquents, speaking of the subject, adds, "It cannot be affirmed that the corporal and psychical peculiarities noted in a prison population only accompany criminality, that they are never found in individuals who pass as normal in the community in which they live; we cannot affirm, through data gained at the post-mortem table, that they are due to subjective causes that operate in the individual to produce a criminological diathesis." Dr. Baer denies the criminal type altogether, in the anthropological and biological sense, or that the criminal face has any distinct peculiarities or international resemblance, and that the psychological difference between the criminal and the lower classes, from whom he descends, is only quantitative, not qualitative.

With this divergency of opinion on the part of specialists equally qualified to judge, and regarding the question from a purely racial and class point of view, the
attitude of the Italian and French savants seems dogmatic. Conditions that go in modification are not
taken sufficiently into account. Moreover, it must not
be forgotten that the Old World offender is not in all
points the histological counterpart of his brother in the
New; social, civil, and economic conditions bring about
with them marked anthropological changes by the
blending of heterogeneous elements, and after a few
oscillations become gradually settled, and in process of
time evolved into a new and distinctive race type. Environment undoubtedly has its effect in shaping individual character, which in time is individualized and
becomes itself transmissible, exaggerating its good and
bad qualities into ethnic peculiarities, which, when unfavorable, may become the ready vehicle of degenerative tendencies. Some criminologists contend that
crime is not distinctively an individual, but wholly a
social, phenomenon, and consequently that its abolition
presupposes the readjustment of the conditions in which
it thrives. Though undoubtedly there is truth in this
view, nevertheless, the bulk of criminality, in the sense
of the genuine offender, must be regarded as inhering
primarily in the anthropological rather than in the collective organism.

It is highly probable that the general changes and
differences observable among races extend as well to
the interpretation of the special criminal characterization, and are found in him in varying and accentuated

forms. In this respect, it is therefore probably true
that the Italian offender differs from criminals of other
races precisely in the same manner and to the same
extent as the normal members of such races differ from
one another, preserving each their main racial characteristics modified only by local conditions. Max Nor-
deau comes near this idea when, in his " Degeneration,"
he cites his master's "born criminal" as "being nothing but a subdivision of degenerates." [1] Had he in-
serted the word "racial" before "degenerates," he would
perhaps have conformed more nearly to the explanation
here ventured.

A glance at the physiognomies of the inmates of a
cosmopolitan prison population serves well to illustrate
the phase of the subject above mentioned. Analyze the
heterogeneous mass of incarcerates in almost any of
the jails and penitentiaries in the United States, upon
racial lines, and select from them the Italian element,
and you have a fair representative of Lombroso's stereotyped criminal habitué. Separate the Gaelic constit-
uency, and we have a good illustration of what the
neurotic offender of that versatile race must of necessity
be. The Germanic and Anglo-Saxon, belonging to the
more phlegmatic temperament, hand down in their
degenerates their heavier physiognomy unimpaired;
while the prognathic jaw, voluminous cheek-bone, and
superciliary ridges of the Celt are preserved in the
Irish criminal. An admixture of racial affinities modified by new environment gives us the latest evolution of
the American type, whose recalcitrant member breeds

[1] p. 17.

true to its ethnic root. Thus each exceptional subject accentuates himself along lines of transmissible race eccentricities to which alone he proves true, and not to any exceptionally vague physio-psychological archetype.

Lombroso's typical criminal may be strong in his provincialism, but he is weak in his universality. The characterization cannot be regarded in the light of a composite portraiture of the conventional criminal absorbing and assimilating into itself the illusive outline of every other into a homogeneous whole. The picture fits the criminal better than the criminal fits the picture. The negatives are too illusive for tangible realization. Dr. Laurent, in this connection, has very sensibly remarked that out of 1022 portraits of offenders, it was impossible in many cases to pronounce one a criminal from his physiognomy.[1] To what do these facts point, but to indicate that the criminal inherence does not exclusively reside in any particular form of physiognomical or anatomical configuration, save only in exceptional cases, and then as the acquired or entailed mark of class inheritance or ethnic distinction shared in common by both normal and abnormal man.

Crime is not, as Lombroso and his coadjutors would have us believe, wholly either a disease or a neurosis, in the sense of a direct absolute physiological pathognomonic, though doubtless not infrequently closely associated with physical, anatomical, and nerve degeneration, as above conceded. To presuppose absolute and necessary brain lesion, or diseased nerve action, or anomalous physiog-

[1] "Archiv für Anthropologie," 1889.

nomical or anatomical diathesis as the inevitable precursor of any form of moral deflection, is an assumption
wholly unwarranted, and is nowhere substantiated by
facts, though its advocates have sought to lay their
foundation deep and wide in the materialistic hypothesis.
Most criminals present unusually sound physiological
conditions, and no unusual death-rate, considering their
habits and mode of life, as we shall hereafter see, and
hence their moral cannot be associated with physiological instability in the absolute sense. The defection
(physical) must be either reversionary or incidental,
rather than absolute.

The theory of type, therefore, as applied to the subject of criminal characterization, has been pushed to
extremes by the ultra school of criminologists, who have
sought to place upon its accumulated data a weight of
construction it will hardly bear. As a working hypothesis it is almost wholly impracticable. Class distinction
offers the explanation, at least in part, and that sustains
little practical relation to criminality *per se*, save as found
in the tendency of the lower classes, who, through stress
of circumstances, or for other reasons, yield a larger
percentage of the criminal infusoria than either the
higher or intermediary walks of life. To assign to
such generalization the nature of an infallible criminal
criterion seems unwarranted, and is the dictum of the
study rather than the conclusions of common sense or
experience.

That certain external conformation, or physical characteristics, degenerative or otherwise, may at times
associate themselves with corresponding psychical mani-

festation is readily conceivable. That such conditions on the part of one invariably set up necessary and corresponding changes in the other, so that all who fall thereunder are thereby of necessity predestined criminals, is quite another proposition, the length of which I cannot go, and I do not believe is borne out by facts. The criminal character is limited to no special bio-physiological or psychological state or condition, is confined within no social or individualistic bounds, but overlaps all classes and conditions of men irrespective of social or intellectual distinctions, or physical or organic asymmetries. The finer as well as the grosser type of organizations, the higher, intermediary, and lower classes, contribute indiscriminately to swell its ranks; the symmetrical and the unsymmetrical, the epileptic or nonepileptic, neurotic or phlegmatic, alike come under the ban. Whether one class or type preponderates, is largely a question of social, climatic, or economic preconditions, plus ever the inherent moral subjectivity of the individual himself.

Type, as such, transmits itself unerringly. The criminal resemblance, so-called, not so. An Italian, or an Englishman, or a Teuton, may be picked out among a thousand; a criminal, with peril. Heredity is the essence of type. The power to transmit itself here admits of no contradiction. Exception is fatal to the theory. Not one of its criminological advocates would go to the extent of affirming the persistency of criminal type as an unerring biological fact in its law of transmission. To say that the instinctive criminal propensity and psychological equipment is congenital, and to affirm that it is so only in association with invariable, well-defined, and preordained physiological and biological type from which there is no escape, are two distinct propositions, one of which holds true, the other is governed by exceptions as numerous as the rule, and for that very reason is vitiated as an indispensable precursor of the criminal propension.

Professor Lombroso and his coadjutors concede that the full description of the criminal is rarely, " perhaps never," realized in the true sense, and that " in practice two or three good, reunited, physical characteristics are sufficient to establish type." The asseveration is not helpful, since the query still remains, Are the " two or three characteristics " left over, to be deemed infallible ? If not, it but leaves the subject where it finds it, and all such insignia remain without any special force or fixed moral or anthropological significance, except as already pointed out.

Like most iconoclasts, opponents to the ultra type theory have no fixed substitute to offer in place of the positivist attitude with reference to criminal identification and type. It is doubtful if any is needed. As the assumptions of the latter seem to fill entirely its mental horizon, it is perhaps as well to leave that of the classical school unobstructed, lest the central fact, — that of responsible moral conduct, — the real substance involved, be lost sight of or endangered amid the crush and grind of purely materialistic forces, and which is made entirely too little of in the marshalling of facts by the modern anthropological school of inquiry. Conduct, upon the appreciable basis of motive in attestation of character, and under ordinary judicial tests, presents the only true rational basis upon which the offender may be brought to judgment. Whatsoever is more than this, is, to say the least, hypercritical as it is ultra-scientific, falls short of the tests of inductive reason, and must await the verdict of further experience.

CHAPTER III

CRIMINAL CLASSIFICATION AND THE CATEGORIES

WHILE insisting upon the impracticability, if not the impossibility, of evoking type as the outcome of criminal anthropological unification, the generalization of the criminalistic element into a well-defined class, upon the basis of psychological distinctions and sociological modifications, is the natural result of the experimental method, and gives us the criminal categories which are the chart and framework of modern empirical criminology.

As heretofore laid down, the science of criminal anthropology views the recalcitrant man primarily in his psychological and sociological constitution; and secondarily, as to his physiological and organic relations, which latter sustain an indirect, oftentimes conformative, correspondence to the psychological, to the extent at least that both not infrequently answer to the etiological inquiry ever in the foreground, Whence is criminal man? Is he normal or abnormal? and if the latter, in what do his anomalous characteristics consist? Are they morphological, or impromptu? To what extent does the physical sympathize with the psychical, and which are predetermining? We have but imperfectly traversed these grounds, and must leave the verdict to the synthetic judgment after proper arrangement of all the facts.

Man is as much a wonder in the majesty of his ruin

as in the plenitude of his power, and to the well-organized mind affords as mournful food for contemplation in the one instance, as for unfeigned admiration in the other. To know him at his best, it is necessary to know him at his worst, since both equally sound the depth of his potentialities, and test the range of his possibilities. The aim of the moralist is to celebrate him at the climax of his capacities; the task of the criminologist is to register him at their zero — the breaking-point in the chain of moral continuity; and thence, if possible, to trace him in the devious windings of his bio-psychological self to his ultimate genetics in the obscurities of moral causation, and the will.

Compelled to the conclusion that there is no such thing as criminal type, in the anthropological sense, there is, nevertheless, a distinctively criminalistic element susceptible of classification on the basis of ethical differentiation as expressed in concrete acts. The province of special criminology opens up a wide field for discussion in a science but yet in its polemical stages. Much preliminary work is necessary to be done to clear a path for scientific inquiry that will lay bare and so systematize the whole subject as to ultimately entitle it to the dignity of an accepted branch of sociological science. The whole scope of the biological and the zoölogical must be made contributory thereto, including comparative anatomy and physiology; the range of pathology, and the abstruse realms of psychiatry and metaphysics; the field of historical survey, including the study of laws and customs; as well as the exclusive work of the specialist and the expert in their several spheres, — all, lending their aid to the study of abnormal man in his objective and subjective capacity, both as an individual, and as a factor of the social and civic community. The law of disease, scientists tell us, is as beautiful as the law of life. The former is but the line of progression reversed, more difficult perhaps of explanation in proportion as the origin and play of disintegrating forces are found to be the more obscure and mysterious. The law of progression is from the homogeneous to the heterogeneous in ever increasing complexity. The law of degeneration is from the heterogeneous to the homogeneous with general and specific tendency toward first principles in ever increasing simplicity. The task of the criminologist, like that of the physician, is therefore along the line of retrogression in the interpretation of morphological changes. One is in the nature of an evolution, the other an involution; one is confined to the realms of the normal, the other is limited to the field of the abnormal and the morbid. The psychologist, the criminologist, and the expert are collaborators in this field of knowledge, in that they are a unit in the task of reducing to a minimum the anomalous and the morphological in the sphere of morals and physics, thus winning bloom from decay, and snatching life from death. Their lines, *diverging* in the initiative, *converge* ultimately upon the personality, the criminologist taking upon himself the twin labor of physician and metaphysician, dealing equally with the material and the immaterial, — with body and soul.

The sympathetic factors that enter into the personal make-up of the criminal offender are : (*a*) Cosmic — that which may be said to stand associated to his dietic, atmospheric, and climatic surroundings, and which strongly affect the bulk of crime ; (*b*) Biological — comprehending his personal characteristics, whether psychical, anatomical, or physiological; and (*c*) Social — his economic, industrial, or social surroundings proper, as custom, habits, etc. The first of these are largely under the domination of race determinism, and fall back upon class distinction for their essential interpretation and meaning, in this connection. The second is predetermined by heredity, and by the modifying power of postnatal influences, or both, as the setting up of acquired habits closely associated with nerve action and often accompanied with organic functional changes, which might be called the direct agencies in the formation of criminal character; while the third is under the sway of environment, and social surroundings, which, while indirect, are nevertheless the field in which degenerative tendencies are cultivated. Broadly speaking, and in its individual sense, the first may be said to embrace both the instinctive criminal and the impulsive recalcitrant; the second, the congenital or instinctive and the habitual offender; while the last is usually considered the natural source and limitation of the so-called criminal by occasion, who might also without violence be called the true social offender, inasmuch as that is largely the etiological source and vehicle of this class of delinquents, as we shall hereafter see. Each of these will be more fully developed under their proper categories.

The personal factors of crime remain the proper and legitimate field of anthropological criminal speculation. All empirical research must be focussed upon them, as Dr. Benedikt has said, "In order to acquire and spread abroad a sensible view, and before all, that it may be clearly ascertained whether and how criminals can be corrected, and how society can be best protected from the scourge of crime, it will be necessary for criminalists to adopt the method of naturalists." Enrico Ferri, in his able treatises, has more minutely outlined these essential concomitants of criminal sociology along similar scientific lines.

To be more particular, the anthropological characteristics inherent in the individual offender are the primary factors of criminality, and, as a matter of fact, therefore, necessarily take the first place in his systematic study and analysis. They are divided into three subclasses, according as the criminal may be regarded organically, physically, or socially, the latter including his psychical conditions. The organic constitution of the criminal comprises all anomalies of the skull, the brain, the vital organs, the sensibility, the reflex activity, and all the varied bodily phenomena taken together, as physiognomy, bodily and anatomical defection, external markings, etc.

The mental constitution comprises all peculiarities of intelligence and feeling, the comparative capacity of the will, the intellect, the imagination; their morbid manifestations and allied functional derangements; the moral powers, especially of the moral sensibility, their imperfect and defective operations under degenerative impulsations; the specialties of writing, slang, etc.

The personal characteristics of the criminal comprise his purely biological conditions, such as race, age, sex; bio-social relations, as civil status, profession, domicile, social rank, instruction, education, sexual relation, etc.

The physical factors of crime are climate, the nature of the soil, the relative length of day and night, the seasons, average temperature, meteoric conditions, agricultural pursuits, racial and ethnic peculiarities.

The social factors comprise the density of population, public opinion, manners, and religion, family circumstances; the system of education, industrial pursuits; alcoholism and morphinism, economic and political conditions; public administration, justice, and police; and in general, legislative, civil, and penal institutions.[1]

These are the first steps toward scientific classification with a view to a proper understanding of abnormal man, and the conditions underlying his bio-psychological genesis and identity. Perhaps a more special classification under the head of sub-topics, is that of Benelli, Tamborini, and Lombroso, as furnished by the eminent specialist of the Bureau of Education, at Washington, in his "Abnormal Man"; which may not be out of place in this connection, as giving a comprehensive insight into the vast array of detail and general scope of the subject, that must be laid under contribution by the successful student. An outline will furnish the reader a consensus of detail that blazes the path for a more extended criminal pathology as a science.

[1] See "Criminal Sociology," Ferri, p. 53.

Generalities. — Name, age, country, profession, civil, state.

1. *Anthropometrical Examination.* — Development of skeleton, stature, development of muscular system, weight. Color: of skin, hair, iris, uniformly colored, double coloration, peripheral and central, non-uniformly colored, color predominant, color not predominant, beard. Piliferous system. Tattooing. Craniometry: face, height, bizygomatic diameter, facial type, facial index; nose — profile, dimensions, direction, anomalies; teeth — form, dimensions, anomalies; eyes. Neck; thorax; lungs; heart; genital organs; disfigurements.

2. *Examination of Sensibility.* — Touch: electric current, left hand, right hand, tongue; æsthesiometer of Weber — right hand, left hand, tongue. Pain: algometer of Lombroso — left and right hands, tongue. Sensibility: muscular, topographic, thermic, meteorologic, magnetic, metallic, hyrrotic, hypnotic, credulity, visual, acoustic, olfactive, gustative, chromatic, sensual, (generative); first sensual relations, aberrations, anomalies.

3. *Examination of Motility.* — Voluntary movements: gait, speech, language, writing; reflexes; muscular force; dynamometry; manual skill; anomalies.

4. *Examination of Vegetative Functions.* — Circulation, respiration, thermogeny; digestion; secretions — saliva, urine, sweat.

5. *Psychical Examination.* — Perception (illusions); ideation (hallucinations); reasoning; will (impulsion); memory; intelligence — works, writings, slang; conscience; sentiments — affective, moral, religious; pas-

sions; instincts; sleep; moral sense; habitual expression of physiognomy; psychometry; anomalies.

6. *Anamnestic Examinations.* — Family, parents; state of family, daughters, sons; age of parents; history, diseases, crimes of parents. Precedents; education, instruction, intellectual and political developments; traumatic accidents, crimes, habitual character, occupation preferred. Latest information: last crimes, cause of crime, repentance, admissions, nervous diseases, and mental anomalies intercurrent; inquiries. To fill up this outline chart of criminalistic propensities to bloom into flesh and blood, with the hectic flush of the social taint upon its cheek, is the self-imposed task of the criminal anthropologist. The initiative is ethical. Its ultimate bounds are the undefined zones of physiological incitation and psychical cognition, with all the subtle and co-related phenomena, and intercurrent forces and operations, into much of which the investigator can only enter with imperfect apprehension and uncertain soundings.

Systematic criminological classification, as the result of ethical empiricism with its co-related phenomena, is the desideratum of the special and practical criminologist, toward which all his labors converge, and with which his theories must ultimately conform at the dictates of experience upon the basis of ascertained facts. Its ultimate realizations may be but imperfectly attained from either objective or subjective points of view, in that the conditions precedent, already pointed out, are bound to intermingle, and the generalizations to overlap. For instance, it may be observed that the criminal of passion, as portrayed, may readily be assimilated with the criminal by occasion, and the latter shades imperceptibly through force of repetition into the ordinary habitué, while all in turn may share esoterically in the sad heritage of the hereditary taint through pregenital influences, to a greater or lesser degree. The representative of one class may therefore not incorrectly be frequently classified with either, or all the others, without violence to any. The zones of criminality are designated by arbitrary lines, and the passage from one to another is by imperceptible degrees. This is the reason why no criminal category, any more than an hypothesis of type, may be considered as absolute and unvarying. The impulses and characteristics that distinguish one class of offenders may also possibly be present in more or less degree in another class, even be shared in common by criminal and non-criminal man, without necessarily bringing either under the ban of any special category. Thus, the thief, or the criminal by a single offence, may also be the "criminal by passion"; while the instinctive offender may combine in himself the attributes of both, or all, without being specifically classified under either — a sort of "jack of all crimes," as frequently happens. Indeed, to discriminate between criminal and non-criminal men is often as delicate a task as to determine between a criminal and non-criminal *act* — the question of time and opportunity, self-control, and even the trivial fact of accident being sufficient, at times, to determine superficially the concrete character of both the act and the actor. While motive sounds the legal, and freedom the moral, tenor, an undefinable territory indicates where lines of conduct intermingle and distinctions vanish, or become vague and compromising, in a just discrimination of character.

Criminal classification has been essayed upon various grounds. Topinard suggests a segregation along the special professional lines of the subject, as artist, mechanic, the professional, the laboring man, and the literary classes, a distinction without particular force, inasmuch as the incentive or sub-relation of the particular employment with distinct forms of wrong-doing is enigmatical, obscure both in origin and fact. Distinctions are also formed on the basis of neurosis, as the insane, epileptics, kleptomaniacs, pyromaniacs, necrophyles, alcoholics, etc., whose criminalistic tendencies are fanned by degenerative nerve functions, sometimes betraying themselves through anatomical and cerebral anomalies by development, accident, birth, etc.

Dr. Laurent submits three categories, to correspond to cranial conformation, — frontal, parietal, and occipital, viz.: (1) Criminals of thought, or insane criminals, arising from the superiority of the frontal, as the seat of intelligence; (2) Criminals by impulsion, allied with parietal stratum, where he somewhat arbitrarily (as yet) assumes to localize the functions of activity and character; and (3) the criminal by instinct, or real offender, associated with the instincts. Thus, in connection with the now generally accepted theory of brain localization (though disavowing the same), he unwittingly associates the normal sense, an assumption which is not by any means clear.[1]

[1] "Les Habitués des prisons de Paris," Dr. E. Laurent, Paris, 1890.

The classifications of M. Joly, Lacassagne, Badeck, and Marro rest upon purely descriptive criteria of the organic or physiological characters of criminals; Liszt and Mendeun, upon the curative and defensive influences of punishment; Töhring and Starke, upon certain judicial points of view, as recidivation, or a tendency thereto, which is chiefly effective in conjunction with judicial and penological prevention. The judicial subdivisions of the criminal group adjust themselves naturally into grooves worn in the course of time by civil procedure with reference to purely legal forms, regardless of causal relations. Stephen, in his "Digest of the Criminal Law of England," defines the crimes known to the law under which the offender might, without violence, take his stand: (1) offences against public tranquillity; (2) the obstruction or corruption of public authority; (3) offences against public morals; (4) offences against the persons of individuals, and the rights annexed to their persons; (5) offences against the property of individuals and rights connected with property. It would not be far-fetched to associate the criminal of passion with the first, and Ferri's political offender (so called), with the second group; the third would readily comprise the criminal by occasion, while the instinctive and the habitual recalcitrant might share the remaining two divisions respectively.

In the hands of the scientist and criminological experimentalist, the categorical ideal slowly assumes more tangible proportions. Under their inspiration, Professor Tyndale arrayed these unclassified elements for the first time into three fundamental groups that come with

any degree of accuracy near the true criminal conception in its more concrete forms; viz.: the criminal
by occasion (accident) but of essentially sound morals;
criminals of the plastic type, that is, such as can be
readily moulded through predisposing influences or external circumstances; and lastly, the incorrigible, whose
mental and moral attitude is one of fixity, answering
generically to the latter assumption of type, under ultra-
scientific theories.

Taking these as the starting-points and germs of
the newer generalization of the experimental school,
subsequently broadened and summarized into the five
categories of Colajanni and Ferri, and now universally
adopted by the doctrinaires, they fall under the following five heads; viz.: (1) the Criminal Madman; (2) the
Born Criminal; (3) the Criminal by Contracted Habits;
(4) the Occasional Criminal; (5) the Criminal of Passion. Each separate category is self-explanatory to a
degree, but owing to the psychiatry involved, an arbitrary consonance of the forms here laid down with the
facts involved cannot be insisted upon, since the moral
elements blend to a more or less extent, hence any arbitrary attempt to confine them within the bounds of any
single category would, as in above instances, prove fatal
to the whole. They are hedged about with the difficulties
attached to all purely psychical and moral phenomena,
and already animadverted upon. The tools employed
for dissection are usually borrowed from the materialistic workshop, hence inapplicable to the task in hand.

The nature of the above categories, it is observable,
is etiological, grouping the several subjects about which

they centre with special reference to *origin*, and the causes that have operated to fix the criminal disposition. An accurate examination and comparison of the data involved fails to carry out altogether the theory at the instigation of which the above categories are formulated. It is observable at a glance that, separately, they present a hopeless interblending of causal relations that preclude the possibility of intelligent specialization. The Criminal of Passion, for instance, represents a varying quantity whose criminalistic manifestation cannot always be limited to its own special category. The isolated manifestation of nerve effervescence that relegates him to that particular sphere may be merely an incident in his real underlying criminosity. He may be really much more a deliberate offender than a neurotic, and in reality may prove as susceptible of classification upon some such basis as upon the other. The principle is capable of similar application indefinitely along other lines of esoteric wrong-doing.

The Criminal Madman, as we will hereafter show, belongs rather to the defective classes, and can have little place in a category of true moral delinquents. Ferri himself thinks the insane and the habitual criminal are oftentimes, in the biological and the anthropological sense, criminals born. Confounding the categories in this respect destroys the ensemble of each and the force of all. There can be no vicarious relation between the madman and the criminal in a true ethical sense, and the first category can hardly stand for more than a euphemism, or less than a contradiction. He *must* be either a criminal or a madman.

The Criminal by Occasion is a patent ambiguity. How many overt acts must suffice to establish the fact of criminality? If a single one, then he cannot be a criminal by occasion; if more than one, how many are requisite to transfer him from the role of the "*accidental*" to that of the "*habitual*" offender? What constitutes the dividing line between the latter and the congenital? Both the habitual and the instinctive criminal, as well as the criminal of passion, are in a sense genetical; but the offender by occasion ostensibly answers to no such sweeping designation, his disorder being symptomatic and impromptu, rather than organic, due, as we shall hereafter see, as much to social conditions as to any chronic inherent disorder of moral centres. His moral defalcation may traverse indiscriminately the border-line of either the neurotic, the criminal by passion, the homicide, or the merely social defalcant. His criminalism is incidental, not generic.

No formal distinction is made in the enumerations of the specialist, so far as I have been able to gather, of the strictly *single offender* under the categories, save under the various vague nomenclatures of the "Occasional Offender," the "Criminal by Occasion," etc.; though he represents by all odds the most numerous in the whole range of legal defaulters, and with reference to whom criminologists are generally agreed there is no distinguishing mark to differentiate him from the rest of mankind. To denominate him as the "criminal by occasion," does not cover the ground; is in fact misleading. To designate him as an "occasional offender," is to classify him fatally near, if not actually within, the grasp of the habitué. The question therefore is pertinent, How *many* repetitions of the act are necessary to constitute him an habitual offender, and how *few* will keep him within the pale of the " criminal by occasion " ? The majority of offenders, by far, are such by virtue of an isolated act, — a single offence, — and are thereafter possibly as free from the anti-social taint as the average man, among whom they are not always by any means the worst or even exceptional cases.

We have usually recognized the single offender as standing at the minimum of the criminological scale, as the antipode of the repeated offender — the " recidivist." I would know him simply as the " Single Offender " — a classification at once generic and accurate, and fairly descriptive of the unfortunate who, while perhaps no worse oftentimes than the generality of men, is compelled nevertheless most unfairly to carry the stigma usually associated with the professional class. This term will be employed throughout these pages to designate him in contradistinction from his more pronounced colleague. His personality will be more fully discussed in a chapter by itself.

The Political Criminal, mentioned by some of the schools, notably by Ferri, will hardly bear the designation, his effervescence being nothing more than an exaggerated form of partisan zeal which, to just the extent that it is leavened with the criminal leaven, must bear the opprobrium of that particular offence, and no more. They, by reason of such ambiguities, are manifestly entitled to no separate place in the categories but belong rather to that certain clinical form of mental alienation termed "mattoids" by Lombroso, and better designated as "cranks" in America. They sometimes infest the civil, literary, and religious walks of life, and are most active in seasons of political or psychical disturbance.

For all practical and scientific ends, a primal classification, therefore, of the criminal element under three general heads seems all sufficient, since such a division ostensibly combines more harmoniously both the genetic and concrete descriptions of the true criminalistic concepts, without the continuous overlapping so characteristic of the ultra refinements of the schools, that serve only to confuse the subject.

The criminal category, therefore, may properly be reduced to three general heads, preserving the outlines of the central figures in tolerably clear perspective for all purposes of practical and scientific illustration, thus reducing the embarrassment touched upon to their minimum while preserving all the essential features, viz. : —

I. The Instinctive Criminal.

II. The Habitual Criminal.

III. The Single Offender.

I. *The Instinctive Criminal* — with predisposing bent toward innate criminal wrong-doing, whose instinctive proclivities lead him preternaturally to immoral overt acts and into anti-social environment. His biological, moral, and intellectual equipments are the results of hereditary entailment from prenatal sources, mediate or immediate, and in varying degrees of modification and impressiveness. This class represents the instinctive congenital criminal proper, and is *sui generis*.

II. *The Habitual Criminal* — verging closely upon the instinctive offender in general description, differing from him chiefly in origin, possibly in degree rather than in kind, since he draws his inspirational forces from subsequent environment rather than parental fountains, though how far such postnatal tendencies may be implicated, genetically speaking, is a question that must remain unsolved. As a comparative moral quantity he stands as a compromise between the single offender on the one hand, and his more accentuated prototype on the other, into either of which he shades by imperceptible approaches through repeated acts of misconduct or the reverse, as the case may be.

III. *The Single Offender* — the legal defalcator and essentially social misdemeanant, accredited with a single isolated act of overt wrong-doing, is most frequently dis-associated with any serious antecedent immoral conduct or distinctive evidence of pregenital taint, but is often-est the impromptu exponent of vitiated tendencies or of his own sporadic impulsations. He may be an offender by passion, impulse, overt act against person or property, and makes up the largest class of misde-meanants. He is a criminal because the law declares it.

Lombroso's and Ferri's criminal of passion may well be eliminated from the catalogue, since he may readily be accounted for under other heads, belonging as he does to no particular active criminal sphere, but is rather the victim of spontaneous nerve explosion, and who, in the event of repeated acts (especially when associated with nerve lesion), may well be relegated over to the alienist and to the specialist as the victim of degenerative nerve function and deranged cerebral action, hence a *defective* rather than a delinquent, at least from the professional standpoint. The lines of demarcation between the normal and the abnormal, in this respect, are often hard to define, and present one of the chief difficulties to the scientific criminologist.

Recidivists by reason of pure passion are comparatively rare, as will be hereafter noticed, — a rareness that obviates the necessity of a special category for their preservation. Their digression, as may be surmised, is largely temperamental; while, of course, their association with any of the graver offences would properly serve to assign such more distinctively under the head of either the instinctive or habitual criminal, as the case may warrant, and as his revealed moral antecedents or essential character would seem to indicate.

CHAPTER IV

THE INSTINCTIVE CRIMINAL

Psychological

THE instinctive criminal is a sufficiently accentuated personality by reason of well-defined moral retrogressiveness and anti-social proclivities to entitle him to special consideration in the categories. He stands first and foremost, under the head of genera, as a distinctively moral anomaly; a being at variance with the innate instincts of humanity and in antagonism to the altruistic sentiment of mankind as evolved from primitive elements to ultimate expressions of benevolence and justice. The criminal is an anomaly in civilization, because he represents primitive conditions under modern forms and an instinctive savagery not yet eliminated in past racial evolution through the process of selection. He is an enemy to the elementary moral sentiment of humanity, and to its innate sense of self-preservation. Whatever difference of opinion may prevail as to his anthropological relations and origin, his self-revelation through the law of consciousness and the processes of experience presents the unmistakable evidences of his essential moral nature, which is not, like any mere physical insignia, subject to numerous ambiguities, but is self-evident.

The interpretation of the true criminal is a moral one; his self-revelation, like that of other men, is a simple unfoldment along channels of common experience, gauged by ordinary tests and impulsation. This is the only satisfactory approachment to the real man, whether normal or abnormal, and is the true test of his moral and social characterization.

The genuine criminal is a pronounced individuality by reason of his accentuated moral pathology and mental bias. We know him through his intellectual and ethical personality under the inspiration of premeditative conduct and instinctive acts. Underlying impulsations manifest themselves in many ways. It is not always the enormity of the offence that marks the true moral delinquent; though it is usually the outbursts of impromptu savagery that assign him his place *sui generis*. While it is undoubtedly true that the graver rather than the lesser offences more seriously violate public conscience and bring their perpetrators under general condemnation, nevertheless they do not thereby necessarily relegate such offenders to a more distinctively criminalistic rôle than their less pronounced colleagues, whose acts, though less forceful, are more diffusive, but thereby none the less dangerous.

It might be questioned, Which is the greater menace to society, that form of moral disease which makes its onset through slow persistency, or that which endangers by sudden shock? The bulk of the mischief on the whole seems to lie against the former, who may be said to be the greater enemy to society, inasmuch as we have him ever with us. To this class belong all that numerous hoard of petty offenders who, with feebler intellects and depleted vitality, ally themselves to instinctive vagabondage and bristle with a promiscuity of indifferent offences that render them a pest to society and a veritable thorn in the flesh. The petty habitué is as intrinsically a criminal as his more meteoric colleague, whose moral offshoot and feeble imitator he affects to be. He is the author of the bulk of offences charged against this class of moral and social perverts.

The sporadic criminal, however, is generally held to be the true moral anomaly and representative of his kind. Superficially, he may be known by the degree of spontaneity with which he commits the act, which is largely against the person, and not infrequently the finale of a career not particularly marked by any previous moral shortcomings. Overt acts without premeditation indicate the more instinctive criminal. It reveals the purely animal nature unmodified, and thus far traces the retrogressive shading successively through savagery into animalism,—the groundwork and basis of the true criminal characterization. He interprets the anti-social proclivity at its fountain-head and presents the best example of precipitation of allied primitive instincts into present environment.

True to historical antecedents, the existent criminalistic predilection of the instinctive offenders runs largely into homicidal tendencies, perhaps associated at times with crimes against property, and not infrequently allied with sexual pathology.

Subjectively, the premeditative criminal, whose conduct is incited by the more complex motives of civilization, is, on the other hand, less suggestive of primitive propensities than those whose actions imply pure impulse, since he finds his inspiration in more deliberative centres, which, being nearer the sources of moral responsibility, necessarily renders him the more culpable, if not always the more dangerous. However, the difference is rather quantitative than qualitative, their origin being the same.

The mental and moral evolution of the true criminal is potentially foreshadowed in the child, and in the savage. The psychology of the child is the psychology of the man plus the educative and repressive agencies that go in modification of innate tendencies. Education is the equivalent for selection in the ethical evolution. All repressive forces are merely substitutional. Arrested development is degeneration begun, and is in part explanation of the criminal phenomenon. The criminal is the child atrophied in the man, — racial retrogression exemplified in the individual.

Criminalistic precocity has a place in its dynamics. Incipient tendencies are here the prophetic germs of all subsequent moral fulfilment, and it may perhaps be not too much to say that the earliest manifestations of child life hold in embryo the future man. Innate instincts in rudimentary man always unfold themselves in analogous order. For instance, in the adult criminal we see reproduced all those ruling impulsations of the child heretofore referred to, its impulsiveness, its innate cruelty and destructiveness, the retaliatory and revengeful disposition, the tendency to truancy, natural mobility of character and emotions, the propensity for

lying, love of pleasure and display, vanity, impatience
of restraint, the proclivity toward theft incident to the
growth of the property instinct, and, above all, the
singular lack of foresight, and tendency to a purely
vegetative life, all of which attest to an arrested development when existing in the undeveloped man.
"The germs of crime," says Dr. MacDonald, "are
met with in a normal manner in infancy. A familiar
fact that if many embryonic forms should cease to
develop they would become monstrosities, so a child,
if it retained some characteristics, would either become
a criminal or a person with little moral sense." The
psychological evolution of man is apparently analogous
to his embryological metamorphosis, as where, in the
latter case, we see him pass alternately through all
the lower rudimentary stages, so in his moral psychological evolution he develops successively from the
animal, through the savage into the barbaric, and ultimately culminates in the highest form of civilized and
enlightened life. Thus, while on his physical side man
illustrates the doctrine of the survival of the fittest, on
his anti-social side, in this respect, he emphasizes the
survival of the *unfittest*, and is therefore a social
anomaly and a moral monstrosity cast upon the shores
of the present by the receding waves of past racial
retrogression.

The complete delineation of the criminal man, as to
his actual psychical and physical descriptions in detail,
is of the essence of the subject, and belongs to the province of the criminologist, as that of nature to the bota-
nist, or the domain of physical and racial life to that of

the naturalist and the ethnologist. As the studies and observations of the latter lay bare all the great abiding characteristics, and as they deduce their general conclusions and laws therefrom, so the observations of the anthropologist, psychologist, and criminal statistician have grouped together the salient features of these organic and moral anomalies, and out of these generalizations have given us the conventional criminal.

The Criminal — His Psychological Distinction

Moral Insensibility is the radical characteristic of the criminal degenerate. The distinction is vital, since it goes to the foundation of his mental and moral constitution in explanation of his true moral diathesis. While it may not be fully determined in what abnormality consists, the true criminal may be broadly defined as the persistent offender against the accredited moral sense of humanity expressed in its judicial functions. Aside from all refined distinctions, he is simply a being in revolt with his environment. This constitutes him, *a priori*, a deviation from the normal, and presents this grave anomaly of the moral sensibilities, the true functioning powers of the soul that hold the conscience to the dictates of probity and justice. So marked at times is this pronounced ethical defection, that the delinquent seems to be totally unable to discriminate correctly between right and wrong. The apparent unconcern in which criminals hold their offences, the manifest indignation with which they view their punishment, and the sincerity with which their every offence is condoned, all bear silent testimony to this moral anæsthesia. Where operative at all, it is feeble and eccentric, frequently at the dictates of caprice or of some form of self-interest or hypocrisy. His immorality becomes food for his vanity, and the grosser crimes but ideals for emulation. Great homicides and habitual offenders show inclination to exaggerate their offences, even to the extent, oftentimes, of assuming a vice where they have it not. They recount their unnatural deeds with apparent relish, and are able to look with equanimity upon the face of their victim, as in the case of Bellew, the fratricidal poisoner who soothed the dying moments of his brother and sister, and shed maudlin tears at the funeral. Murder, in the case of the instinctive homicide, incites to the sexual desire, both passions acting reflexively, as in the cases of " Jack the Ripper," and the " Demon of the Belfry " atrocities in San Francisco.

At the Elmira Institute, New York, where a thoroughly scientific anthropometric system prevails (and the inmates are felons), fully 75 per cent are reported (1897) as below the average in susceptibility to ordinary moral impulses; while out of a total of 8319, 3989, or 39 per cent, were positively non-susceptible to moral impressions; 3196, or 38.4 per cent, possibly some; 1759, or 21.2 per cent, were ordinarily susceptible ; and only about 375, or 4.5 per cent, were specially susceptible.

The moral paralysis may not always sweep the whole scale of active premeditative conduct, as, for instance, it not infrequently happens that the homicide is otherwise a man of ordinary probity, and the criminal of passion is oftentimes a person of average morality, even susceptible of keen remorse and finer impulses, — the cataclysm passed. The thief and the robber may prove true to certain ideals, as is frequently evidenced in their contempt for a certain class of offenders, and their scorn of particular vices.

Moral insensibility also explains the tendency, so universal among all criminals, to extenuate their offences. It is not, as generally supposed, so much an exhibition of insincerity or hypocrisy in the real criminal, but rather an expression of the low state of moral susceptibility, that causes him to minimize the wrong done to the level of a commonplace affair. It is a fundamental defect in the moral constitution of the offender that renders him impervious to a proper conception of the enormity of his deed.

Cruelty is psychologically associated with moral insensibility. It stands for the positive, as the former for the negative, side of the criminal temperament — the man in action at the call of opportunity. It is a well-known fact that the sight of blood arouses the latent thirst therefor, even in natures hitherto unsuspected of such sanguinary predisposition. History furnishes numerous instances of this trait. Savages drink blood before engaging in conflict. Mobs are incited to frenzy at the flow of blood, and crowds catch the infection, thus accounting for the barbarous lynchings so frequent, as well as the cruel excesses of vendetta and revolutionary bands, and the horrors of the Inquisition. The immunity from punishment that attends collective crime discovers the native passion, while the frenzy and unnecessary torture, as well as the uncontrollable impulse to a repetition of the first attack in almost all cases of homicidal acts on the part of criminals, amply testify to the innate cruelty that underlies the criminal character. It sometimes manifests itself in strong contrast, however, as where, in seasons of calm, unusually cruel murderers have been frequently known to evince marked tenderness and compassion for animal life, or otherwise in cases of suffering or of distress, etc.

A Lack of Remorse is the logical corollary to the above. It is cumulative, in explanation of criminal characterization. The same moral obtuseness that originally incites to criminality refuses to respond, the act once committed — the mainspring, conscience, being wanting. Such moral reaction would manifestly throw the whole character out of harmony and render it self-contradictory. *With it*, the criminal disposition could hardly exist. It accounts in part for the manifest sincerity with which capital offenders deny their guilt, and the equanimity with which they meet their doom, protesting their innocence, even in the face of apparently sincere religious profession. Leconaitre, the French criminal and assassin, declared on the scaffold that he had never known what remorse was. Of more than a score of executions witnessed by myself, not one subject has ever been known to give evidence of genuine remorse. "Oh, you are differently constituted," replied a youthful homicide, otherwise of fine organization, in answer to inquiry as to whether he felt any compunction of conscience for having taken a human life. "*Time*," rather than *crime*, troubles the average immured. Not one in a hundred evinces remorse for wrongs committed, or injuries perpetrated, conversing with apparent indifference upon the subject of their offences, while the graver crime of murder, to them, rarely rises out of the commonplace. The genuine criminal feels no remorse.

Lack of Foresight is among the most marked traits in the mental equipment of the average recalcitrant. He acts with all the native impulsiveness and natural confidence of a child. Cause and effect are rarely brought face to face. Prescience is not an attribute of his "prophetic soul." This peculiarity is due, analytically speaking, to a lack of the imaginative faculty of the mind. This wanting, and the subject is unable with any sense of clearness to precipitate himself into the future, or to forecast results with any realizing sense. Its existence as a mental attribute safeguards conduct by throwing out its warning rays upon the pathway of hidden danger. The ordinary criminal is radically defective in this essential, hence his recklessness and want of deliberation in wrong-doing. This quasi-ethical faculty might thus be termed, without violence, a sort of "false" conscience, with fear as its conserving factor. Its absence accounts for much of the overt wrong-doing of this class. It helps to account also in no small degree for the apparent unconcern with which the condemned faces futurity, the barrenness of the imaginative faculty failing to clothe the future and people it with attributes that, in the more richly endowed, cannot fail to "make cowards of us all."

Mental and Emotional Instability is a factor in his psychological equipment. He is easily moved in his tastes and affiliations, both intellectually and morally, ever looking for something new, and never long satisfied with existing conditions. His range of emotions and impulses, not broad, are ever upon the surface, waiting for the troubling of the waters. If he responds tentatively to the claims of society or morality, however sincerely, relapse is almost as certain. His resistant powers are impaired. He is constitutionally incompetent to give moral battle. In so far as the nervous system may be said to sustain a sensory relation to the emotional nature, experimentation through mechanical devices has been applied to test the state of the emotions under given conditions. For this purpose, the instrument known as " Plethysmograph," invented by Masso, has been employed to ascertain the state of the mental feelings from the arterial circulation. The sight of blood or of a weapon, or a suggestion, thus reveals the emotional state, and indirectly gives a clue to the moral impressionability of the subject received therefrom. The " Kymographion " is also used to register similar results by the movements of the chest, as indicated by certain wave lines registering the impressionability. Lombroso thought the strongest indications produced by them were by cowardice and vanity. The facilities afforded for deception and tricks on the part of the subject, who would be liable to be moved by a variety of motives, would seemingly render these appliances of doubtful utility; though Ferri thinks them a great aid in discovering guilt, and Dr. MacDonald has employed them to advantage in the case of Holmes.

Spasmodic outbreaks occur among criminals, individually and collectively. It is the logical sequence of this
inherent mobility of temperament. There is no regularity attendant upon the criminal manifestation, since
its moving causes are quite as much dependent upon
the variableness of social and economic conditions, as
upon its own psychical aberration. The power of suggestion, in this connection (and more particularly
referred to in another chapter), is well known, and
epidemics of crime under the inspiration of example,
through the agency of the public press and otherwise,
are well-ascertained phenomena. One or two suicides
of prominent persons, or perpetrated in a peculiar
manner, an atrocious murder or violation, leads to
fulsome emulation even to the verge of mania. These
nerve storms occur most frequently among youthful
offenders, and females at the menstrual periods.
Twenty in six hundred are subject to them, says an
authority. It is also observable among the defective
classes in asylums. Perhaps it may not be far removed
from certain epileptic tendencies, to which, in its outbreak, it presents certain neurotic relations.

Similar phases are familiar in all prison experiences,
where an explosion is periodically expected, and a calm
is usually looked upon as the precurser to a storm.
Cosmical conditions undoubtedly exert no small influence upon this neurotic and emotional class. Ferri
thinks the extremes of weather cause corresponding
diminution of violent assaults, homicides, and *vice
versa*. Lombroso finds them more sensitive to changes
of weather than ordinary men, and " more quarrelsome

in the spring." Out of 29 in Elmira, 9 became quarrelsome before storms. The general condition of the health, as well as of the nervous system, must have something to do with this condition.

Fidelity to "pals" (within the limitations of self-interest) seems to have a place in their character. The average criminal makes much of it, and a violation of its unwritten code is constructive heresy in the craft. Startling contradictions reveal themselves in depraved, as in ordinary, human nature, and instances of generosity and fidelity are here by no means rare.

Blushing, which might be termed nature's barometer of the sensibilities, is not a weakness of the criminal nature. Among 98 young offenders 44 per cent did not blush; and out of 122, 81 per cent did not respond. The same is observable among idiots and savages.

Untruthfulness is the one peculiarity common to all. Where, in ordinary natures, this feature is exceptional, here it is the general rule. The proclivity is simply the outcropping of the broken-up moral substratum that, in its integrity, forms the basis of the normal character. Whether instinctive or acquired, its growth is doubtless traceable in the unrepressed tendency of childhood, strengthened by defensive necessity, and gradually hardened into habit. The whole phenomenon is in strict accord with the balance of his nature. The true criminal character is consistent only in its inconsistency.

Vanity plays its role among his leading idiosyncrasies. He is felicitous in the possession of his mental and bodily equipments and qualifications; is proud of his sagacity, his prowess, his ability to avoid detection and effect escapes; all of which is self-complimentary. His petty accomplishments come in for their share of laudation. Great criminals are interested in great crimes, and seek to emulate them. They enjoy their notoriety, and pride themselves upon their success. Their vanity sustains them upon the scaffold; the desire to "die game" is a desideratum.

Caste displays itself in prison life upon this line. The pride of the homicide prompts him to ignore the thief; the highway robber despises the petty offender; and all together execrate the ravisher; while the forger and the embezzler congratulate themselves that "they are not as other men." Imaginary crimes are even conjured up from the vasty deep of a vitiated imagination to help fill up the cup of their iniquity, when not otherwise complete, and to satisfy their unnatural vanity. Holmes confessed to crimes he was not guilty of, and others have regretted their inability to realize their hideous ideal. This is the logical sequence of that moral insensibility already discussed, and of which it is but the active expression.

Sentiment, in its lower sense, is not wholly wanting, though crude and lustreless. Mottoes upon the walls, tattooing upon the body expressive of religious symbolism or of affection, as well as attempts at crude doggerel, exhaust their repertoire. They sometimes evince family affection, and love of animals and pets.

The Intelligence of the conventional criminal is of a low order, and verges rather upon the cunning of the savage, the simplicity of the child, and the instinctiveness of the animal. His mental grasp is narrow and feeble, and its range confined to immediate surroundings. His thoughts and groupings of ideas are illogical, as a rule; his knowledge is confined chiefly to passing events and desultory facts, with a superficial dabbling of historical and geographical data, the latter acquired usually through personal contact, for he is a great traveller. His philosophy is crude, running chiefly into quasi-political and socialistic themes, his arguments bristling with sophistry and half truths, and aimed chiefly against the rich, with a recklessness of prophecy and dogmatic felicity only equalled by his ignorance of fundamental principles. The sense of right being rudimentary, and intensely unipersonal, his legal notions are held together by the straw of self-interest, and nothing will provoke a sneer so quickly as the bare mention of concrete justice. Patriotism is not a spontaneous sentiment with him. How can he love a country whose laws have been so manifestly unjust? Both his literary tastes and attainments are extremely meagre, being chiefly confined to a limited familiarity with flashy novels and such as savor of the erotic and the sanguinary. History, poetry, and the higher fields of literature are wholly unexplored; though there have been exceptions among the more intelligent criminals, like Wainwright, Eugene Aram, the boy Pomeroy, and the New York murderer, Thorn, all omnivorous readers; and Rulof, who was profoundly versed in the Greek and Latin classics.

According to the United States Census Reports on Education and Crime, for 1890, the number of defectives in intelligence was given at 19 per cent; 33 per cent showed fair intelligence; 38 per cent were good; and 5 per cent showed excellent intelligence. The professional criminal's educational capacity and qualifications are deficient, though sometimes taking advantage of his incarceration to acquire the rudiments of an education. The youth of Elmira Institute, for the year 1897, showed an illiteracy of 18.3 per cent; simply reading and writing with difficulty, 43.3 per cent; ordinary common school, 35.2 per cent; and high school, 3.2 per cent. The report of the United States Bureau of Education, above mentioned, showed that 13 per cent, out of 27,103 criminals in the penitentiaries of the United States, could neither read nor write; 1 per cent claimed to have been in college, and 4 per cent in high schools or academies; 48 per cent in grammar school grades of public schools, and 20 per cent in private elementary schools. Of those discharged, 3 per cent were unable to read or write. Of the total 82,329 prisoners in the United States, at that time, 19,631, or 23.83 per cent, were illiterates, and 59,422, or 72.23 per cent, could read and write, inclusive of 25,019 colored persons, who comprise nearly 69 per cent of such illiterates. In Italy, 6.50 per cent of criminals have a superior education; in France, 6 per cent; in Austria, 3.6; and in Bavaria, 4 per cent. About 90 per cent of the English criminal population are able to read and write, leaving, perhaps, 10 per cent of illiterates. In her local prisons 25 per cent are illiterates and 72 per cent can read and write. The illiteracy in English prisons in 1887 is given by Mulhall at 31.4 per cent.[1] Of course those from business and professional ranks are usually better educated. It must be remembered, in this connection, that the above enumerated figures embrace all classes, both professional criminals and those by a single offence, a large number of the latter being presumably normal, — forgers, embezzlers, poisoners, and murderers ranking in education in the order named; 33.43 per cent of the latter being unable to read or write, by the last United States Census; the number of those who have received the higher education among this class being but 3.44 per cent. Thieves are usually ignorant. The burglar is more intelligent, with faculties better trained and more alert. Highway robbers are likewise a grade higher in general intelligence and courage. The latter is always expecting to make a stake and "quit."

Slang is the court language of criminals. Rich in tropes, and picturesque in rough metaphor, it constitutes the jargon of the rank and file. We are told the French criminal possesses 44 different terms in which to express drunkenness, 20 for acts of drinking water, 8 for wine, 72 in all; and 36 for money. Signs and hieroglyphics are employed in its signal corps, and are used mainly in predatory and prison life. The chirography peculiar to criminals, and mentioned by Lombroso, is without much force. Only experienced penmen impart their identity, to any degree, in their handwriting. That of the criminal is usually clumsy, and betokens little more than his immediate illiteracy.

Analgesia — insensibility to physical pain — is notice-

[1] Ed. 1892.

able in them more than among ordinary men. It is physio-psychological in its nature, and within its manifestation lies the mysterious boundary between nerve and psychic phenomena where incitation becomes sensation. "On his physical insensibility rests his moral insensibility," says Mr. Ellis; a position I would hardly wish to maintain, since its insistence would go the whole length of the materialistic hypothesis, which is untenable. The relation, however, is organic, and, like others in our complex being, is to a greater or lesser degree retroactive. It is undeniable that criminals on the average manifest greater obtusity to pain, and recover more readily from desperate wounds, than ordinary men. It is no uncommon thing for a prisoner to mutilate himself by inserting a member in the machinery; or to deliberately chop off a finger for the sake of avoiding some disagreeable task, or to obtain a coveted favor. Ramlot found, out of 27 normals and 103 criminals, obtusity in 20 per cent of the former and 44 per cent of the latter. Their resistant and recuperative powers are doubtless hardened by rough outdoor contact, as farmers and day-laborers, who likewise become indifferent to pain. Females, notwithstanding their finer organization, are known to endure pain with much more fortitude than men; and while savages are apparently impervious thereto, the more effeminate Hindoo is equally so, enduring the most appalling suffering with equanimity. Lombroso says suicides from physical pain and want are greater among men than women, and "females stand misery better."[1]

[1] "The Female Offender," p. 271.

Dr. MacDonald has made some interesting experiments upon the functions of the nervous system with reference to the more exact determination of disturbances of motion and measurement of pain. In his early experiments on 1412 persons, he found that females are more sensitive to pain than men; that American professional men are more sensitive than American business men; that the laboring classes are much less sensitive than the non-laboring classes; that women of the poorer classes are less sensitive to pain than those in more comfortable circumstances; that the wealthier classes, in general, are more sensitive than the poorer classes, and that the left hand is more sensitive to pain than the right. His experiments with the "Temple Algometre" comprised 899 persons, confirming largely his former conclusions with the additional fact that the sensibility to pain decreases as age increases, with general variations in the different ages among the youthful classes.[1] Professor Lombroso, however, seems to have come to opposite conclusions by similar experiments with the "Electro-algometre," by which he ascertained that woman is inferior to man in the matter of general insensibility to pain, a position in which he seems to have been sustained by eminent physicians in Europe.[2] And yet, what that eminent authority has called inferior sensibility may not be so much a lack of sense perception as quick responsive reflex nerve action to sustain and rally from the first shock of pain.

The *sensorium* of criminals presents much like con-

[1] *Boston Medical and Surgical Journal,* February 9, 1899.
[2] *Fortnightly Review,* March, 1892, p. 356.

tradictory data for speculation. Lombroso affirms, in his work last quoted, that only 3 in 15 of born criminals possess normal vision; hearing normal in 86.68 per cent in thieves, and 54 per cent in homicides. Smell was three times duller in criminals (6 per cent) than in normals (2 per cent). Taste in 50 per cent of normals and 15 per cent of criminals showed delicacy. Touch was greater among criminals than among normals. Bono found the vision of 49 per cent criminals superior in comparison with an equal number of normals; Brekaloff found them inferior. Ottolenghi found color blindness very rare among them; Dr. Bono says it is frequent. Biliaker discovered 50 per cent of murderers color-blind. Dr. Gradinger ascertained 72 per cent defective in hearing, and among females 53 per cent.

Religion, in its relation to the pronounced criminal, is among the incongruous anomalies that go to make up his peculiar psychological endowment. Crime and religion stand for his moral antithesis, and are not infrequently found blended in him in glaring contradiction. Rev. I. W. Horsley states that out of 28,351 prisoners in English jails and prisons, only 57 described themselves as atheists. Lombroso records that 61 per cent of the violators, and 56 per cent of assassins, frequent churches; and of 500 criminals and 100 normals, in Italy, 46 per cent of the former were regular attendants at church, and 57 per cent of the latter; 38 per cent of the former were absentees, and 29 per cent of the latter; 25 per cent of the criminals were irregular, and 13 per cent of normals.

Among Italian murderers, M. Ferri found none irreligious; and Garofalo says of Naples, the most religious city in Europe, that "no other city can boast of such frequent processions, no other is perhaps so zealous an observer of the practices of the church." But unfortunately as illustrious an historian (Sismondi), speaking of the Italians of that day, wrote that the murderer, still stained with the blood he has just shed, devoutly fasts even while he is meditating a fresh assassination; the prostitute places the image of the Virgin near the bed and devoutly recites the rosary before it; the priest, convicted of perjury, is never inadvertently guilty of drinking a glass of water before mass. "These words," Garofalo adds, "are true to-day as when they were written." A notorious criminal of Milan, also cited in Dr. MacDonald's work, who was guilty of 34 murders, attended mass every day and preached Christian morality continually. Another stole to found a chapel, and a strangler gave his mistress absolution *in articulo mortis;* then sold the proceeds of his theft to have mass said.[1] "It was the good God who placed her in my path," exclaimed Luccheni, the wretched assassin of the Austrian Empress, as she sank beneath his cruel weapon.

The philosophy of crime and religion is not far to seek. Dr. Wines gives us the key, when he divides the religious type into four heads, viz., Theological, Ritualistic, Emotional, and Humanitarian, and very properly groups the equi-balanced religionist under a union of the four, and makes the test of religious abnormity to con-

[1] "Criminology," p. 98.

sist in a preponderancy of any one of these at the expense of the balance. Omitting the theological, which represents the intellectual; and the humanitarian, which stands for the moral; and the instinctive criminal's religious affinities have a tendency to associate themselves with either one of the remaining two; *i.e.*, he is liable either to become an emotional or a mechanical devotee; and as the natural tendency of either being not to make much of the essentials, religion leaves him largely where it finds him. There are, of course, remarkable exceptions to this rule. The writer recalls the instance of one who, though up to a certain period had been seven times the habitué of the prison, has been for many years a true and faithful Christian man, and a useful and law-abiding member of society. Jerry McAuley was both an instinctive and habitual criminal up to the period of his remarkable conversion and change of life. The generic explanation of the origin of the religious phenomenon above presented, is simple enough. The germs of the religious and criminalistic instincts of man belong to his original nature. Their explanations are theological, and are entirely in consonance with facts. As far back as human history extends we find them associated in his organic constitution. The most ancient historic document reveals them side by side, — the religious instinct and original sin, — prime factors in the earliest recorded human tragedy. The first juridic homicide sprang into savage prospective under the protest of the primitive religious instinct.

The religious prison statistics of the United States

Bureau of Education and Crime, for 1891, give us a nominal ratio of 42 per cent Catholics; 33 per cent Protestants; 0.8 per cent Jews; and 16 per cent of "no faith." About the same relative proportion exists throughout the various prisons of the land.

As to actual accredited church relation, the average prison record is misleading. It is not by any means to be presumed that all those "giving themselves in" as "Protestants," or "Catholics," etc., are, or ever have been, thereby necessarily actual members of such organizations. Misconception, desire to palliate offences or to curry favors, usually account for the above fact. Careful inquiry convinces me that, so far as nominal Protestant prisoners are concerned (to which class my inquiry has been more particularly directed), not one-half of one per cent of the total prison population held actual membership in good standing with any Protestant Evangelical church at the time of committal to prison ; and as to the habitual criminal, or recidivist, I have never known such an instance.

CHAPTER V

THE INSTINCTIVE CRIMINAL

Physiological

CRIMINOLOGICAL literature abounds in descriptions of the physiological and anatomical side of the true moral delinquent; indeed, the bent of present scientific inquiry seems mainly directed along the familiar lines of his bio-physiological genetics and external configuration.

The illustrious man who honors me with an introductory to this work, in apologizing to the assaults of his critics for the meagreness of his descriptive details along the spiritual lines of the subject, assigns as a reason that he "deemed it unnecessary to prove that the sun shines." But by *that* light alone is the recalcitrant revealed on the anomalous side of his moral delinquency, all other indicia being but indirect, and hence liable to lead astray. And yet it is also true that its very uncertainties entitle it to an abundant hearing, and as lending to the physiological side the burden of proof. I will briefly follow out the example set by its chief exponents along well-known paths, in the following pages of this chapter.

The physiological inquiry enters upon an important and interesting field of investigation, the scientific import of which has already been sufficiently outlined in the preceding pages; and it remains for us to take up the thread of inquiry in parallel order and thus obtain a more nearly perfect understanding of the man as he stands revealed in the completeness of his objective and subjective anomalies.

The stereotyped criminal has already been sufficiently described by the master hand of the chief delineator of the Italian school; it remains for the pupil, who would take up the task, to analyze and fill in the details until they reach the proportions of a symmetrical and synthetic whole.

Cranial Asymmetry may be said to stand first and foremost in the order of physical investigation as characterizing the anatomical structure of the ideal criminal. Cranial configuration is held by mental physiologists to be largely indicative of a corresponding state of cerebral development and conformation. The shape and capacity of the skull depend upon cerebral growth. The organ gives rise to the function, the function in turn reacting upon the organism, together shape the cortex. Osteological malformations due to fœtal or other causes are exceptional, and are said to affect the relative development of the cranial content or its functioning capacity but little. That cranial capacity and cerebral activity are indications of intelligence is shown to a certain extent by a comparison of the cephalic variations of the different races, taken in connection with brain weight, facial index, and lower maxillary. Whether this cerebral superiority is due to civilization, or is in itself the cause that renders some races more susceptible of cultivation than others, is a

question. The following table, gathered from various
sources, serves to illustrate these ethnic distinctions : —

TABLE I

RACES	CEPHALIC INDEX	SIZE OF SKULL (cu.in.)	MEAN CAPACITY	WEIGHT OF BRAIN (oz.)	FACIAL ANGLES (degrees)	JAW
Caucasian	Mesocephalic. 79.9	* 87	* 90–6	* 49.50	† 80°	Orthognathic
Oceanic	Pure Dolichocephalic. 72⁻	85	83	46.5	§ 74°	Prognathic
Esquimau	Pure Dolichocephalic. 71	87	83		76°	Prognathic
African	Pure Dolichocephalic. 77.7⁻	83	83	45.6	70°	Prognathic
Mongolian (Tartar)	Pure Brachycephalic. 88+	82	82		75°	Orthognathic
Indian (American)	Sub-Brachycephalic. § 80+	79	84		§ 73°	
Gorilla	Brachycephalic			20	61°	Prognathic
Minimum			30	30.32		
Maximum				64		
Idiots (10)	Microcephalic			34	47.5°	
‡ Mean	Mesocephalic	78				

* Dr. Morton.   † Camper.   ‡ Broca.   § Smithsonian Institute.

The size of the cranium is to some extent modified
by environment. Retzius asserts that the skulls of
town and country people in Sweden differ in size owing
to different modes of life ; and Wilson states that

those of ancient barbarian Scots were smaller than those of modern civilized peoples. Even the testimony of missions in South Africa, according to Bruce, in his " Races of the Old World,"[1] is that in the third generation the shapes of the heads of the children begin to change. That the size of the cranium appears to have altered through the process of civilization seems to be indicated from the skulls of the Middle Ages, taken out of the tombs, 125 of which gave mean capacity of 84.777 cubic inches, comparing them with those of the eighth century, which gave 86.901 cubic inches. A. de Quatrefages, however, thinks that, notwithstanding these facts, but slight differences exist between the crania of the oldest peoples and the moderns, and that the " troglodytes of the *Caverne de l'Homme-Mort* would be superior to all races enumerated in the table (M. Topinard's) including contemporary Parisians " ; and concludes that " there can be no real relation between the dimensions of the cranial capacity and social development," and " the fact which already clearly results from the comparison of different races, namely, that the development of the intellectual faculties of man is, to a great extent, independent of the capacity of the cranium and the volume of the brain." The latter has even shown from Morton's table that the Creole negroes of America fall below the African negroes in the lesser development of the cranial capacity, though far more intelligent, showing that intelligence may increase while cranial capacity diminishes.[2] That the cranium develops independently of the brain contents seems to be

[1] p. 478.   [2] "The Human Species," pp. 381–384.

indicated to some extent in the fact that certain idiots possess large (long-headed) cranial structures with but slight brain mass.

Among the great collection of aborigines' skulls in the Smithsonian Institute, Washington, tabulated and averaged by myself (manuscript on file in Leland Stanford Jr. University), I find out of a total of 143 Mound Builders (16 different tribes), an average head length of 172.21 millimetres, and head breadth of 142.85 millimetres, with a circumference of 500.21 millimetres, a zygomatic breadth of 136.62 millimetres, and a facial angle of 75.12°; and 343 crania comprising Apaches, Sioux, Californians, and Pawnees, etc., gave an average of 177.26 millimetres in head length, 143.24 millimetres in head breadth, 509.65 millimetres in circumference, with a zygomatic width of 136.03 millimetres, and a facial angle of 72.76°; figures that may be of interest in making comparisons hereafter as between the crania of civilized and primitive man and those of criminals divided into special classes.[1]

The capacity and circumference of the average criminal skull is smaller than that of ordinary men, according to the positive school of experts. Lombroso found that crania of small volume exceed, and those of very large fall below, in this class; while the weight of the cranium itself is greater in them, indicating a commensurately larger bony structure. Dr. Baer, in his "Criminal Anthropological Relations," after a careful study of the criminal cranium, reaches diametrically opposite conclusions from the eminent Italian, and de-

[1] Tables I, II, III.

clares he finds that the capacity of the skulls of criminals does not materially differ from those of normals. He concludes that the " criminal skull does not show anything specific; the anomalies are mostly pathological ones, and the so-called atavisms are safe and exist also otherwise." Ranke considers their cranial capacity equal to other men's, with the difference in the minimum and maximum, as applying to assassins; and Berdier finds in the latter a superiority to normals. The cranial capacity of thieves is said to be less than that of murderers.

The architectural form of the cranium is perhaps to a large extent a racial peculiarity. The positivist school employs it in confirmation of criminal type.

The " Cephalic Index " supplies the standard of comparison in the study of cranial anthropometry.

The criteria of cranial configuration is obtained by comparing length with breadth, on the scale of Retzius and Broca. The following figures, indicated by the letters A, A, A, showing vertex of the skull as viewed from above, will more fully illustrate the method of obtaining cephalic measurements.

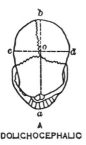
A
DOLICHOCEPHALIC

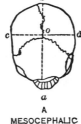
A
MESOCEPHALIC
CEPHALIC INDICES

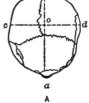
A
BRACHYCEPHALIC

Let o represent the bregma of the cranium; a the frontal; b the occiput; and c, d the parietal regions. A line drawn from a to b represents the longitudinal antero-posterior diameter, while the distance between $c\ d$ at the widest portion will give the transverse diameter. Taking 100 as the longitudinal base line, and 80 for mean breadth, the variations of the latter give us the several cranial subdivisions into *Dolichocephalic* (long heads); the *Brachycephalic* (round heads); and a compromise between the two, the *Mesocephalic*, or medium head.

The following scale, formulated on Broca's plan, will better illustrate the method employed in estimating the Cephalic Index, the proportion being found, of course, by dividing the breadth by the length in millimetres.

CEPHALIC INDEX

(Broca's plan)

DOLICHOCEPHALIC, smaller than 77.7,	*a.* Pure Dolichocephalic, less than 75.
	b. Sub-Dolichocephalic, ranging from 75–77.7.
MESOCEPHALIC,	Ranging from 77.7–79.9.
BRACHYCEPHALIC, from 80–90,	*a.* Sub-Brachycephalic, ranging from 80–84.
	b. Pure Brachycephalic, 85 and beyond.

The average length of the British skull is a little over 7 inches; its breadth, 5 inches; its height from the plane of the foramen magnum to vertex, about 5 inches; its greatest circumference, 21 inches; and its average capacity in males, 92 cubic inches — the same being usually obtained by filling the skull with sand or shot.

The cranial capacity of man ranging from 1000 cubic centimetres to 1800 cubic centimetres, for convenience of classification the calvaria are grouped according to their relative capacities. Thus all beneath 1350 cubic centimetres are termed microcephalic, those between 1350 and 1450 cubic centimetres are mesocephalic, and those of 1450 cubic centimetres and over are megacephalic. The European races fall under the latter head.

The brachycephalic head is usually designated as predominating among criminals; although Lombroso more properly cites it as an indication of a tendency to exaggerate ethnic indices. Others attach little value to the shape of the skull, even as a mark of race distinction. Thus Dr. Meigs is quoted[1] as giving his conclusion from the observation of 1125 human crania, "There is a marked tendency of these forms to graduate into one another more or less insensibly; none of these forms can be said to belong exclusively to any race or tribe." Professor Huxley, in comparing the Engis and Neanderthal, and a number of skulls with English crania, comes to about the same conclusion, viz., that "cranial measurements alone afford no safe indication of race."

The cephalic index in revelation of criminalistic anthropological tendencies gave, out of 394 thieves, 74 dolichocephali, 129 mesocephali, and 191 brachycephali; of 106 homicides, 21 were dolichocephali, 31 mesocephali, and 54 brachycephali; of 92 sexual offenders, there were 18 dolichocephali, 30 mesocephali, and 38 brachycephali; of 54 swindlers, there were 19 dolichocephali, 15 mesocephali, and 30 brachycephali. Lom-

[1] "Prehistoric Man," p. 245.

broso's table gives also 7.5 per cent oxycephali heads
(sugar loaf) to criminals, and 2 per cent as against the
same of normals. The same authority also found 13.5
per cent of this class among female offenders, 26.9 per
cent among prostitutes, and 22.9 per cent among murderers. Dr. Von Hölder attributes the increased height
of cranial structure that characterizes this class to the
contemporaneous premature closing of sutures at the
expense of width, and in the same manner accounts for
the retreating forehead and projection of orbital arches
(superciliary ridges), by the premature closing of the
frontal sutures. As osseous development varies with
age, this may be true, as it has been shown that in
infants the particular cranial development period is
occipital; in the child, temporal; and in the adult,
frontal. The fact that, while in childhood the negro
is precocious and intelligent, but his maturer years do
not fulfil the promises of youth, has been held accountable for this premature closing of the coronal sutures.
The same may be true in many cases of idiocy.
Quatrefages attached more importance to the anterior
parietal angles formed on both sides of the skull by
two lines tangential to the most prominent point of
the zygomatic arch, and to the fronto-parietal suture.
By taking the most prominent point of the parietal
eminence as the second extremity, he obtained the
posterior parietal angle, to which the term "pyramidal
(Prichard) skull" has been applied, and which the
above named authority held to be not incompatible
with great intelligence and genius. Topinard found
in New Caledonians the most pyramidal heads. The

negative parietal angle is regarded as the result of a cessation of development. Benedikt considered it an evidence of a defective organization. The most pronounced criminals not unfrequently come under this class. However, as has been justly observed, a close comparison of the tables of M. Pruner Bey, M. Broca, Morton, and others, relative to cephalic, facial, and other variational indices, cannot but strengthen the conclusion that these anthropometric variations so overlap and intercross one another as to lose much of their individual, and even racial, significance, taken specifically.

For our purpose, a summary of head measurements of five special classes of criminals (697), compiled by myself from the Bertillon system, furnishes the following table : —

TABLE II

No. Crime	Cephalic Measurements				Cephalic Index	Stature Height	
	Head Length		Head Width				
	Metric	Continental	Metric	Continental		Metric	Continental
44 Murderers (26 executed)	182 mm.	7.16 in.	152 mm.	5.98 in.	83.51	1686 mm.	66.4 in.
33 Erotics . . .	191 mm.	7.51 in.	151 mm.	5.94 in.	79.05	1695 mm.	66.7 in.
120 Robbers . .	190 mm.	7.48 in.	153 mm.	6.02 in.	80.52	1709 mm.	67.2 in.
250 Recidivists (pronounced criminals) .	189 mm.	7.44 in.	152 mm.	5.98 in.	80.42	1712 mm.	67.4 in.
250 Single offenders (normals)	190 mm.	7.48 in.	153 mm.	6.02 in.	80.52	1669 mm.	65.7 in.

The above table would thus seem to indicate that where the head of the murderer is considerably shorter than that of the other classes, its width is within one millimetre as broad as those of robbers and single offenders (the broadest) and equal to that of recidivists; while his cephalic index is the largest by a fraction over 3.

A compilation of average measurements of two thousand white male adult convicts, under the Bertillon system of measurements, made by myself, and a similar one completed by the Director of Physical Instruction and Sanitary Inspector of the Elmira Institute, of an equal number of white male reformatory inmates, kindly submitted for these pages, together with Dr. Hitchcock's summary of measurements of Amherst College students (about the same age with the latter), furnish us the following table as a basis of comparison, to which reference may be had hereafter : —

TABLE III *

	College Students, Amherst College		2000 Inmates, Elmira Reformatory		2000 Prisoners, San Quentin, Cal.	
	Metric	Continental	Metric	Continental	Metric	Continental
	mm.	in.	mm.	in.	mm.	in.
Stature height . .	1726	67.9	1694	66.7	1696	66.8
Outstretched arms .	1794	70.6	1740	68.4	1767	69.6
Right ear length .			61	2.4	62.4	2.5
Left foot length . .	260	10.2	257	10.1	258	10.1
Middle finger length			116	4.5	115	4.3
Left finger length .			89	3.5	94	3.7
Left forearm . . .	449	17.7	454	17.8	462	18.2
Cephalic length . .	189	7.44	191	7.52	189	7.43
Cephalic width . .	154	6.1	151	5.9	151	5.9
Cephalic Index . .	81.48		79.00		79.84	

* 25.4 millimetres equal to 1 inch.

The measurements of the Amherst students were taken from the glabella to the occipital protuberance; those of the prison and reformatory inmates (Bertillon) from the root of the nose to the furthest projection of the occiput, making a difference between the two measurements of about 5 millimetres or .20 of an inch. The heads of the Elmira inmates show an excess of 7 millimetres or .28 of an inch in head width. The two groups of delinquents taken together give us 5.9 millimetres or .23 of an inch in excess of head length over the Amherst students, while the latter exceed the combined average of both delinquent classes in head width by 3 millimetres or .12 of an inch, the prison and reformatory classes separately presenting a remarkable unanimity in this respect, each group of 2000 yielding an average head width of precisely 151 millimetres or 5.94 inches. The Amherst students, it will be seen, thus present a cephalic index of 81.48 per cent, bringing them within the range of sub-brachycephali; while the Elmira inmates, with a cephalic index of 79.00, and the San Quentin prisoners, with a cephalic index of 79.84, hover over the dividing line between the dolichocephalic and mesocephalic.

The following table (p. 94) will more fully illustrate the variations between the cephalic measurements of the heads of Amherst students and the inmates of the Elmira Reformatory and the San Quentin prison.

The dolichocephalic form of cranium supposedly constitutes the lowest geological stratum of population in Europe, and which, according to latest authorities, was anciently distributed with great uniformity throughout Europe, as evidenced by the remains of the Neolithic

INSTITUTIONS	CEPHALIC LENGTH		CEPHALIC WIDTH	
	Metric	Continental	Metric	Continental
	189 mm.	7.44 in.		
	* 5 mm.	*.20 in.		
Amherst College	184 mm.	7.24 in.	154 mm.	6.06 in.
Elmira Reformatory	191 mm.	7.52 in.	151 mm.	5.94 in.
Amherst { Greater			3 mm.	.12 in.
Lesser	7 mm.	.28 in.		
	189 mm.	7.44 in.		
	* 5 mm.	*.20 in.		
Amherst College	184 mm.	7.24 in.	154 mm.	6.06 in.
San Quentin, Cal.	188.8 mm.	7.43 in.	151 mm.	5.94 in.
Amherst { Greater			3 mm.	.12 in.
Lesser	4.8 mm.	.19 in.		

INSTITUTIONS	CEPHALIC LENGTH		CEPHALIC WIDTH	
	Metric	Continental	Metric	Continental
Elmira Reformatory	191 mm.	7.52 in.	151 mm.	5.94 in.
San Quentin, Cal.	188.8 mm.	7.43 in.	151 mm.	5.94 in.
Elmira { Greater	2.2 mm.	.09 in.		
Lesser				
	189 mm.	7.44 in.		
	5 mm.	.20 in.		
Amherst	184 mm.	7.24 in.	154 mm.	6.06 in.
Average Elmira and				
San Quentin, Cal.	189.9 mm.	7.47 in.	151 mm.	5.94 in.
Amherst { Greater			3 mm.	0.12 in.
Lesser	5.9 mm.	.23 in.		

* Amherst measurements are from glabella to occiput ; Elmira's and San Quentin's (Bertillon), from the root of the nose, a difference of 5 mm.

Age, even when populated by the brachycephalic type. Dr. Herman Schaafhausen, honorary professor of the Anthropological Society of London, as expressed in his lecture, " On the Primitive Form of the Human Skull," delivered before the Archaic-Anthropological Congress of Paris, August, 1867, reaches similar conclusions, viz., that the dolichocephalic head may be held to be an imperfect and primitive form, because observations made during the growth of this skull have shown that its final increase in width is commensurate with the increase of intelligence, and thinks the Mongolian exception is explained in the fact that their head width lies mainly between the parietal protuberances, while the width in relation to mental capacity lies over the base of the cranium. Indeed, there is a whole series of facts which go to prove that a very pronounced dolichocephalic is a primary and less developed form of the human skull. We see its decrease with the progress of civilization, as Broca found, in the population of France. Similarly, the ancient German dolichocephalic has given way to the brachycephalic tendency, or more properly speaking, the mesocephalic or middling head, as shown by the observations of Welcker.[1] Ecker observed the same thing when comparing Alemannii with their descendants, whose skulls have diminished in length but increased in breadth.[2] Physiological and anatomical causes are doubtless somewhat responsible for these conditions, as Blumenbach has shown that spasmodic muscular contractions and exertions, as well as the

[1] *Anthropological Review*, London, January, 1870.
[2] " Crania Germanice," *Merid. Occid.*, Freib. i. p., 1865, p. 82.

premature closing of sphenoccipital sutures, and pressure of brain growth, causes the lateral sutures to remain open, thus expanding the skull and producing brachycephaly.[1] Professor Ripley holds substantially the same view, and finds that the broad-headed layer of population was not contemporary with the earliest stratum, but superimposed upon it geologically, and confined to but a small portion of Europe. This ethnological feature in Europe is thus seemingly secondary, the result of the crossing of the extreme primary types, probably resulting gradually through social evolutionary processes in a distinctively intermediary or mesocephalic type, — the ideal cranium and ultimate cephalic type of civilization. The study of the 889 crania of male aborigines in the Smithsonian Institute, already referred to (summary made by myself with reference to comparative head length and width of this number) representing in all 96 different tribes, gives an average head length of 174 millimetres, and a head width of 143 millimetres, presenting thus a cephalic index of 80.20, slightly above the dolichocephalic, which may be accounted for substantially upon the same hypothesis that Professor Ripley advances, of the possible ethnic invasion of Asiatic affinities for the subsequent partial occupation of Europe, in connection with the dolichocephalic (Africanoid) type,[2] the modern American Indian being doubtless preheralded by a still more ancient and dolichocephalic race, as is evidenced by existing types and the yielding up of the most ancient tumuli.

[1] *Anthropological Review*, London, October, 1868.
[2] *Popular Science Monthly*, January, 1898, p. 14.

The *Vertical Index*, an important factor in estimating the capacity of the skull, is the diameter from the base of the skull to the bregma from a back view (normal occipitalis). The length is about five inches in the average British cranium. Bordier considers it greater in criminals than in normals. Heger thought it less. Lombroso found no difference.

Cranial projections are emphasized in considering the anatomical description of crania in both normal and abnormal man. Frontal, posterior, and coronal configuration are usually held to be more or less determinative in varying degrees as to mental and moral qualifications and physical endowments. To ascertain their relative proportions, Broca's method of auricular angles is employed.

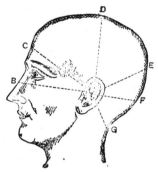

A represents the auricular (ear) centre of measurement, from which the lines of the angles diverge. *B* is the alveolar; *C* the suborbital; *D* the bregma; *E* the lambda; *F* the inion, and *G* the opisthion. The angle *ABC* represents the facial or nasal orbital angle, its slope being the facial angle, measured by degrees. *CAD* comprises the frontal region; *DAE* the parietal; *EAF* the occipital, and *FAG* the cerebellum.

According to Bordier, exaggeration of the parietal regions characterizes the largest number of criminals. Lombroso thinks there is no distinction here. Asymmetry of the frontal region has been made a distinguishing mark of the criminal head, Albrecht noting fifty-two per hundred anomalies of the frontal series. The retreating forehead was found in 28 cases out of 100, and Lombroso mentions 11 per cent among female criminals as against 8 per cent normals. He calls special attention, however, as more distinctively criminalistic, to the undue asymmetry of the median occipital fossa, caused by the thickening of the bones. The *Superciliary Ridges*, generally associated with the retreating forehead and producing the " beetling brow," are unduly developed among criminals, giving 15 per cent among the latter as against 8 per cent among normals. Dr. Marro, however, compared the foreheads of 539 delinquents with those of 100 ordinary men, and found a smaller percentage among them than among average men.

Anomalies of the Sutures are more common among criminals than among normal men. The presence of notched sutures are said to be frequent, and, as they are embryonic, they are suggestive. Premature growing together is noted, with effacement of parietal sutures. Von Hölder calls attention to the parietal closing of coronal sutures and resulting asymmetry, already noted ; Benedikt, to the bilateral elevation of the sagittal sutures, which he regards as " significant of profound perversity of brain function." An *Excess of Wormian* (floating) bones in the sutures is particularly remarked by leading experts as being characteristic of the craniums of delinquents. This is especially manifest in the regions of the median and lateral posterior, and fontanels. Dr. Corre and Lombroso found these anomalies to exist in 16 per cent in normals and 23 per cent in criminals. Out of 114 crania, Drs. F. Marimo and L. Gambara discovered 24 per cent with anomalies among normals and 71 per cent among prisoners.

Ferri, in his "Criminal Sociology," gives us the following as the result of cranial observations of homicides, which may be helpful: —

TABLE IV

Persons in whom Detected	Homicides Sentenced		Soldiers 711
	Penal Service 346	Imprisonment 363	
Number of anomalies of skull	11.9 %	8.2 %	37.2 %
One or two anomalies . . .	47.2 %	56.6 %	51.8 %
Three or four anomalies . .	33.9 %	32.6 %	11.0 %
Five or six anomalies . . .	6.7 %	2.3 %	0.0 %
Seven or eight anomalies . .	0.3 %	0.3 %	0.0 %

Criminal anomalies, according to Lombroso, are more manifest than cranial measurements, the difference, according to this authority, being so small between normal and abnormal beings as to be discoverable only to the most careful investigation. Female skulls, he holds, approximate more nearly to those of males, both criminal and normal, than to normal women, especially as to the lower jaw and occiput, which are more pronounced in the female offender.[1] Both Bishop and Topinard found the differences in weight between the two classes but little noteworthy. Manouvrier, who examined the

[1] "Female Offender," p. 28.

same series, declares he saw no difference. Heger, the Belgian expert, detected no difference from the skulls of the race to which the delinquent belongs, which accords with the theory heretofore advanced, that criminal type is but class distinction under patronage of race differentiation. Mr. Ellis holds that criminal and cerebral characteristic "is not so important as formerly, the average size is the same in normal and abnormal men "; and thinks, with some show of reason, that "both small and large heads are found in larger proportions among them." [1] Mr. Wines properly thinks that anthropometry is an aid to anatomical study only, and its importance slight.

The *Brain* is the chief seat of intelligence. The criminal brain has been the subject of much investigation and study among experts, with varying results as a whole, due no doubt, in a great measure, to the present imperfect state of knowledge relative to the physiology and anatomy of this important organ, as well as of its pathology and disease. Progress has been made within the last few years with reference to its functional relations, with due regard to concurrent nerve incitation, localization of brain functions, and kindred phenomena, which is only a preparation for a deeper insight and the precursor of more important discoveries into its physiological and pathological conditions. While it may serve to shed light upon the mysterious organic relation it sustains to mental and psychic phenomena, we can never hope to solve the mystery of the relation, or go beyond the obscure boundary line where the scal-

[1] "The Criminal," p. 50.

pel gives place to the metaphysical process, and the material fades into the spiritual. They stand in juxtaposition, and are mutually, though incidentally, correlated. To affirm more is hazardous. We can at the best but stand baffled before its mysteries. Every effort on the part of the scientist to hew a pathway for physical experimentation as the ultimate test of the psychological, has failed, and *must* fail, in the necessity of the case. The relation of the brain to the criminal problem sustains the same inscrutable relation, and in the same degree, as in the phenomena of ordinary life. The task of the anatomist and the criminologist has been directed toward the discovery of anomalies in differentiation of brain and cranial type in contradistinction from the normal, in explanation of criminal man, with perhaps less satisfactory results than in the more distinctively pathological lines of investigation. Few distinctive characteristics of importance, anatomical or otherwise, have been discovered in the brains of criminals who have been subject to the clinical test of the post-mortem, outside the fact of accident or lesion. Messieurs Lombroso, Benedikt, Bischoff, Manouvrier, Tenchini, Topinard, Drs. Corre, Lacassagne, Flesch, Baer, Von Holst, and many other eminent men have taken up the task at various points of observation, often with conflicting and rarely with either harmonious or satisfactory results.

Brain area is supposed to determine largely the measure of mental capacity. Nature economizes space in the form of convolutions and fissures of varying depths, in attaining this end. Thus, the size of the brain is determined by the number and depth of such convolutions. These have been shown to be decidedly less numerous and complicated in the savage than in the civilized and more intelligent races. The area of the brain, from a purely physiological point of view, is thus supposed to correspond with the degree of mental activity, and the organ of an educated person is presumed to be commensurately larger than that of an ignorant one, the same expanding with the development of the function ; and *vice versa ;* since, as we have seen, psychical activities are concurrent and retroactive. The brain of the Hottentot Venus, for instance, was found to be the simplest ever observed in an intelligent being ; while that of Cuvier was ascertained to be the most complicated and possessing the profoundest convolutions of any ever examined. The volume of gray matter, together with the minute white febrils thrown off from the under portion of these convolutions, gather into bands and finally pass out below in the form of nerves, and thence, ultimately joined to all the organs of sense in the periphery, form the registering mechanism that records sensation through the optic thalamus (the receiving central), transmitting thought and volition through the corpus striatum, the distributing office of the brain. It forms thus the chief physical organ and medium of communication of the mind, whose surface, quality, and density must all be considered conjointly in order to an intelligent comprehension of its relative efficiency as a corporeal agent of the thinking soul. Mere size itself is insufficient as an indicium of mental activity. The average weight of the brain of the adult European male is about 49.50 ounces; female 44.45 ounces (Wagner's tables give 1410.36 grammes — 49.74 ounces for males, and 1262 grammes — 44.48 ounces for females, between the thirtieth and fortieth years, up to sixty years of age, when it begins to diminish in weight — males to 45, and females to 41 ounces). Below 30 ounces (Wagner says 975 grammes — 34.39 ounces) it is incompatible with intellectual power. The Australian and African brain, the lowest among the races, averages from 42 to 45 ounces, though 141 negro brains examined by Mr. Sandford Hunt averaged 1331 grammes (46.98 ounces). Weight is not necessarily a criterion of intelligence. The brain of Cuvier weighed 1829.96 grammes (68.43 ounces), while that of common working-men were found by Bischoff to weigh from 1650 to 1925 grammes. The ordinary weight taken at 49 ounces (1350 grammes), that of idiots has been known to reach 62 ounces, and the brains of geniuses, abnormals, and defectives have been frequently known to exceed the normal in both cranial capacity and weight, owing doubtless to the chronic state of cerebral congestion incident upon its morbid activity. The weight of Webster's brain at seventy was 53.50 ounces (1520 grammes), and his cranial capacity and horizontal measurements very large; while that of Byron's brain though small, weighed 1807 grammes (63.73 ounces). Cromwell's brain weighed 2231 grammes (78.69 ounces), while Gambetta's, of equal mental activity, weighed but 40.9 ounces. The brains of Descartes and Dante were both sub-microcephalic, while those of a Chippewa squaw in the Smithsonian Institute ("1031. b.") weighs 73.5 ounces. Bischoff

found small-sized and medium brains about equally
common among both classes of the 137 criminals and
422 normal brains he examined, and the heavier ones
among the former were from 1400 to 1500 grammes
— above that of Liebig, and just below Webster's.
Benedikt, the eminent specialist in craniology of Vienna,
in his study on brains, gives us as a summary, in his
work on "Anatomical Studies upon Brains of Criminals," that "the brains of criminals exhibit a deviation
from the normal type, and criminals are to be viewed
as an anthropological variety of their species, at least
among the cultured races." He did not, however, appear
to have compared his researches among criminal brains
with an equal number of normals in the same line of investigation, which must materially weaken his conclusions. He emphasizes strongly the fact of the existence
of confluent (continuous) fissures in the brains of criminals, and also lays stress upon additional convolutions in
the frontal lobes in excess of those found in normal
persons. Broca adds his testimony to the fact of
confluent fissures, and maintained that, while not in-
consistent with intelligence, they were defective only
where too frequent. Benedikt discovered confluent
fissures among 19 criminal brains; though Tenchini,
who examined the brains of 32 criminals, did not. Dr.
Giacomini found as many anomalies among normals as
among abnormals. As to brain weight, Bischoff found
no striking differences between those of criminals (137),
and ordinary men (422), and Dr. Baer ascertained that
the brain volume of the born criminal does not exceed
that of others, and in 69.53 per cent cases the forepart

of the head was superior to the posterior. Topinard discovered an inferiority of some 30 grammes in criminals. Lelart rated them as below normals in weight. Veraglia and Silva ascertained the average weight of 42 brains of Italian female delinquents to be 1178 grammes; while Pfleger and Wechsel's results were 1189 grammes. In 120 normal women the maximum ascertained by Giacomini was 1530 grammes and the minimum 929 grammes.[1] The brain of Ruloff, the Rochester murderer, weighed 59 ounces, and his skull was the thickest on record. Hallam's, the congenital assassin executed in Illinois, weighed 52 ounces. Kavalev's, the Russian assassin and exile, executed at Folsom, Cal., weighed 50 ounces. Post-mortems, in France, give to the worse class of criminals 55 to 60 ounces.

Not infrequently one lobe is larger than the other. Thus, out of 42 homicides, 20 were found with the right side heavier, and 18 with the left; and in 4 others, equal (Giacomini). The large percentage of superior right lobes, it has been suggested, probably accounts for the greater number of left-handed and ambidextrous persons among criminals, as hereafter noted, as cerebral hemispheres control opposite sides.

On the whole, the question of cerebral anomalies as indicative of anomalous psychical conditions has not been sufficiently proven on scientific grounds to warrant any definite conclusions. It is as yet undemonstrated as to what constitutes a true normal brain. Indeed, Dr. Bardeleben, the eminent German specialist, affirms there is no such thing as a normal type of brain.

[1] "Female Delinquent," pp. 36–40.

Moreover, the matter of size and weight is largely a question of relativity, depending very much upon the age, weight, and *height* of the individual, all of which must be taken into consideration in order to institute intelligent comparison. Of the 964 brains examined by Rud. Wagner, it was ascertained that the weight of the same varied proportionately to the height of the individual. That defective brain organization and cranial asymmetry are oftentimes closely interrelated with moral and mental degeneration, is undeniable; but that a causal relation is thereby proven to exist between such organic degeneration and the criminal propensity, or that mental alienation and moral defection necessarily verge one upon the other, is a position that cannot be maintained, and few would venture to affirm. Cranial asymmetry, and brain lesion, have been associated with the best of men from Pericles to Dante, and from Kant to Descartes and Hugh Miller, the former of whom was ultrabrachycephalic, and the latter (Descartes) submicrocephalic.

Closely allied to the brain and its cortex, *Physiognomy* has long held a foremost place as guide to the moral content of both normal and abnormal man. From the earliest philosophers down to the modern physiognomist and phrenologist, facial expression and peculiarities have counted for much in aiding to form the consensus of opinion with reference to the *real* man. The positivist school cast the die upon a conventional order of physiognomical criminal type from joint facial and cranial indicia. For purposes of accurate analysis, various methods have been resorted to for a physiological basis of physical and psychical comparison in connection with facial and cranial anthropometry.

The *Facial Angle*, a term proposed by Camper, is a method usually employed to determine the relative superiority of the frontal over the posterior brain mass as determined by the variation of the angles. It is obtained by drawing two lines as represented in the figures *A*, *B*, below : —

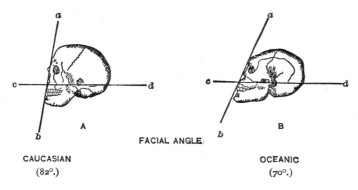

FACIAL ANGLE.

A
CAUCASIAN
(82°.)

B
OCEANIC
(70°.)

The line *ab* is drawn from the most prominent part of the forehead (glabella) to the front of the upper jaw. The line *cd* represents the base line of the brain, and runs from the orifice of the ear along on the floor of the cavity of the nose, the variation of the angle thus being regarded by Camper as the measure of the posterior brain mass (and consequently of intelligence) in a graduated scale from the Greek and Roman profile (100°–95°) to the white (80°) and yellow race (75°). This position has been called in question by other anthropologists, and to some extent disproved by pathological facts that go to show that angularities of 90°

have exhibited no undue intellectual superiority over the ordinary, while a difference of more than 16° has been shown to exist, by Quatrefages, between the educated whites of Paris, that is to say, 6° more than the distance established by Camper as separating the negro from the white.[1]

The *Facial Index* is the method usually employed to aid in estimating the maximum breadth (bi-zygomatic) of the *Face* as compared with its vertical length. It is obtained by multiplying by 100 the length of the face, and dividing it by the breadth. The breadth of the average normal face from one zygomatic process to the other is about 5 inches.

The *Nasal Index* gives the maximum breadth of the *Nose* in connection with its length. It is ascertained by multiplying the breadth of the nose at the opening of the nasal fossæ by 100 compared with the length from spine to naso-frontal articulation. M. Broca estimated the mean nasal index at 50.00. Its variation in races is comparatively small, being about 16.05, while among individuals it gives a maximum variation of 36.51. A comparative study of Dr. Corre's Table of Facial Characteristics gives a simple length of face, normal 87 millimetres as against 92 in criminals ; and a zygomatic width of 132.2 millimetres in normals, as against an average of 132.7 in criminals. It is larger in assassins (133.6), most voluminous in murderers considered with theft (135.0). In female criminals, Lombroso found 19.9 per cent, and 14 per cent in normals. The nasal indices in normals are less than those of crimi-

[1] "The Human Species," p. 394.

nals. The nose, generally rectilinear, large, and frequently crooked or malformed, with large wings and orifices, sometimes undulating and with uplifting base, is peculiar to them. Among habitual criminals, I found, upon examination, 44 per cent possessed noses deviating to one side or malformed; among thieves, 46 per cent crooked; among sexual offenders, 30 per cent, and among homicides, 42 per cent. Lombroso found 25 per cent crooked noses among female offenders, and 8 per cent among prostitutes; flat noses, 40 per cent in normals, 12 per cent in homicides, and 20 per cent in thieves. Malformations are doubtless largely due through accident, attributable to their wandering habits, drunken brawls, and general recklessness. But slight satisfactory results are derivable either from nasal or facial indices, for similar reasons as already stated with reference to facial indices and cranial capacity. M. Broca thinks the variation of nasal indices observed in the same races may often be referred to the arrest of development, or evolution.

The *Palatal Index* shows the relation of width to length of *Palatal Vault*. The table shows the difference between 74.7 millimetres in normals, and 81.5 millimetres in assassins. The absence of the palate is frequently observable in the feeble-minded. I do not think its absence is noticeable among criminals oftener than among ordinary men.

The *Criminal Jaw* is prognathic. Manouvrier gives the average weight of the lower jaw in Parisians at about 80 grammes, while he assigns to murderers about 94 grammes. Large jaws prevail in normals to the extent of 29 per cent; in criminals, 37 per cent. Ferri and Manouvrier also found a greater development of the lower jaws, and this fact was so noted by the earliest experts. Dr. Baer, in the work already quoted, found the breadth of the lower jaw in most criminals only medium. Among females, 15 per cent prognathism was found in offenders, 26 per cent in prostitutes, and 9 per cent in normals. Prognathism characterizes the Oceanic and African races. Quatrefages referred prognathism to atavism.

Lombroso notes the undeveloped form of *Teeth* in criminals, a fourth molar being peculiar to apes, and also found among criminals; though his table, as given hereafter, shares an asymmetry among normals of 6 per cent, and among criminals of but 1 per cent. The canine form of teeth is notable in assassins. The tables of Lombroso and Amadei (p. 111) may be of interest here, as illustrating the above asymmetries.

The *Criminal Ear*, its voluminous and projecting shape as a peculiarity in the criminal physiognomy, has been much dwelt upon by all writers and experts upon the subject. The latter feature doubtless receives its emphasis from its supposed similarity to the anthropoid ape and the several lower races, as well as to other animals, to which it bears analogy. Its size has been made to do duty alike for the just and the unjust as a revelation of both good and bad qualities. Lombroso found it prominent in 28 per cent of his criminals, and in 9.2 per cent among female degenerates, as against 6 per cent of normals. Marro did not think it more frequent among criminals than among normals; and Von Hölder makes the small ear a sign of degeneration.

TABLE V

TABLE OF ASYMMETRY (3000 CASES)

(Lombroso and Amadei)

	MALES		FEMALES			
	Normals %	Criminals %	Criminals %	Normals %	Savages %	Insane %
Plagycephalic heads	20	42	21	17.2		24
Cranial sclerosis	18	31	31	17.2	100	50
Sutures ("soudées")	25	37	26	13.3	8	28
Suture (metopique)	9	12	5	10	5.1	9
Wormian bones	28	59	46	20		68
Epactal bone	5	9	1.7	6.8	5.4	3.8
Fusion of Atlas with occipital bone	0.8	3	3.2			2.7
Middle occipital fossa	4.1	16	3.2	3.4	26	14
Hollow of Civini	27	15	8.1			
Receding forehead	18	36	6.8	10		
Frontal apophyses of temporal bone	1.5	3.4	6.6		12	2.3
Superc. ridges and developed sinuses	25	62	29	19	100	67
Anomalies of lower teeth	6	2	3.2	0.5	40	
Large jaws	29	37	25	6.5		
Very large jaws	4.5	10.6			100	
Traces of intermaxillary suture	52	24	3.3			
"Oxycephalic"	2	7.5	3.3			60
Double suborbitary fossa	6	18				
Subscapohcepalic	6	6				
Prognathism	34	34	32	10	100	
Projecting zygomaticapophyses	29	30	7.6	6.9		
Nasal Glabella much depressed	13	31				
Platycephalic	15	22	33	0.1		
Asymmetry of face	6	25				
Asymmetry of teeth	6	1				
Projection of temporal bones	27	43				
Frontal beak of coronal suture	2	9				
Depression of coronal glands	29	50				80
Wormian bone of pterion	16	23	3		66	18
Anomalies of occipital fossa	2.5	10	11.5			0.5
Feminality	15	6				
Virility			9.2			
Projection of orbital angle of frontal bone	15	46	7	6.9	100	

(From "Criminology," Dr. MacDonald.)

Dr. Lannois examined the ear of 43 young offenders, and found them as free from anomalies as those of others. Out of a given number from the following classes examined by myself, the percentage of asymmetries given were as follows: Among robbers, 42 per cent had large and projecting ears; among recidivists, 71 per cent; and 57 per cent projecting ears. Among homicides, 52 per cent had large and 32 per cent projecting ears. Out of 600 criminals and 200 normals, Ottolenghi found 20 per cent among the latter and 39 per cent among the former, with large ears. The ears of Thorn the New York murderer, Durrant (56 millimetres), and Holmes (60 millimetres) were all small and unsymmetrical, with lobules especially so. The Darwinian tubercle is most common to the criminal ear, also the absence of helix.

As to the *Hair*, an abundance in both male and female has been noted (the latter virile), and is given by Lombroso in 15 per cent of offenders, as against 5 to 6 per cent in normals. The texture is coarse, with tendency to curl in the cases of homicides. In color, the dark predominates in the proportion of 49 to 39 per cent among criminals and 33 per cent in normals, except as to sexual offenders, where the blond and curly prevail. There is no tendency to *turn gray* among criminals, except in case of swindlers. Lombroso found it in only 25 per cent of criminals, as against 62 per cent of normals; while among females, 60 per cent of honest women showed gray hair, against 45 per cent delinquents. *Baldness* is rare among them. It occurred in 2 per cent of thieves, 13 per cent of swindlers, and

19 per cent of normals. The *Eyebrows* are thick and close, especially in thieves. *Scantiness of Beard* exists in the male criminal, with a tendency to the contrary in females, and decidedly so in male sexual offenders. Marro gives 1.5 per cent cases of absence of beard among normals, 13.9 per cent among criminals.

The *Orbital Index*, for estimating the variations of the orbital opening, is usually considered to be large in criminals. Quatrefages thought them characteristic of primitive types, the yellow races, including the Chinese, presenting an arrest of evolution, and diminishing with the progress of evolution. It remains in all races greater in the woman than in the man. The Orbital Index is obtained by Broca by multiplying the vertical diameter of the orbit by 100, and dividing the product by the horizontal diameter. The three divisional groups range from 83 to 89, the highest mean index rising to 98.8. Its value as an indicium of either mental or moral qualifications, are open to the same strictures as heretofore. The *orbital capacity* is said to be greater among criminals than among ordinary men. Dr. Topinard gives 88.4 millimetres in criminals and 83.7 in normals. The writer has noted the marked orbital capacity in the most pronounced criminals.

The *Eyes* of the Habitual Criminal are usually small and uneasy; in the homicide cold, fixed, and nystagmus; in the sexual offender, generally light, and projecting in their orbits. I have noticed the congested state of the eyelids as peculiar to this latter class, noticeably in the case of certain pronounced sexual offenders and congenital homicides.

The *Arms* are sometimes longer in criminals than in normals, similarly as in the case of negroes. *Left-handedness* prevails among the former. Carriere found 33 per cent left-handed. Ottolenghi discovered in 100 criminals and 50 normals the right hand long in 14 per cent of the latter, and only 5 per cent among the former, and in none of the thieves and pickpockets. In 350 of the latter he found the left hand larger as compared with normals. The same peculiarity prevailed as to *fingers*. The hands of assassins are short and large; those of thieves, long and thin. In 58 cases the left *foot* was reported larger than the right, and in 12 cases both equal. In 54 instances the left arm was larger than the right.

Wrinkles, according to Ottolenghi and Lombroso, are more frequent in criminals than in normals. It has been ascertained that the former show them earlier in life than in case of the latter. In the examination of over 700 of each class, Lombroso observed that they occurred from two to five times more frequently in criminals. In persons under the age of 25, wrinkles of the forehead appeared in 7 per cent normals and 34 per cent criminals; the wrinkles from each side of the nose to the corners of the mouth appeared in 22 per cent among the former, and 69 per cent among the latter. Forehead wrinkles in those between 25 and 50 were present in 62 per cent of normals, and 86 per cent of criminals. He lays much stress upon the "*zygomatic wrinkle*" as a special identification of criminals; finding it in 75 out of every 100 faces in the " Rogue's Gallery," and 33 per cent of instances upon personal examination, as against 18 per cent of normals. This peculiarity has heretofore been made to do duty as a sign of good nature.

" *Tattooing* " has been made much of, as a special practice peculiar to criminals. Both Lombroso and Ferri take great pains to enter into elaborate tabulation in corroboration thereof, and all authors scrupulously refer to it. The former found it to prevail among delinquents to the extent of 26.2 per cent among male and only about 2.15 per cent among 1175 female offenders. Among 100 children in the reformatory at Turin, he found 40 per cent tattooed, and among 235 other juvenile delinquents, 32 per cent. Among 80 murderers, 20 per cent; 141 thieves, 14 per cent; 11 violators, 9 per cent, and 191 recidivists, 26.2 per cent, bore the indication. The habit is not peculiar to criminals, but is the mark of the wanderer and the idler the world over. It is fully as common among soldiers and sailors, on the whole. It usually takes the form of religious symbols, sentiment, initials for identification, etc. No special significance attaches to it.

The average *Height* of Criminals is claimed by Italian experts to exceed that of ordinary men; 67 inches being the mean stature of the Caucasian. I have not found it so. Two hundred and fifty pronounced criminals summarized by myself (Table II, p. 91) gave an average of 67.4 inches, with the maximum in favor of recidivists, and the minimum in favor of single offenders (normals). The 2000 criminals measured (Table III, p. 92) give an average of 66.8 inches (1696 millimetres) in the stature height of prisoners confined at San Quentin, and 66.7 inches (1694 millimetres) of the inmates at Elmira Institute. The Amherst student averages 67.9 inches (1726 millimetres), an excess of 1.2 inches over the Elmira youth of about the same age, and 1.1 inches above the more mature inmates of San Quentin. The average height of 318 Londoners was 66.72 inches (Dr. Beddoe); and 300 London criminals averaged 54.70 inches. Knecht says the German criminal presents no difference in this respect from ordinary men.

Average *Weight* is also considered greater among this class than among normals. The London criminal has been quoted as inferior in this respect to the average artisan population in large English towns, as a whole, the former being 136 pounds on the average, and the latter 138 pounds.

The *Health* and general vegetative functions of the criminal in general exceed the normal. The advantage he derives from incarceration (where his pathological conditions are more particularly revealed), through better care and systematic employment and living, is perhaps counterbalanced by vicious habits and secret vices contracted in prison life, the sense of confinement, and the prison atmosphere combined, all of which tend to break down the physical and mental organization prematurely. The United States Educational Bureau reported 82 per cent of its 27,103 prison population in 1891 as in good health; 11 per cent fair, and 6 per cent bad. Of the total number of prisoners, 88.99 per cent were in good health, and but 6.26 per cent were ill. By the Census of 1890, of the 97,175 inmates of both penal and reformatory institutions, 90.33 per cent were in good health, and 5.47 per cent were in ill health. In Elmira Institute, New York (1897), out of a grand total of 8319 inmates received, 91.5 per cent were in good condition, and but 3.3 per cent in ill state of health. The death-rate in English prisons is reckoned on the basis of 7.2 per 1000; and convict prisons, 10.6 per 1000, inclusive of alcoholics;[1] and among ordinary classes, from 1888 to 1889, 7 per 1000. In Italy, of 567 homicides and 143 thieves, respectively, 53 of the former and 19 of the latter were in delicate health. Prevailing diseases are tubercular and syphilitic, with jail fevers and heart-disease, the latter common among them. Flesch thought 20 per cent afflicted with it. The prison pallor is due to cerebral congestion incident upon cellular confinement. His *Muscular System* is said to be weak. His inability to long continued exertion and hard labor seems to bear it out. The *Osseous System* is represented as weak in thieves and strong in homicides and robbers. The habitual and instinctive criminal is rarely of suicidal inclination, but clings to life. He is seldom depressed, but rather given to hilarity. He is not *long lived*.

The total percentage of *insane* to the criminal population of the United States is about 1.77 per cent, and inclusive of reformatory institutions, 1.51 per cent or 150 per 10,000. The total number of insane in the United States, 1890, was 106,485, or 17 out of every 10,000 inhabitants. In Germany, about 2.07 per cent of her prison population were insane. In England, by

[1] Commissioners' Report for 1897.

the last prison report (1897), in table of convicted prisoners in custody on a given day, and length of time they had served in prison, the number of convicted prisoners in prison on such given day was 11,512, which shows a ratio of 37.3 cases of insanity per 10,000 of such prison population. During the year 1895, 18,251 of the general population over fifteen years were certified insane and admitted into lunatic asylums, giving a ratio of 9 per 10,000 of the general population. The fluctuation in prison is much greater, however, than that of the general population, which may change these figures somewhat.[1]

Lombroso points out an anthropological resemblance between *epileptics* and criminals, and Ferri refers to the fact that in Italy the districts that furnish the greatest quota of criminals also supply the largest number of epileptics. Among 23,333 male criminals confined in Turin prison, 0.66 per cent were epileptics, and 0.22 per cent out of 3358 female offenders were so afflicted. In Germany, 1881, 22 per cent epileptics were discovered among 65 male lunatics. Clark finds crime to prevail among 11 per cent of epileptics. The well-known tendency in this disease to weaken the mental faculties, and consequently the resistant powers, may help to lay the foundation for moral delinquency. It is undoubtedly more noticeable in older countries where race-stock may have more or less opportunity to degenerate. The theory of Richter, that more crimes, especially murder, audacious burglary, common theft, etc., come by epileptics, or those with a tendency thereto, is

[1] "Report of the Commissioners of Prisons," 1897, p. 37.

not well founded, at least, as applied to the criminal of the New World, if facts count for anything.

The *Physical Habits* of the criminal vary with his industrial, economic, social, and cosmical environments and temperament. Under the first head, it may be said the habitual and instinctive recalcitrant rarely belongs to the *trades* or *professions*. Such as do are the exceptions, not the rule. Their very natures preclude the necessary technical skill and perseverance required, which is essential to qualify them for such employment. The criminal's whole traditional tendency and training are averse thereto. He is ever on the verge of vagabondage, and vagabondage is the open invitation to crime. But 9.50 per cent of the total prison population of the United States, in 1890, were mechanics, and 77.28 per cent were without trade, or "trade not stated." Of the penitentiary population, reported by the Board of Education, but 38 per cent were regularly employed (and perhaps the great majority of these but transiently) at the time of their admission. Dugdale says that 79.4 per cent of criminals examined had never learned a trade. The burglar may attain a certain degree of mechanical dexterity, and the professional forger an imitative skill, while the balance are usually guided by natural cunning and adroitness. In the physio-social sense, the true criminal is lazy and debauched, with the proclivity for gambling and sexual pleasure hard upon him. Swindlers and professional gamblers are, as a rule, abstemious as to drink, luxurious livers, prodigal and generous, especially toward those in distress and for religious and moral purposes. Thieves are proverbially ignorant and gamblers are superstitious. Thieves are gregarious, even to the extent of forming combinations and sharing their plunder. They place confidence in one another to a remarkable degree, implicitly trusting one another where they would hesitate to confide in a reputable person. Criminals lack in *Courage*, at least as to its higher forms, as is evident by their furtive attacks upon life and property. Burglars and highway robbers are more bold and courageous, with keener intellects and more foresight, possessing greater decision of character than ordinary criminals, and hence more readily reform at a crisis in their career. They are sometimes well informed; may have respectable families (as swindlers and gamblers), and sometimes return to society as law-abiding citizens.

The *Use of Intoxicants* is an almost universal habit among criminals, and may well bear special examination elsewhere as entering into their personal idiosyncracies, or as an element in their social retrogression.

Tobacco is almost universally used among this class. One authority found it used among 45.8 per cent of male recalcitrants, as against 14.3 per cent in normals; and 15.9 per cent among females of the same class, as against 1.5 per cent normal women. Among 603 juvenile delinquents between 8 and 15 years of age, 51 had acquired the habit; and out of 300 over 30 years of age, 279 smoked.

Morphinism, or the *Opium Habit*, next to alcoholism, is fast becoming the prevalent vice among criminals, as it has touched the higher strata of society. The habit is deadly to all the nobler instincts and possibilities of humanity.   It is a neurosis that undermines virility, depletes vitality, paralyzes the will, and totally destroys the moral integrity, reducing the victim to absolute inanity.   Its subtleness and the facility it presents for smuggling and handling in the prisons render it a fearful accessory as a criminal-producing factor.   Frequently introduced as a therapeutical and medicinal agency, its use and inroad is a serious menace to all classes, especially to those whose conditions and environment, as well as weak inhibitory powers, render them an easy victim to the habit.   A hint of its existent and prospective inroad may be gathered from the published report of a leading penitentiary in the United States.[1] Out of a prison population of 1392 inmates, 614, or 44.10 per cent, were addicted to the use of opium upon their admission to prison ; while the same is assigned as the ostensible cause of committing crime in the cases of 560, or 40.22 per cent, of the inmates.   When it is observed, by the same report, that 49.07 per cent out of the same totality were alcoholics, it may readily be seen that the innovator is pressing hard upon the older habit as the prevailing vice of the criminal classes.   Pederasty and onanism are practised among prisoners.

As to his *Conjugal Relations*, as may readily be presumed, the celibate state is more favorable to crime than the marital.   Out of the total criminal population in the United States, 61.54 per cent were single, 29.15 per cent were married, and the balance were either widowed, divorced, or " relation not stated."

This completes the criminal delineation in detail, as

[1] San Quentin, Cal., Prison, Report of 1891–1892.

its subject stands out in savage perspective from the canvas of anthropological asymmetry — harsh in its discordant outlines; filled in with glaring colors drawn from the pigments of a sedimentary humanity; abnormal, viewed as a whole; startlingly familiar upon closer inspection (though no less repugnant), its synthetic outline may yet be said to rarely find its complete counterpart in actual flesh and blood. The real man, as he exists, fits into the ideal prototype only piecemeal and in fragmentary details. Though illusory, its advocates nevertheless claim to have enshrined him permanently upon a pedestal by himself, and so unmistakably transfixed his identity that the wayfaring man, though a fool, need not err therein. Its scientific exploration remains the work of experimentalist and scientist, whose unfinished task it is to pursue the illusory research with ever varying success and never wholly satisfactory results.

CHAPTER VI

THE INSTINCTIVE CRIMINAL—HIS ORIGIN

Heredity

THUS far we have passed in review the criminal personality as revealed through the interpretation of his internal and external self on the basis of moral conduct. Were his defection less pronounced, and the relation sustained to sociological and personal environment more manifest, the cause and origin of his peculiar endowment might be traceable with less uncertainty, if not wholly accounted for upon esoteric grounds and contemporaneous influences. The force of example, the power of suggestion, the stimuli of direct association, and the subtle currents that flow through the mental and moral channels, are in themselves sufficient to account for him to a certain extent. Unfortunately the scope and power of these educative forces are qualified, perhaps more or less modified, by strong predetermining factors never wholly eliminated from the play of personal forces. However that may be, it is evident, if the problem were hedged about by no further and unaccounted forces, the anomalies in question might be readily explainable upon the basis of the well-known axiom that man is the creature of his environment. Unfortunately for this simple view of the subject, the individual, introspectively, finds himself in the field already equipped with certain mental and bodily qualifications and endowments that give predisposing bent to his impulses and largely tend to shape his subsequent career. This is a feature that must be counted with in taking stock of his spiritual capital, and in point of importance has precedence over every other factor. Environment goes only in modification. Preëndowment, already alluded to, stands for the original stock the individual starts out with in life — whatever comes after only subtracts from or adds to. He stands in the middle of a current that bears him onward, having its source elsewhere than in the sum of the influences that spring up and affect him from without.

Instinct plays a foremost part in his psycho-physiological make-up. It is the germ of incipient intelligence, anterior to all rational experience, since it lies beyond the scope of purely contemporaneous educative agencies. It stands at the converging lines between the intellectual and animal domain, which latter, as has been already pointed out, is at the basis of the criminal characterization. Instinct is not a particular acquirement in the individual meaning of that term, but stands as the aggregation of such acquirements in the form of transmitted tendencies in the species, though Wallace bases it rather upon variation of the germ, due to natural selection, than upon actually inherited experiences.[1] It is automatic in action and limited in time and space. Standing thus close to the bio-genesis of the criminal man, it gives first insight into the subject of his origin.

[1] " Darwinism," note, p. 442.

That solution must be sought in the simple law of transmission by which species and individuals transmit themselves in unbroken succession. The fact itself is a familiar one, and is inferred from the phenomena of life as presented in all its varied detail.

Heredity may be briefly designated as the sum of those transmitted qualities which descend from progenitors to descendant, and are reproduced in the latter as the blended and modified qualities of the former. Weissmann defines it as "that property of an organism by which its particular nature is transmitted to its descendants." Ribot tersely summarizes it as "the tendency of a being to repeat itself in its progeny." Like begets like, is the familiar aphorism under which it operates. The mystery surrounding its active attributes, as employed in the generative process itself, has thus far yielded but little satisfaction to the accurate inquirer. In the microscopic germ all the primordial elements lie hidden, the central nuclei or protoplasm of which contains both the potential pattern and material out of whose mysterious fecundity the copy reproduces itself unerringly from perfected organism to minutest fibre and nerve centre and molecule in the offspring. All attempted explanation of the phenomenon of reproduction upon a physiological basis is unsatisfactory, and hypothetical. Darwin advances the theory of *pangenesis*, by which each and all of the individual germ-cells in the body give off lesser ones, each possessing the power of reproducing itself in kind, and which being collected in the generative cells are thus capable of continuing themselves in the form of a new organism similar to the parent's. Weissmann's theory is, that the reproducing substance does not arise out of *all* the germ-cells of the body of the individual, but proceeds directly from a single original germ-cell, and at every act of generation gives off a portion of this germ-plasm in the parent egg, when fertilized, the remaining portion being reserved to produce subsequent cells for following generations. His continuity of the germ-plasm is substantially the theory of Haekel, who makes it to consist in the spontaneous subdivision of the unicellular germ, much as in the plant or zoöphyte of the simplest organization. These theories, it will be observed, are merely confined to a mechanical elucidation, and are largely conjectural. Simplicity is in favor of the unicellular explanation.

In its economic value, the law of heredity may be termed the *conserving* principle of life that holds it true to its ideal, while it perpetuates indiscriminately its vices and its virtues, its normalities and morbidities; the former series in progressive ratio, the latter as containing within themselves potentially their own self-limitations. Nature is chary of her prerogative and jealous of her workmanship.

In its functional operation, the law of heredity asserts itself under twofold aspects, viz.: —

I. The *Law of Uniformity,* under whose patronage may be grouped all those similarities of traits that spring immediately and directly from the parental stock, sometimes repeating the whole in unbroken pattern down to minutest detail, at other times in vanishing series, or in blended modifications. Here, heredity is the rule ; non-heredity, the exception. It is the most familiar exemplification of the law.

II. The *Law of Diversity*, representing the law of transmission in its eccentricities under the guise of spontaneity, as where the uniformity of the law is seemingly marred : at times overleaping a generation or two, to reappear in a later ; or, in the sudden appearance of apparently entirely new characteristics in the descendant. This is reversional (or *atavistic*) heredity, where the current of transmission has apparently vanished, to reappear in another generation. This special feature is of important and ever recurring interest to the criminological student, and affords food for his rarest deductions and experimentations in the phenomena of criminal entailment. Its collateral phases also take place, though more rarely, by transmission through indirect ancestral channels, as uncle, nephew, etc. ; and even the influence of previous sexual relations, through magnetic influences, seemingly remain to modify the offspring of a subsequent union, as is so frequently noted in the breeding of the lower animals.

Character in the male and female progenitor may be similar or dissimilar under the operation of above laws. In case of the latter, there is a mutual and reciprocal neutralization of the two, the qualities under the stimulus of the generative act resulting more or less in the modification of each other, or in the creation of attributes *apparently* differing from the originals. Under this law of *opposites*, heredity reaches its highest perfectibility. It is nature's effort toward maintaining a fair average. Absolute uniformity in the parental stock tends to operate as a bar in the law of transmission. The tendency of integral resemblances in both parents are inhibitory, the augmentation of similarities residing in both the male and female parent tending toward exaggeration in the offspring, an error nature seeks to avoid by setting bounds. It is doubtless for this reason that ties of consanguinity and strong similarities of temperament are often barren, or result in degeneration. The sterility of hybrids is illustrative of these opposite tendencies, and is nature's line of demarcation between *species*. Mr. Spencer, calling attention to the above facts, notes that "Fertilization does not depend on any intrinsic peculiarities of sperm-cells and germ-cells, but depends on their derivation from different individuals. It explains the fact that nearly related individuals are less likely to have offspring than others; and that their offspring, when they have them, are frequently feeble. And it gives us a key to the converse fact, that the crossing of varieties results in unusual fertility and vigor." [1]   The Principal of the New York Institute for the Deaf and Dumb finds it most common for children of parents thus afflicted to possess the faculties of which their parents were deprived. Dr. Beniss reports, as the results of 833 such consanguinary marriages, of 3942 children 1134 were defectives, as follows: 308 idiots, 145 deaf and dumb, 98 deformed, 60 epileptics, 85 blind, 38 insane, 300 scrofulous, and 883 died young.

Dr. S. G. Howe, in his statistical tables upon the causes of *Idiocy* in Massachusetts, found 114 idiotic per-

[1] "The Principles of Sociology," p. 289.

sons whose parents were known to be habitual drunkards; 419, of scrofulous families; 211, some of whose near relatives were either insane or idiotic; 49, with one near relative idiotic, and 50 whose parents, one or both, were idiotic or insane.[1] Dr. Strahan found that the forms of degeneracy most directly transmissible are insanity, imbecility, epilepsy, drunkenness, deafmutism, blindness, cancer, scrofula, tubercular disease, gout, rheumatism, and instinctive criminality.

The interesting and important question as to the *Specialization of Gifts* belonging to both the parents, in the matter of their relative distribution to immediate descendants, is not definitely determined. Schopenhauer thought that the fundamental endowments of the descendant, such as character, talent, passions, and the moral tendencies, are inherited from the father; and that intelligence and mentality are derived from the maternal side. Special talents seem usually attributed to the male line of descent. Men of great intellectual qualifications have almost uniformly had like endowed mothers, and strong-minded fathers with mediocre wives proverbially propagate ordinary sons. History furnishes ample attestations in the mothers of the Gracchi, the Wesleys, the Adamses, Napoleon, Cromwell, and many others more obscure, but equally strong-minded. The mother of Cromwell possessed rare executive ability, which was transmitted to her illustrious son. His wife was a weak woman, and while the sons of such a union possessed none of the talents of the father, as is well known, the daughters had all the

[1] Dr. Howe's Reports, 1848, p. 45 of Tables.

courage and independence of the father, so that Bishop Burnett said, in comparing them with the brothers, "If those in petticoats had been in breeches, they would have held faster." Napoleon's mother was a woman of great force of character, while *his* wife in turn was a person of but feeble powers, hence the son proved a weakling. However, no certain rule can be deduced from the mass of evidences, much depending upon the state of the parent or parents at the time of generation and the accidents of gestation.

The law of heredity is bilateral, with a tendency to preponderance on the part of one of the parents. Theoretically, its ideal implies "the absolute equilibrium in the physical and moral nature of the infant of the integral resemblances of the parents." [1]   Practically, this is never realized, the vigor and nutrition of the individual egg and the vitality of the germs being probably largely determining factors therein.   The transmission in unilateral direction from father to son, and from mother to daughter, while more common than when passing equally from both parents, is perhaps on the whole less frequent than transverse inheritance from father to daughter, and from mother to son.   The latter realizes nature's highest approximation, and is her guarantee against excessive grossness through accumulative transmission of the coarser male qualities on the one hand, and ultra attenuation of nerve fibre through the female channel to its own sex, on the other.   Nature thus perpetuates a healthy balance between sex extremes, and maintains the equilibrium of nerve tissue

[1] " Heredity," Ribot, p. 148.

and psychological qualities possessed by the two and transmitted to their descendants in conserving order and equilibrium.

Direct heredity is the form under which the criminological student must here chiefly pursue his task, though in numerous instances the reversional type alone can furnish the clue to the anomalies presented. The whole individual unit passes under the survey of the law: (a) *Physiologically* — most familiar, because directly appreciable by the immediate senses. It covers the whole physical cortex, organically and functionally, in its racial, family, and individual peculiarities. Resemblances in physiognomies are strong alike in race and family descent, especially as to the nose, contour of face, color and expression of the eyes, etc. The Roman and Grecian profile, the Jewish and many other types of countenances, have preserved themselves intact through ages. Similarly, family resemblances perpetuate themselves along many generations. Anatomical and physiological peculiarities, both normal and abnormal, are maintained without deviation — large osseous structures, coarse organizations or the reverse; either parent breeding true to kind, or in modifying degree where opposites are involved. Physical peculiarities (not accidental) repeat themselves with remarkable accuracy, as deformed nose, strabismus, deaf and dumb, blindness, Daltonism, the sensorium, supernumerary digits, shape and condition of teeth, club-foot, harelip, etc. Diseased and pathological conditions, both organic and constitutional in the parent or parents, or the predisposition thereto; depleted vitality; scrofulous or other constitutional taints, — reproduce themselves directly, or lay the foundation in the physical organism or constitution of the offspring for like or other disorders, culminating usually at about the same age and period in life as in the parent thus affected. Dr. Burrows found 84 per cent of instances with such tendencies present, out of the whole number passed in review. Longevity, in like manner, with remarkable precision and uniformity, is transmissible, the last forming the basis of tables as a guidance for vast business interests.

The law of heredity asserts itself : (*b*) *Psychologically* — here, with more far-reaching results and momentous import than in the purely physiological sphere. As to whether one exists in causal relation to the other has already been sufficiently noticed, and need not here be further entered upon. Suffice to say, the law of heredity implies facts in connection with which the sweep of its operation is all-embracing, comprehending as it does man's physical, intellectual, and moral natures, and his volitional powers as well, all with equal pertinacity and impressiveness.

The *Intellectual Faculties* come under the direct domination of the law of heredity. Great intellectual powers are oftentimes handed down as they existed in their progenitors, either those of the reason, the imagination, memory, or volition ; whether of the æsthetical, judicial, or administrative faculties ; literary, artistic, or musical talent. Thus the family of the Bach's were musicians of a high order through eight generations, the genius manifesting itself in each individual at a very early age. In 1750 as many as 150 members of the family attended a musical family reunion. In Mozart's family there were 5 distinguished musicians, and the infant prodigy showed decided musical talent at three and astonished the court circles at six years of age. In the family of Mendelssohn there were 4 musicians. Out of 42 great painters, Galton shows that 21 had illustrious progenitors in the art; and in the family of Titian there were 9 painters; while both the parents of Raphael are represented as artists, "the mother delighting in the finer representations, the father excelling in strength, and the gifted son in both," as evidenced by his creations. Shelley, Chatterton, Southey, and Pope, all "lisped in numbers," and with Keats, Byron, and Burns, were all descended from mothers strongly possessed of the poetical temperament and endowed with fine nervous organizations. The Coleridges inherited their literary talent from the father, who was a prodigy and a neurotic. Statecraft, the executive, judicial, and oratorial departments, all lay claim to marked inheritable tendencies, as witness the great names of ancient and modern history, notably in our own land those of the Adamses, which furnished four generations of statesmen, two presidents, and a candidate in a third; the Bayards, Fields, Ameses, Beechers, and others. The scientific field also boasts its share in the Darwins, Owens, Herschels, Mitchells, and many other shining examples not necessary to enumerate.

Anomalous *Psychical Characteristics* are held with equal firmness within the grasp of this ubiquitous law, transmitting themselves with as uniform facility and precision as in the spheres of the purely intellectual and the physiological. For instance, those forms of vice and moral disorder that stand closely related to the nervous organization are among the first and strongest to impress themselves upon the descendant through the law of bio-genesis. Dipsomania scarifies the nervous system, and as such entails its dread inheritance upon the unfortunate descendant of alcoholic parentage. One-half to three-fourths of the dipsomaniacs are such by reason of hereditary entailment, defects which, upon the best medical authority, are irremediable, since it implies moral and physical degeneracy, alteration of tissue, and decided nerve disorder. It is a form of mental alienation that pushes itself irresistibly in the direction of excess, and while it may not always be shown to be an efficient direct cause of crime, it is at least the true patron, as well as indirect provocation, of a large share thereof. These forms of neurosis are sometimes transformed from one phase into another, as where dipsomania in the ancestor may subsequently show itself as mania, or epilepsy, or idiocy in the descendant; and conversely, the latter may lay the foundation for drunkenness in the descendant, though perhaps not appearing in some instances for a generation or more. Marro rated over 40 per cent of criminals as descending directly from such drunken parents, as against 16 per cent of normals. Marcot tells of a father who was a drunkard, and who had 16 children, 5 of whom were born dead or died early, and the rest were epileptics. Instances are common of idiot children begotten of drunken, though otherwise normal, parents; and offspring has been known that was fairly intelligent only when intoxicated, but silly when sober, as the result of such criminal coition while the germ was intoxicated. Of 300 idiots examined by Dr. Howe, 145 had drunken parents, and out of 95 epileptics, Voison found 12 to have had parents who were intoxicated during the period of their honeymoon. Alcoholism, as a disease, has a tendency to repeat itself with remarkable precision, coming to the surface frequently at the precise age when it originally made its appearance, or reached its climax, in the parent. Instances are known to the writer, where individuals hitherto of sound habits, and even possessed of a revulsion to drink, up to a certain point of their lives, have subsequently become confirmed dipsomaniacs at precisely the same period in life where the father had become such, the habit disappearing in the son at about the like age as in the parent's case. Ribot records a similar instance in which a family was afflicted with hereditary blindness, the same occurring throughout three generations invariably at 17 and 18 years of age in the successive descendants.

The question of the transmission of *Acquired Characteristics*, resulting in the formation of habits from the experience of the individual, is a mooted one, with opposite conclusions. Weissmann contends in the negative, and accounts for all such seeming examples upon the ground of selection. Wallace agrees with him, claiming that the molecular structure of the germ-plasm is already determined within the embryo. Lamarck holds to the affirmative, and incorporates his conclusion in his fourth law of evolution, that "all that has been acquired, begun, or changed, in the structure of individuals in their lifetime, is preserved in reproduction and transmitted to the new individuals which spring from these who have inherited the change." Whatever may be the contrary view, it seems undeniable that acquired tendencies being non-transmissible, a large proportion of the accredited phenomena of the entailment of habits known to have been hitherto confined to the single original ancestor, remain unaccounted for; as, for instance, the subject-matter of alcoholism, just discussed, that must have made its *first* impress as an *original habit* upon some *one* individual, and been thus transmitted by him to his descendant, either in its direct or metamorphosed state. Habit fixes itself in the organic and psychical constitution of the individual; heredity perpetuates it in the race. Why a habit, long indulged in, should not eventually effect a molecular change in the germ-plasm, and in that form impress itself permanently upon the embryo as any other inheritable quality, is not made clear. Acquired tendencies must in the nature of things account, in a large measure, for the law of heredity as to its inceptional stages, which law must, primarily, fall back upon this very fact for its initial point. That such habits, or even spasmodic and volitional impulsations, thus impress themselves upon the fœtus *in utero* is unquestioned, as we shall hereafter see.

The records of families noted for their criminal propensities have been carefully collated by all eminent authorities upon the subject, and serve to illustrate the fact of the *Entailment of Degenerative Functions* and tendencies upon descendants, the details of which it will be unnecessary to enter upon largely in this connection. M. Ribot mentions the Chrétien family, starting with seven and continuing to breed criminals through many generations, down to the present time. Mr. Dugdale has gathered, with remarkable patience and labor, the records of the celebrated Juke family, whose antecedents in New York were traced back through the genealogies of 540 persons in seven generations and 169 related by marriage or cohabitation, to one " Margaret " and her drunken husband, of which 709 persons, 280 were paupers; 140 were criminals and prostitutes, encompassing 115 different kinds of crimes, including highway robbery, and seven murders; incurring a direct cost estimated at $1,308,000, to say nothing of indirect damages to society, which were incalculable. Many similar instances afford convincing proofs of the propagative power of criminality through the direct operations of the law of hereditary entailment. Of hereditary insanity and epilepsy, at Elmira Institute, New York, the total ancestry among inmates thus calculated averaged 11 per cent; drunkenness was clearly traced to ancestral sources in 37.6 per cent, and doubtful in 51 per cent.[1] At Auburn penitentiary, New York, 23.03 per cent of the inmates were of neurotic stock. Morro found 90 per cent of morbid inheritance from parents on the whole among the criminals he examined. Mr. Dugdale found, out of 233 offenders in the New York prison, 17.16 per cent were of criminal families, 22.31 per cent were of pauper stock, 42.49 per cent of intemperate, and one out of every four, born of neurotic parentage,

[1] Report of 1893.

in one or both. Sichard, Director of Prisons in Germany, concluded that out of several thousand prisoners examined in the prisons of that country, some form of inherited neuroticism, or suicidal tendency, prevailed among thieves, to the extent of 28.7 per cent; sexual offenders, 23.6 per cent, and among incendiaries, 36.8 per cent.

Of studies made by the State Board of Charities of New York, and given in Mr. Warner's valuable work on "Charities and Corrections in the United States,"[1] of 12,614 persons in the almshouses, 397, or nearly 3.15 per cent, were offspring of pauper fathers; 1361, or 10.79 per cent, were of pauper sisters; 143 pauper uncles, and 133 pauper aunts. Of 10,161 different families represented, the total number, including three generations, who were known to have been dependent upon public charity, was 14,901. Total number of insane in the same families, 4968; total number of idiots, 844; inebriates, 8863.

"The heredity of the tendency to thieving," says Ribot, "is so generally admitted, that it would be superfluous to bring together facts which abound in every record of judicial proceedings." In the House of Detention at Perth, Dr. Thompson found 109 prisoners belonging only to 50 families. Virgilio ascertained that 195 out of 266 criminals were affected by hereditary taint.

Avarice in the parent, often leads to theft in the child. Maudsley bears testimony to this feature of moral degeneracy springing from this commonly con-

[1] p. 81.

sidered legitimate source; and a recent writer upon the subject records an instance of a young woman brought up in affluent circumstances, married to a farmer penuriously ambitious to prosper, even to the extent of denying his wife many of the ordinary comforts of life. In the prospect of motherhood, she accustomed herself to the habit of slyly abstracting, at times, certain dairy products, which were disposed of in exchange for the objects of her intense longing, which habit she kept up for several years, in the meantime becoming the mother of four children, every one of whom became born thieves. Kleptomania is undoubtedly the result of an unappeased craving in the mother during the intrauterine period, which leaves its ineradicable mark upon the fœtus, and results in insane and perpetually unsatisfied desire in the child, after birth, even for that for which it has no legitimate use, the disposition being described as one of intense pleasure and excitement, when in activity. Maudsley classifies it as a moral insanity.

The *Sexual Appetite*, when at its maximum, may thus be transmitted to plague the descendant; and a case is given of a man of otherwise excellent qualities, who all his life had been addicted to lust and unnatural crime, and who entailed the curse upon his sons and daughters, with the added propensity to rape. The passion for gambling, gluttony, and kindred abnormalities, especially when inflamed at the generative period, often stigmatize the offspring, and incarnate themselves in living monstrosities of iniquity.

The tendency to *Pauperism* is both hereditary and

induced.   It is simply the phenomenon of depleted vitality in the stock and, as such, has its origin in weakened germ-cells.   "Hereditary pauperism," says Dugdale, "seems to be more fixed than hereditary crime, for very much of crime is the misdirection of faculty, and is amenable to discipline, while very much of pauperism is due to the absence of vital power."[1]   Pauperism is the foster-mother of crime, especially of the pettier order.

Many of the neuropathic conditions of heredity are entailed upon the progeny, reacting by the *Law of Compensation* upon otherwise innocent offspring, who are thus compelled to bear the onus when hardly deserving it.   Uterine influences both before and after birth, as well as at the moment of conception, are allpowerful in shaping the destiny of the unborn infant for good or evil, almost at will, as has been actually demonstrated in numerous instances that might be cited with profit. The mother of Zera Colburn, the infant mathematical prodigy who, at the age of six years, astonished the learned world by his marvellous feats of computation, herself an ignorant woman, was intensely puzzled during the period of gestation over the price of a few yards of cloth, which she, however, persisted in working out mentally to her satisfaction, the extraordinary effort accounting subsequently for the mental monstrosity.

The preconditions that make possible the *Instinctive Homicidal Proclivity* may also be traceable in the same manner in the operation of these well-known laws back to pregenital sources, if not immediately asso-

[1] "The Jukes," p. 50.

ciated with the actual mental, moral, and emotional states of feeling present in one or both parents at the time of generation. Hatred, passion, malice, moroseness, melancholy, cunning, determination, courage, self-control, or their opposites in the unborn child may all be clearly mirrored and forecast in the parental psychosis, and are fairly predestined in the germ which is vitalized by the corresponding mental and emotional nature or mood of the parent, or parents, at the time of coition. Napoleon was conceived in a tent within sight and sound of carnage, upon the eve of battle, while the germ was intoxicated with its excitement, and this entailment, combined with strong mentality in the mother, gave to the world at once its most consummate military commander and its greatest congenital homicide. On the other hand, the gentle mother and profound Christian environment, at the crucial moment, gave us the Wesley brothers, the most beneficent religious personalities of the century; in each instance, the exact though accentuated moral potentialities of the progenitor at the moment of conception were minutely photographed upon, and reproduced in, the descendant.

In the light of these facts, thus intensely suggestive, the genetics of the instinctive criminal propension is not far to seek. In almost every instance it is the direct entailment of a precriminalistic stock whose antecedent moral ideals were low, and whose nature had already received the inviolable impress of the pregenital taint to be transmitted to the descendant with the unerring certainty characteristic of Nature in all her ways. It would undoubtedly be an easy matter, could the antecedent life history of every such progenitor be minutely ascertained, to point out clearly and in detail all the subtle lines of convergence of this law of entailment in logical and consistent sequence in the reproduction of the original likeness upon the descendant, thus bringing cause and effect face to face, and clearly account for the result at every step of the process of transmitted inheritance upon bio-genetic law. The process is hidden, — the facts are manifest. Sufficient is known of the operation of these laws to relegate the true criminal psychosis at once to these creative sources for its genetical explanation.

To the depths of the bio-psychological, then, with its co-related physiological and neurotic phenomena, we must go to know him as he is, and to trace the causes and origin of his distinctively anti-social and degenerative functions to their ultimate sources.

The burden with which the congenital offender comes already laden, and from which he draws his inspirational forces, is purely congenital. It is the product of entailed inheritance from ancestral germ-plasm out of whose mysterious depths they are evolved, possessing all the potency that moulds the embryo into the image of the original, elaborating and imparting to it its very essence and individuality, even carrying in its current and inoculating that new life with the very germs of theft and murder already stirring in the blood of its progenitor ages back, and waiting but the call of opportunity to spring into sentient life in the scion, and expend itself at times in wanton joy at the incitation of the savage nature:

As if to further accentuate this law, and thus aggravate the case, all such as come under the ban instinctively seek a criminal environment in which to nourish and fructify the latent germ, thus complicating by so much the problem of Nature's struggle to perpetuate her biological ideals, good or bad, even to the "visiting of the iniquities of the fathers upon the children to the third and fourth generation."

Nature, religion, and history join to celebrate the inviolability of that law upon whose dictum, modified, or altered by subsequent environment, is largely written the fate, as well as origin and perpetuity, of her handiwork — good or ill.

CHAPTER VII

THE HABITUAL CRIMINAL

THE personnel of the habitual offender has already been sufficiently delineated in a previous chapter, under the head of the "Instinctive Criminal," whose natural coparcener in crime, to a certain extent, he is.

The criminal by habit, and the instinctive offender, cannot be said to differ materially, either as to their physical or moral constitution, since they share sympathetically in the sad heritage to which they have come by diverging steps: one by way of the beaten path of heredity, the other, as we shall presently see, through the more tortuous windings and indirect course of a vicious social and personal environment.

Precisely to what extent the habitual himself may have been the recipient of the prenatal taint is, of course, not always possible to say. Where facts are ambiguous, conjecture alone can supply the place of certainty, though overt acts in the main afford the safer guide. The character and nature of the offence, in the absence of direct congenital proofs, will determine with reasonable certainty the nature and origin of such active criminalistic propensity, whether it be inherited, or is the sum of acquired characteristics through association. If, for instance, the act belong to that distinctively anti-social group and be directed against the person, if it vent itself in spontaneous acts of bloodthirstiness and impromptu savagery, particularly when accompanied with sexual passion, or when perpetrated with sufficient spontaneity to preclude the possibility of premeditation, such an act may safely be set down as atavistic, answering genetically to that form of perverted egoism that lies at the basis of the true criminal character. The actor is to be judged apart, as possessing an instinctiveness and juridic identity all his own, whose sole authenticity is traceable primarily to ancestral fountains. Such carry the virus of pregenital criminalism in the blood, ready to strike the moment the criminal hunger is on — the appetite whetted by what it feeds upon. The moral antecedents of such are clearly prefigured in the unnatural deed in whose emotional depths their moral instability lies mirrored.

The other class of delinquents presents a milder type of the criminal obsession. The diathesis of the ordinary habitué is manifestly not so virulent nor precipitous. The nature of his offence, as a rule, is less against person than against property, with a tendency toward crimes of mendacity and theft, suggestive of depleted vital force (as indicated by the absence of animal ferocity), and clearly with a touch of premeditation that indicates contracted habit through progressive initiatory steps to an ultimate determination of the will. It is the distinctiveness between the latent ferocity of the tiger and the secondary wariness of the fox, with glimpses now and then of a traditional soundness in the interval — an apparent return to normality, however, with

L

the moral certainty of ultimate relapse. Such generally exhibit a passivity rather than an aggressiveness of
disposition, in direct contradistinction to the instinctive
criminal. The one comes to his inheritance at a bound,
the other furtively and under covert, with a sense of in-
decisiveness that bespeaks primarily broken-down moral
centres and progressive degeneracy, usually at the instance of secondary depraved social initiatives. Thus,
while largely inferential from the nature of the offence,
the moral state thus set forth is to a great extent its
own interpreter, and may be relied upon with a tolerable
degree of certainty for diagnosis.

Categorically, a correct generalization would assign
the criminal by habit a place midway between two
extremes, *i.e.* with the criminal by instinct at one end
and the single offender at the other, toward either of
whom he shades by imperceptible gradations from first
offence through successive stages of repetition until he
emerges into the full-fledged professional and hardens
into the genuine habitué.

One of the most curious studies within this special
range, is that singular but mournful phenomenon not
infrequently presented, of a single recalcitrant in a family composed of otherwise normal members, the offshoot exhibiting all the symptoms of a genuine moral
pervert. He is a true anomaly who apparently cannot
seek refuge under the direct hereditary plea. There is
presented one of two alternatives to account for him, —
atavism, overleaping a generation or so to account for
itself in the life of all that is past; or, *acquired habit*,
tracing his moral antecedents directly to the sum of

those conditions with which he stands vitally associated in his immediate surroundings. In this instance, it is not unusually the latter.

The firstborn (if at all), according to Dugdale, is usually the criminal of the family; the last one the pauper. The generalization (if it be correct) doubtless is due to the fact that the first receives all the excess of native vigor in the original stock which, when perverted, runs instinctively into criminality; while the latter stands for its depleted vitality, where, both parents having passed the climactrix of their powers, endow the offspring with an impoverished inheritance. Marro found the preponderance of the criminal issue, by far, to have descended from elderly parent stock, especially so in cases of criminals of violence, as homicides, assaults, etc., a fact corroborated by Dr. Körösi.

The distinctive characteristics as between the two classes of offenders as thus above noted, lie, as we have seen, in the intensity of the act, one pointing to instinctive criminality for its origin and tracing its lineage to the loins of its progenitor, the other, as certainly, finding its explanation in the bosom of environment. The criminal by instinct is born, not made; the criminal by habit is made, not born. The one is a question of heredity reënforced by a self-sought environment; the other, of environment modified (or unmodified) by an unsought heredity. Heredity is the mother of crime; environment is the father. The diagnosis of the *habitual* is easier, and his genetics less obscure, solely because the metamorphosis goes on before our eyes. The spectacle of a clean youth with a sound stock behind it is not infrequently the condition precedent of the criminal by acquired habit; the reverse is more liable to be true of the born offender. It is the difference between predetermined criminalism under bio-genetic conditions, and unrestrained moral degeneracy under the guise of free will as the ostensible outcome of the ethical miscarriage. The instinctive criminal *ab initio* is a moral *defective ;* the criminal by acquired habit is a moral *delinquent ;* the etiological distinctions fading away into that mysterious twilight that hangs low upon the horizon both at the entrance and exit of all such anomalies.

Environment is the tentative field of the criminal exploitation. It is a far-reaching and comprehensive term. With reference to its essential bearing upon the individual character within its present practical meaning, it may be briefly understood to be the sum of those immediate surroundings that go in modification of the personality. Among these may be classed education, personal association and example, religion, manners, customs, family, social and civil relations, climate, mode of life, etc. It shares with heredity the prestige as a paramount formative agency among life forces, whose value and importance in this respect are attested in every department and avenue of progressive experience, and is the inspiration and essence of its vast accumulative entities, private, public, social, and institutional.

Eminent authorities differ as to its comparative value side by side with its initial coefficient, heredity. Ribot regards heredity as the predominant factor among life forces, with environment as an indifferent second, applicable only to "mediocre natures, attaining its maximum in average minds in the middle of the scale from idiots to geniuses; a glossy varnish as in case of educated savages, education only a covering underneath which the savage nature of man continually burns." Dr. Hirsch, on the contrary, assigns the educative faculties first place in the list of efficient agencies, and declares them as "of great importance for the development of character, particularly in the case of geniuses. Education is the foundation upon which the whole man is built."[1]

The educative faculty, whether voluntary or involuntary, holds the key that commands the avenues of power, and reduces and assimilates the whole mental and moral pabulum it accumulates from external impressions until it absorbs them into its life forces in the form of ideals that become to the individual both substance and spirit,—character-building factors that make him ultimately what he is. Conscience itself bears testimony to the efficiency of this primary formative agency in human character, it being equally with other attributes the sum of educative process both past and contemporaneous — a plant of slow growth, its absence testifying to arrest of development in the moral evolution, as exemplified in the case of the criminal by instinct. It is this that Aristotle meant when he called man the "most imitative of animals, and makes his first step in learning by aid of imitation," a fact taken up by all great teachers of men, and made the cornerstone of the constructive processes, giving it first place

[1] "Genius and Degeneration," p. 50.

in the evolutional chain, providing ever no actual organic or functional impairments exist to negative its value.

If, upon scientific grounds, in the process of selection, organism be held to be in the grasp of environment which goes to set up certain alterations and changes, it is presumable that moral conditions and socio-ethical development may be held to be equally impressionable as well as susceptible of modification under its metamorphosis. In other words, it is probable that the continuity extends from the realm of the physical into that of the moral; and if the law of purposive selection thus fastens upon environment to effect its changes in the bio-physical sphere, it will equally so in the bio-psychical, progressively or retrogressively.

Habit is the chief neuro-psychic agency that mediates between the external world and self — the process at least by which impressions are permanently infixed in the character to act with automatic regularity and precision. In its perfectibility it may be said to be that form of *established* conduct that ultimately acts without the direct intervention of the will. Habit is an acquired tendency. In its physical sense it is simply a form of nerve energy reduced to automatism, the unconscious operation of secondary nerve centres acting independently of higher brain control. Every inferior nerve ganglion possesses a memory of its own, and is "conscious and unconscious after its own fashion," all the differing degrees of mental operations encroaching upon each other.

In its higher moral and intellectual manifestations,

habit is a mode of action as applied to conduct. The mechanical operations of the mind are largely operative along the line of unconscious automatic cerebration involving all the higher activities of judgment, ratiocination, memory, and willing. Education is summarized in habit, the sum of all acquired tendencies in this respect may be said to be perfect in proportion as they are self-operative. The secret of moral training lies herein, as well as the whole chain of retrogressive activity as illustrated in the phenomena of degenerate man. The elder philosophers viewed morality entirely in the light of acquired characteristics. Virtue, according to Aristotle, was neither a passion nor a capacity, but a *habit;* and man became just, he declares, by performing just actions, and temperate by performing temperate ones.[1] Originally associated with the volitions, it loses its essential moral quality the moment it becomes subversive to degenerative influences and ends. When it reaches that point of auto-activity where the will is no longer master of its moral functions, but becomes itself enslaved through the tyranny of self-imposed habit, the individual has reached that "last infirmity of evil" wherein the moral nature has become the victim of an automatism that implies the disintegration of the personal integrity, because of the submergence of the will — the unifying centre of the personality.

The nervous organization is the physical basis of acquired habit. "A nerve shock is the unit of consciousness," says Spencer. If so, sensation is its primary psychological coefficient. Its physical mechanism

[1] "Ethics," pp. 39, 42.

is becoming more clearly understood. An object comes into contact with an afferent nerve. The incitation flashes to the lower brain (science informs us, at average velocity of 30 metres per second, visual and auditory sensation one-fifth to one-sixth of a second, and simplest acts of thought one-sixteenth of a second, differing in different persons and at different periods), thence to the upper brain, where it is transformed from a simple nerve vibration into a sensation cognizable in the brain (though located in the periphery), — the primal act of consciousness, accompanied at the same instance with a rush of blood carrying nutriment to the brain cell, where it decomposes the substance while the stored-up energy in the cell is then expended, or thrown off in the act of consciousness.

Localization of the brain surface, in accordance with its mental and functional operations, though an accepted fact, is as yet but imperfectly understood. That the higher frontal region is the seat of reason, and that the lower controls the animal economy, is known. It is also now definitely ascertained that each individual sensory has its special brain area, separately mapped out and set apart in certain portions of the motor surface, where all communications with a given primary sense are duly elaborated and registered. This is brain localization of the functions. The seat of the sensorium has been definitely assigned to the lateral posterior surface below and on each side of the median occipitalis. Even the *modus operandi* of the now ascertained separate nerve centres and independent fibrils, and their intermittent relation at the incitation of special nervous impulsion or act of the will (like a telephone connection), are all tolerably well understood, since the experiments of Golgi and Cajal, in 1889. It is a step in advance toward the solution of vaguely understood facts now partially demonstrated by experiment, promising to overturn the crude theories of phrenology while opening the way to a more thorough knowledge and comprehension of the mechanism of brain action, if not (approximately) the physical relation of the mind itself.

Repetition is the mechanical operation by which impressions are conveyed along the nerve fibres to be permanently registered upon the gray matter of the brain, there to be transmuted into thought. The thoroughness with which this is accomplished is dependent wholly upon the degree of attention bestowed upon the object, or the importance, consciously or unconsciously, attached to the subject. Thus, for example, out of a multitude, attention may be attracted only to a single person or thing to the entire exclusion of all the rest, which one will be ever after permanently retained in the memory.

With every repetition of an act, concentration decreases inversely as the tendency of the act to repeat itself increases, until perfect accuracy, coupled with absolute unconsciousness, indicates the perfection of habit. At that point the operation of the will proper is apparently suspended, and the action repeats itself unconsciously and independently. A good example is found in the case of the rope-walker, who, through stimulation of the nerve centres and concentration of attention, coupled with constant repetition, gradually acquires the habit of delicate adjustment of molecules and control of nerve impulses that enables him finally to maintain a perfect equilibrium, and to accomplish his task without apparent concern. The pianist, the engraver, the artist, all learn to do their work subconsciously which erstwhile required infinite labor and painstaking. This principle of activity pervades the whole range of functional activity from the simplest physical act to the highest form of mental and moral abstraction. Man is a creature of habit, and habit is but the registered memoranda of unnumbered repetitions recorded on nerve centre and brain cell to be reproduced and thrown off in endless richness and variety. Habit is the autocrat of the lower sensory ganglia, and the usurper of the highest moral attribute, tyrannizing alike over the very fount of authority and of life. Habit directs the purpose, controls thought, shapes conduct, modifies character; inspires the reason; and when dominated by the lower propensities and vitiated functions becomes a law unto itself at the expense of its own moral and volitional integrity.

Thus, while the physical organism is under the dominion of the lower brain ganglia and reflex nerve action, the higher mental and emotional natures are equally subject to the domination of degenerative psychical forces, both of which tend to set up morbid and anomalous changes from the newest types of neuropathic sclerosis to the subtlest forms of mental and moral alienation. These elements, while sometimes inborn, are oftener acquired — the result of secondary causes supplied by the unmeasured resources that crowd the individual on every hand from without, and that supply the chief formative agencies and incentives in individual character. Two-thirds of the criminal characterization receives its initiative, and attains its perfection through the law of association and imitation under the fixed law of repetition, as conducive to the establishment of permanent habit. Imitation is assimilation by example, by which the individual approximates his living ideal through the operation of the great objective law of experience. Heredity furnishes the capital; environment handles the stock in trade and so modulates it as to meet more or less its subjective requirements, sometimes retroactively, even in the face of protest, for it is by no means rare for the newly environed will to repudiate past preinheritance, free itself from the prenatal incubus, and project itself along entirely new lines, shaping itself, not through entailed bias, but through the intervention of a postnatal crisis that forms the starting-point and basis of a new and reconstructed psychological experience. "Beyond the field of predeterminism there lies the sea of spontaneity," to which unbiased investigation must give equal credence with the hard and fast play of arbitrary causation and ancestral law. Room must always be allowed for the movement of these unaccounted forces in taking stock of the spiritual capital, since much can be explained neither upon the assumption of absolute free will nor yet upon the doctrine of unlimited determinism, but upon a subtle compromise of the two. A true philosophic insight and scientific theory cannot afford to ignore the potentialities of the religious and moral element as supreme and all-powerful modifying factors in the personal evolution — a sort of compensatory moral adjustment in the law of development from first principles. Such phenomena are familiarized in the history of all great collective movements as well as individual experiences, as where profound emotional waves not infrequently sweep across the surface and stir the great deeps of human character, breaking up the old and building for new and better things. That which applies to organized humanity applies also to its parts; and all law and religion, the reinvigoration of social and private morality, and the remoralization of the community, have, at some period or other, felt this quickening and responded thereto.

What is true with respect to this moral uplift is of course equally so with reference to the retrogressive moral phenomena involved in the problem of environmental and postnatal influences. The moral nature is, in a sense, passive, and is sympathetically susceptible to the influence of environment either good or bad. Environment is the atmosphere in which it abounds, and from which it derives its inspiration and life forces. The force of example, the power of suggestion, the influence of surroundings, the appeal brought to bear in the stimulus of direct association through successive steps to final crystallization into permanent character are the dominating historical facts of all life-history, conscious and subconscious, and are accountable for the unnumbered criminal inherence outside the congenital circle whose elect few come upon the stage of action already handicapped and weighted down with the burden of the prenatal taint. This is not always, be it remembered, the logical outcome of free choice, but as frequently of necessity, that pushes the subject inexorably in the direction of outbreaking crime as more favorable environment urges the good man toward a good life.

The fact is incontrovertible, that the moral susceptibilities are inborn in varying degrees in different individuals. Equally true is it, then, that subsequent impressions go far in modification, if not in material alteration, of its inherent genetic qualities. The influence of environment, the educative forces that slumber at the heart of moral and intellectual ideals are all-powerful formative agencies in human character, particularly when recognized early in life, when the power for moral and intellectual assimilation is more perfect, and the ability to retain impressions is correspondingly tenacious.

The great bulk of induction into crime commences at this formation period, as a more complete knowledge of the subject will amply demonstrate. Out of the whole number of those born without especial proclivities to crime, who nevertheless eventually embark therein, a large proportion, it is safe to say, undoubtedly acquire the habit in early youth, during this formative period of life and before the mental and moral character has solidified. The bulk of crime committed during this period is largely of the pettier order, accompanied with brief sentences; while the graver, implying longer terms, come after. It commences usually with crimes against property.

According to criminological tables furnished by experts, we have more frequent precocity amongst various forms of criminalities in Italy and in France, in respect of inborn tendencies toward murder, homicide, rape, incendiarism; or in respect of tendencies contracted by habit, as simple theft, mendicity, and vagrancy,—all these characteristics of precocity being accompanied by frequent relapse, pointing to distinctly acquired habit before maturity, for their moral genetics.

The initial step in vice and crime once taken, the rest becomes comparatively easy, and is almost certain to be repeated if unrestrained by proper influence and instruction. It is the critical period in the life of the embryonic criminal. This is especially true with reference to the thieving habit, which, gradually acquired and slow in its advancement (generally arising out of petty pilferings begun in early life and under the shadow of the home), usually grows until, the sense of ownership once blurred and the lines between *meum* and *tuum* obliterated, it becomes ere long ingrained; the novice becoming first a pickpocket, then a pilferer, afterward by slow gradations a common thief (singly or in company), finally culminating in the genuine habitué, thus passing through all the scales by successive stages to robber, and grand larcenist, who fill, by far, the largest place in the professional rôle. Among petty offenders, theft in some form everywhere gives the most numerous class of precocious recalcitrants, the act itself being fraught with less danger and accompanied with the most excitement commensurate with moderate courage and a low order of intelligence. In Italy, 20 per cent of the habituals are thieves; in France, 24 per cent; in Belgium, 23 per cent; and in Prussia, 37 per cent.[1] In the United States, 39 per cent of crime and 17.13 per cent of juvenile crimes, are included under the head of petty larceny, which form of crime is in excess in the history of all our incarcerates, as per the various prison records. The ratio increases with social and economic changes, oscillating to some extent with varying industrial conditions. The habit, being insidious, is consequently the most tenacious, permanency being the rule; "once a thief always a thief," having become an axiom in crime. The virility and functional activity of this class are usually feeble, while the moral recuperative powers being commensurately weak, contribute to make this the most hopeless, as they certainly are the most pernicious, in the criminal categories. After theft, the commonest form of offence among habituals may be given in their order (and nationality), perhaps as follows, which may be taken as a guide throughout: Italy, vagrancy, 5 per cent; homicide, 4 per cent; swindling, 3 per cent; forgery, 9 per cent; rape, 4 per cent; incendiarism, 9 per cent. In France and Belgium, it is much the same, except as to homicide, incendiarism, and conspiracy, which are less, while rape is more common.[2]

The bolder forms of attack against property prevail in the United States, together with a much larger sprinkling of crimes of violence, as assaults and homicides. Out of the whole number of criminal offenders, June 1, 1890; viz., 82,329, 7386 (35 in connection with other offences) or 8.97 per cent were charged with

---

[1] Starke, 1884.   [2] "Criminal Sociology," Ferri, p. 20.

homicide, 1704 being classed as manslaughter, and 5548 as murder, of which nearly one half received life sentences. We have no way of ascertaining the precise status of these derelicts, but presume they fairly help to swell the ranks of habituals, much being due to the provincial lawlessness prevalent in the newly settled territories whose moral and social environments are unusually favorable toward the creation of this class of offenders.

From conclusions reached in the above consideration of abnormal man in his twofold aspect as an hereditary and as an acquired offender, it becomes a pertinent inquiry: How far, and to what extent, under the above analysis, may and does he occupy the attitude of a free moral agent?

The inquiry, broadly stated, is important as covering the whole field of moral and legal accountability. While not strictly within the province of a work of this kind, a brief consideration of this relation to the central fact is necessary to a proper understanding of the ethical and legal status of the subject, and may not be here out of place.

Free will is the essence of morality and the soul of all responsible conduct. An examination of the personality from any other standpoint is at the risk of greater contradiction than that from which the inquirer seeks to escape. Even the advance school of criminologists, with few exceptions, abound in attestations to the freedom of the will (in necessary consistency with their central postulate in the treatment of the criminal as a legal offender), without which the whole structure of criminal anthropological unification, legal as well as moral, must of necessity fall to the ground, involving every conventional form of punitive legislation and attempted cure in hopeless ruin.

"No crime," says Ferri, one of its ablest exponents, "whoever commits it, and in whatever circumstances, can be explained except as the outcome of individual free will, or as the natural effect of natural causes.

"Therefore it is far from being exact to assert that the positive criminal school reduces crime to a purely and exclusively anthropological phenomenon. As a matter of fact, this school has always from the beginning maintained that crime is the effect of anthropological, physical, and social conditions, which evolve it by their simultaneous and inseparable operation. And if inquiries into biological conditions have been more abundant and conspicuous by their novelty, this in no way contradicts the fundamental conclusion of criminal sociology." [1]

Freedom of will is, to Despine, "the power which decides the good and the evil after a deliberation made clear by the sentiments of duty"; and Naville recognizes the main fact that, if determinism is the postulate of all the physical and psychological sciences, relative liberty is the postulate of all the psychological and moral sciences. Garofalo, however, among the most brilliant of theoretic criminologists, almost alone lays stress upon the absolute non-responsibility of the criminal, on the ground of the incompatibility of freedom with predisposing criminal bent, resting his claims upon scientific grounds, in which sense he is quite right,

---

[1] "Criminal Sociology," pp. 54, 55.

since it deals alone with the physical which knows no force outside of law, and as to freedom, finds no resting-place for the soles of her feet. The moment psychological phenomena become the subservient adjunct of purely physiological causes, freedom ceases; and the soul with its volitional attributes passes under the ban of necessity. That the victim of disintegrating habit *may* not ultimately reach such a point need not necessarily be here denied.

There is a difference between operation and action, causation and volition, necessity and liberty. Nature comes under the sway of the former of these series; man, in his volitional capacity falls under the latter. His physical organization, as representing the first, is conditioned by law, the intellectual and perceptive faculties and the sensibilities sharing therein, since man obviously cannot will to perceive, or feel; neither can the intuitions respond to the volitions, inasmuch as they act independently. We believe twice two are four, not because we *will*, but because *compelled*, so to do. We are not even masters over our beliefs, but draw our conclusions from obvious premises with unerring certainty, not guided by the volitions, which here count for but little and play only an arbitrary part, if any. Belief is responsible from the standpoint of accepted premises, and not on the ground of conclusions drawn. The reasoning faculty is true to itself; the will alone is fickle.

When we pass within the domain of morals, we enter the true field of responsibility where the will attests to conduct, and its authority is supreme, language itself testifying to its autocracy. All material comparisons here fail to throw light upon the central question as to

the origin of an act of the will in its purely causal relation; Edwards's "balances" being but a bungling attempt to illustrate a spiritual truth by a mechanical
analogy.

The will is self-active; usually, but not necessarily,
falling back upon conscience and motive for its prerogative within the domain of morals, and upon impulse
within the range of the emotional for its primal incentives. Theoretically, it is unconditioned save by disease and the abnormal limitations already noted.

A posteriori, it must be admitted that a certain point
of limitation may be reached in actual experience where
the power of independent action of the will has practically ceased its operation, and instead of occupying the
position of controlling centre, is itself brought under
subjection of forces hitherto regarded as subsidiary, if
not inimical.

This is precisely the state of that large class of moral
degenerates who fall under preceding generalizations,
and of whom it cannot be said, after a certain point in
their experience has been attained, that they are any
longer in the *true sense* free moral agents. Here, retroactive physical and neuropathic tendencies, in conjunction with perverted moral and psychic powers, have
set up degenerated functional centres and so vitiated
the ordinary channels and sources of activity as to
reduce the action of the will to a nullity. To expect of
such the same moral responsiveness as of the normally
constituted and sound, would be too much.

Moreover, the dividing line between moral and mental
insanity is not always clear. For instance, the well-

known fact that the first symptoms of insanity are frequently manifest in the perversion of some moral sense (sometimes even involving permanent alteration after recovery), as of an heretofore chaste person becoming lewd, or an honest one a thief, after recovery, etc.[1] Moral degeneration, on the contrary, is also quite frequently the precursor of mental alienation. How closely these morbid transformations may be co-related with diseases of the will, are problems not yet solved. At any rate, it is plain that personal responsibility can reach no higher than the individual functions permit, and these remain largely the creatures of inheritance and education, twin factors that make up the totality of life and qualify and set up mental and moral bounds. As the last above-quoted authority has well said, " The wicked are not wicked by deliberate choice of the advantages of wickedness, which are a delusion, or of the pleasure of wickedness, which is a snare, but by an inclination of their nature, which makes the evil good to them, and the good evil." [2]

To this class belong all those delinquents grouped under previous heads, who have obviously attained a condition that leads persistently in the direction of wrong-doing at the expense of the will and at the instance of perverted spiritual and functional derangements.

Further attempt toward a metaphysical analysis of the subject but entangles in fruitless contradictions where freedom and determinism can be reconciled only upon

---

[1] " Responsibility in Mental Disease," Maudsley, p. 67.
[2] *Ibid.*

the basis of an imperfect and unsatisfactory compromise.

The will presents the turning-point between environmental and hereditary criminal characterization. What throws the determining weight into the scale, whether anthropological or socio-anthropological, is alone a question of circumstance, though ofttimes of great moment as ascertaining definitely the distinguishing characteristic of the subject himself as to whether he may be properly classified as a true criminal, or one by simple accident, or circumstance ("Criminaloid"). That, in short, the congenital and habitual criminal may attain a point of absolute and total moral fixity, is unquestioned. Both Christian philosopher and moralist meet here on common ground and rest their case in the apostolic aphorism that, "It is no longer I that do it, but sin that dwelleth in me." The habitual criminal has his inception in theoretic freedom; his culmination in practical subjugation — a mental and moral servitude under which lawlessness has become to him a law. Provisional liberty, as the starting-point in his career, has become subservient to a tyranny from whose implacable grasp there is, theoretically, no escape.

As to the hereditary criminal, he may be said to represent, in this respect, only a more exaggerated illustration of the above fact, through enfeebled moral attributes handed down through past ages and descended to him through ancestral channels, possibly primitive conditions (atavistic), into whose struggle moral volition may hardly be said to have primarily entered. The congenital and the habitual criminal, at a certain period in their moral careers, thus stand at equi points in the ethical angle. Just how far the moral susceptibilities may remain rudimentary, or to what extent they may continue to be potentially capable of recuperation and rehabilitation, is a question impossible of solution. Facts and the testimony of consciousness alone must here decide, and they practically go largely in attestation of the all but hopelessness of their condition.

And yet, to say that such as give no evidence of moral resurrection are thus hopeless through lack of *potential* recuperative energy, while such as seemingly testify to a cure are reclaimed by reason of the survival of elementary responsive principle, is, to say the least, a begging of the question, and settles little. On the whole, in view of the inability of the mind to grope its way through the tangle into a clearer field of subjective causal relations as to the sources of human conduct, it is, perhaps, as satisfactory to leave the question to the test of facts as to risk ultimate shipwreck in the vain endeavor to steer safely between the frowning cliffs of necessitarianism and the limitless shores of a provisional liberty. We are here unable to ascertain our soundings in either event, and are adrift upon a shoreless sea.

CHAPTER VIII

THE HABITUAL CRIMINAL — HIS ORIGIN

Environment

How much, and to what extent, the organization and equipment of the habitual criminal are due either to prenatal or to postnatal causes, is, of course, a difficult matter to determine. All that is left the experimentalist is to inquire from external observations which set of influences seem to predominate in the make-up and endowment of the persistent offender, so far as traceable directly from either of these sources, or as may be apparent from an analysis of bare action or premeditative conduct.

The lines to be drawn must necessarily be coarse, and often illy and unsatisfactorily defined. We can only make up our verdict from general deductions. The law of bio-genesis already traced, as accounting for the congenital classes, makes but little of the infinitesimal similarities through the selective principle that are carried along in the stream of transmission. It takes cognizance chiefly of such as push themselves persistently to the front as carrying with them reliability and weight in summoning up the concensus of distinctive qualities. For instance, little significance would presumably attach to the appearance of a crimpled fingernail, while a shortened limb, or extra digits, or certain striking peculiarities of bodily or facial asymmetries, unbrokenly transmitted, would point to a decidedly pregenital characteristic. So, in the handing down of mental or ethical endowments, little stress is placed of necessity upon inconsequential peculiarities that incidentally crop out, while importance would naturally attach to those predominating qualities that give tone and emphasis to the moral and intellectual character or conduct.

The safe criterion would seem to consist in properly ascertaining whether or not the determining causes that contribute toward modification of the personality may be reasonably deducible from the parental stock, or whether such forces are clearly traceable to the mediate or immediate surroundings that go to make up the network of appreciable forces, social or otherwise, into which he is subsequently cast, and which, at times, seem quite as capable of definitely shaping and ultimately solidifying the character as those subtler inspirational forces that are primarily the result of bio-genetic implanting.

The general outlying associations, to which the broadly generic and somewhat ambiguous title of environment is given, and which thus focus upon and modify individual character, may be readily grouped under several different heads as they reveal themselves in the relative degree of importance they sustain to the central subject, to each of which must be given more or less emphasis as influential factors in the evolution and solidification of the true criminal character.

As affecting the criminal problem in its mere external numerical form and as a purely local feature, the tide of provincial criminalism will be found to be largely tinged, and its bulk materially affected, first and foremost, through immigration. The influx of the foreign element, in this local phase of the subject, constitutes no inconsiderable contribution both to the character and to the bulk of the anti-social element. It saturates and colors the whole stream of New World criminalism by force of its peculiar contribution. The immigration of the earlier years was composed in the main of unquestionably sound material, largely the offshoot from the most sterling of Old World stock. They formed the physical nuclei as well as the moral and political basis of much of the healthiest and most promising of this New World race. The door was willingly and indiscriminately thrown open to all classes and conditions of incoming population, which rapidly increased in numbers, reaching such proportion by 1820 as to result in the formation of a political party to prevent further influx, which based its arguments largely upon the enormous accretion of crime and pauperism that attached to the train of this promiscuous invasion.

Up to September 30, 1897, the total immigration to these shores reached 18,476,726. The English-speaking races contributed 8,016,402, over one-half being Irish; the United Kingdom, 6,964,815; Germany, 5,003,490; Scandinavia, 1,192,131; Russia, 749,039; Austria, 821,663; Italy, 818,011; France, 388,000; China, 300,000. Great Britain, out of this total, furnished the greatest number of useful craftsmen; with Germany next, which also excelled as agriculturists; Ireland and the Scandinavian peninsula in unskilled labor; and Italy, Poland, and Hungary, " without occupation." Ireland furnished by far the greatest quota of delinquents and dependents.

The census of 1890, from a brief summary of the relative increase of crime to population from 1850, gives us a fair estimate of its proportions, and its effect upon crime and pauperism in this country, up to that period.

TABLE VI

RATIO OF PAUPERS AND CRIMINALS IN UNITED STATES FOR 1,000,000 OF POPULATION

	1850.	1860.	1870.	1880.	1890.
* Paupers (native)	1765	1849	1635	994	836
* Paupers (foreign)	5986	7843	4095	3438	3072
† Criminals (native)	207	371	733	1054	1233
			(Colored 1621)	(Colored 2480)	(Colored 3275)
† Criminals (foreign)	1074	2161	1568	1917	1788

* U. S. Census Report, 1890, Table 201, p. 654.
† U. S. Census Report, 1890, Table 4, p. 6.

While in these periods the native population is far ahead of the foreign element, the proportion of foreign criminals and paupers, as compared with the native, is enormously in excess in the foreign; in fact, it makes up the bulk of the delinquent classes of the United States. In the census of 1890, the foreign white element, counting foreign born (14.77 per cent) and the children of the first generation, comprise about 32.93 per cent of the population, nevertheless, it gives us 56.81 per cent of foreign prison parentage, one-half of whom were unnaturalized, and one-fifth unable to speak the English language; while the native stock is 54.87 per cent, and gives us but 43.19 per cent of native prison parentage.[1] Including the negro (who is virtually a non-native), the disparity is still greater. Thirty and three-hundredths per cent of white paupers were foreign born.[2]

The race features of the criminal population may be succinctly stated in diagram form drawn from government sources, which shows the race and nativity of prisoners reduced to proportions of per 10,000 inhabitants.

TABLE VII

NUMBER OF PRISONERS IN EACH 10,000 POPULATION: 1890

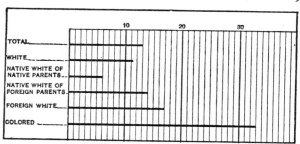

The statistics of two extreme seaboard states show much the same results. The Massachusetts census of 1885 makes a showing of 27.1 per cent of foreign born, who committed 40.6 per cent of its crimes, and gave us 36.87 per cent of its convicts. In the state of California, in 1890, its foreign population numbered 30.31 per cent of the whole, while its foreign prison enumeration in both prisons was 921, out of a total of 2057, or 44.77 per cent. In the prisons of the United States during that year, out of a total of 15,932 foreign prisoners, 34.89

[1] Report of Crime, Pauperism, and Benevolence in U. S., 1890, p. 149.
[2] *Ibid.*, p. 1.

per cent were born in Ireland; 18.61 per cent in Germany; 9.93 per cent in Canada; 12.03 per cent in England; 3.00 per cent in Scotland; 1.75 per cent in France, and 3.56 per cent in Italy. Taking into account only the 105,885 parents whose birthplaces were ascertained, the percentage of native parents is 43.19 per cent, and of foreign parents 56.81 per cent; while the total number of criminal offspring of the first generation of foreign parents is thus 69.60 per cent of the whole criminal population in 1890. In 1860, representing the highest numerical increase of foreign delinquents (2161 per 1,000,000), there were 80,000 persons of foreign birth or parentage supported by the public in the prisons, insane asylums, and almshouses of the United States, the foreign element furnishing one and one-half times as many criminals; two and one-third as many insane, and three times as many paupers as the whole native element. In 1870 this element constituted 20 per cent of the population of New England, and furnished 75 per cent of its crime. In 1890 the total foreign element out of the 340,996 inmates of our public institutions numbered 92,065, or 27 per cent of the whole, while the nativity of 10,523 was unknown.

It will be seen at a glance how perceptibly this depressing inundation must affect the whole moral tone of the New World and key it to a correspondingly lower pitch through the deleterious influence it has upon the whole social economy, affecting even the value of life itself, as seems apparent from the well-known homicidal tendency that has been made to lend its reputation to our new civilization, which must be mainly attributed to this low irresponsible human strata that come to us surcharged with the vices and unrest of the Old World, an inference amply corroborated by tables made up from the statistics on homicide, published by the last census, which give a good idea of the obligation we owe to these sources for our reputation in this respect.

TABLE VIII

COMPARATIVE TABLE OF HOMICIDES TO POPULATION

POPULATION.	PERCENTAGE OF POPULATION.	PERCENTAGE OF HOMICIDES.
Native white	85.23	42.94
Foreign born	14.77	16.50
Negroes	12.00	37.12
Chinese and Japanese	0.17	1.28
Civilized Indians	0.09	1.21

Here aliens, comprising but one-seventh of the whole population, commit one-sixth of the homicides; while the native born, though comprising over three-fourths of the total population, commit considerably less than one-half of such crimes.

The influence of this criminal saturation, to say nothing of its direct contributory result to the criminal element, is immeasurable, and cannot adequately be computed in figures. It serves only to aid in making this ultimately the home of the *depressed* as well as of the *oppressed*, and entails a blight upon the native stock, the onus of which, to this extent, it unjustly bears.

It is thus easy to see that, while immigration is not in itself an organic cause or direct source of crime, it is, at the same time, the most prolific channel of criminal multiplication by accretion peculiar to the United States, through the simple transposition of the integral terms from the congested populations of the Old, to the more inviting fields of the New World.

Foreign countries have but little of this feature of criminal infiltration to contend with, the sediment of foreign element into English prisons being but 2.7 per cent between 1857–1871 ; 2.4 per cent between 1872 and 1881 and 2.1 per cent in 1887; and in Austria (1894) 0.98 per cent.[1] The total foreign population of Great Britain is but 0.36 per cent, and of Germany, 0.94 per cent, which, compared with that of the United States at the same period, was over 14 per cent.

It is worthy of note, as bearing upon this provincial feature, that Professor Ferri, in his late work on "Social Criminology," dictated from his particular standpoint, has naïvely suggested the advisibility of "unrestricted emigration as a safety-valve that carries off many easily driven to crime" — a suggestion it would be well for American statesmen to ponder in formulating future laws at this end of the proposition.

Where the thriftier class of immigrants seek the country, this residuum is cast up and concentrated mainly in the congested portions of our country, in its metropolis, where it thrives best in its banded association in systematic depredation upon organized society.

The city, in relation to this problem, independent of all secondary considerations, affords the maximum of advantage favorable to the cultivation and develop-

[1] "Mulhall," 1892, p. 165.

ment of the criminalistic tendency, not only with reference to this foreign but as well in its domestic aspect. The city presents all the conveniences and inducements held out for systematic wrong-doing upon either a high or a low scale, singly or collectively. It may be truly said to be the host upon which the criminal and pauper parasites feed, whose chosen environments hold out the greatest modicum of advantages for their actual propagation and encouragement. The city's very size and cosmopolitanism is the best guaranty to this end, notwithstanding the comparative perfection of its municipal and judicial machinery.

One of the most significant signs of modern (as well as of past) civilization lies centred in the rise and supremacy of the city, the measure at once of the highest and lowest reach of attainable moral, social, and political power and life. From 1830 to 1880, when the aggregate population augmented in this country 30 per cent, the city showed an increase of over 40 per cent, due in a great degree, as already shown, to the breaking up and scattering of the incoming wave of foreign accumulation, many of our leading cities containing as high as 62 per cent, 80 per cent, and 91 per cent aliens, — sixty-five of them averaging 65 per cent foreigners by birth and parentage. In New York the population has rapidly gravitated toward these great centres. In 1870 its incorporated cities' collective population was 43 per cent of the state's total population. In 1880 50 per cent thereof was incorporated in its great cities; and by the state census of 1892, its cities held 62.3 per cent, since which time it has increased to 65 per cent; and by the time the next census is taken, in 1900, 70 per cent of the population of the state of New York will doubtless be found to reside in its cities, and but 30 per cent in its country districts.

Not only is this urban concentration peculiar to the New World, but it is true also of all civilized countries; is, in fact, expressional of civilization as partaking of its highest centralizing tendency at these great centres of its complex life, where refinement and luxury, as in the days of the Roman and Athenian ascendency, were indicative of their highest political attainment. The most conservative civilized races have felt the swell of this world-tide. The population of Germany, for instance, increased from 1875 to 1895, 12,500,000, that of its cities being almost doubled in the same period, though the increase of its rural districts was but 13 per cent.

The ratio of comparison between rural and urban criminality in France in 1880 was 100 crimes in the rural population to 220 in towns, per million of inhabitants. The cities in Italy stand for 32 per cent of the population and 42 per cent of its crimes.[1]

The city has been well called the nerve centre of the political organism, controlling its functional powers, testing its pulse, and registering its symptoms with utmost accuracy. Like the physical centres, this great political ganglion holds vital connection with every other portion of the body politic, controls its whole corporate existence, both receiving and distributing the alternate shock of demoralization or the attendant glow of health and growth.

[1] " Mulhall," 1892, p. 170.

Bad economic conditions may be set down as among the list of secondary causations that are undeniably favorable to the inroad of the criminal insinuation. The ramification of such evils is far-fetched, implicated with many other forms of social ills. To attempt to trace it in all its bearings upon the subject would be out of place in a work like this; nevertheless, it is full of suggestiveness, the amelioration of industrial ills going far toward the curtailment of many of the leading contributory sources of vice and crime among the non-congenital criminal element. Poverty breaks the backbone of self-respecting manhood. As a direct physiological effect, it makes serious drafts upon the vitality by taking from the individual the stimulus of success, leaving him to contend hopelessly against adverse circumstances. It has been shown by medical authority that poverty curtails life tenure. Charles Ansell, Jr., in his " Tables of Mortality, etc., in the Upper and Professional Classes," for instance, averages the chances of life among the higher, professional, and lower classes as follows : —

TABLE IX

Out of 100,000 born alive, there will be living	End of First Year.	Age of Fifteen Years.	Age of Sixty Years.
" Peerage families " . . .	93.038	85.890	51.166
" Upper class " experiences	91.955	83.392	53.398
" Clergy children " . . .	91.667	79.536	
" English life table " . .	85.051	68.456	36.983
" Carlisle table "	84.610	63.000	36.430

According to Dr. Körösi, statistics reported at the Demographical Congress held at Budapest, 1894, that the average age of the rich classes is 35 years, of the well-to-do 20.6 years, and of the poor only 13.2 years; tending to show that whatever depletes the vitality and degenerates the physical power is favorable to crime. Pauperism is chronic poverty, and poverty is a mild form of the social disease. Poverty may be due to circumstance or accident; pauperism runs in the blood. A discussion of economics being here out of place, the central fact of idleness and want, nevertheless, remains, and may properly be termed conditions precedent to the criminal insinuation and ever favorable thereto.

Though chronic idleness, improvidence, and moral dereliction are unquestionably at the root of many of these economic evils, it is undeniable that faulty industrial relations and unsatisfactory social adjustments are also themselves largely responsible for enforced idleness on the part of the lower and the working classes. That a proper industrial training, at the crucial period, would do much toward stemming the tide of a vicious social current is undeniable; and when these more favorable surroundings fail to supply this essential requirement, enforced idleness becomes Society's most baneful crime-producing contingent. If the struggle out of mediocrity into forehandedness on the part of the healthier and more normally balanced is evidently fraught with so much peril, what can be expected of the mentally and morally unsound, and those with whom the battle for bread becomes direct and bitter? It is significant, as a problem in economics, that the bulk of criminality is recruited chiefly from the ranks of the poor and from those who live face to face with penury.

Whether poverty is the cause of crime or the criminal instinct is the source of poverty becomes merely a matter of casuistry — a transposition of terms, one so largely invades the other in the criminal category. At all events, to the desperately poor, ingratiated in coarse habits and instincts, with gross organizations and all unused to nice ethical distinctions, the clamorous struggle for existence becomes very literal, and it is hardly to be wondered at that they succumb first to temptation and then yield to professional wrong-doing.

Those without trade or permanent employment drift naturally into attacks upon property, under the spur of necessity, coupled, of course, with low moral standards, due lack of the sense of social obligation and weak inhibitory powers.

But 22 per cent of the total criminal population of the United States,[1] including the 60 per cent who owed their offences to circumstances rather than to the criminal propensities, had learned trades; while the number of regularly employed, at the time of arrest, was but 38 per cent, and these doubtless largely accredited to first offenders. At Sing Sing (1897), out of 1243 prisoners, 437, or 35.15 per cent, reported trades, and out of 686 received during the year, 394 were idle and 205 day laborers. At Elmira, New York, only 14.9 per cent were employed at mechanical work and 56.3 per cent were day laborers.

Attachment to soil, trade, and permanent employment are the strongest counteractants to the criminal

[1] Bureau of Education, 1891.

habit; as such, they not only preoccupy the mind but lift the pressure of want and loosen the grip of impecuniosity, the chief inducements to wrong-doing, from an economic point of view.

This floating element is the sediment of population in every city, whose density to the square mile is also the measure of its crime-producing ability. The superintendent of discharged convicts in London estimates the number of idlers ever ready for crime at one hundred thousand in that city alone.

The intemperate use of intoxicating liquors, in addition to the above, is the most commonly associated environment of the criminal habitude. If not always the direct cause, it at least presents all the conditions favorable to the perpetration of the criminal act and the spread of its contagion. It is one of the earliest, as it is the most permanent, of acquired characteristics; is both a cause and an effect, and may be either hereditary or acquired. Aside from its direct bearing upon the subject, it is peculiarly efficacious as laying the foundation of a diseased neurotic condition as premonitory to incipient mental and moral degeneration. Neuro-psychic in its nature, insidious in its advances, and direct in its inroads and effects upon the nervous system, it quickly scarifies both the physical and moral organizations and brings them into subjugation at the instance of a diseased functional activity.

The development from the occasional to the habitual, and thence to the chronic alcoholic (especially in the neurotically inclined or where the inhibitory powers are naturally weak) is rapid. It may be counted upon to develop into settled habit, at times with almost unerring certainty. It will be unnecessary to dwell upon its physiological features. Its stimulation of the vasomotor system, its paralyzing effect upon the motor and nerve centres, and its deleterious influence upon the brain, are all familiar facts and account for much of the rapid increase of nervous derangement. Nervous diseases in Europe from 1864 to 1868, it has been pointed out, aggregated about 196,000; and from 1884 to 1888, about 260,558; while diseases of the heart in 1859–1863, were 92,181, which increased in the period between 1884 and 1888 to 224,102. The insane in the United States in 1860 numbered 1 to every 1310 of the inhabitants; in 1870, 1 to every 1100; in 1880, 1 to every 570. Between 1850 and 1880 (30 years), the population doubled, and insanity increased sixfold. In the decade between 1870 and 1880, the increase in population was 30 per cent, and the increase in insanity was 155 per cent. The increased ratio of lunatics in England and Wales between 1859 and 1800 was 186.7 per 100,000 as against 279.4, and in Scotland was 157 as against 217 per 100,000 of population.[1] Professor J. Holt Schooling, Fellow of the Royal Statistical Society of Great Britain, declares that 1 in every 306 of the population of Great Britain is a maniac, and that the ratio is constantly increasing. He declared that liquor is the cause of nearly one-third, or 33.6 per cent, of such cases.

It is at least noteworthy that the increase of consumption in alcoholic beverages, per capita, records a corresponding increase therein, as in France, from 1.33 litres to

[1] " Encyclopædia Britannica," Vol. XIII, p. 117.

4 litres in a little over two decades. Although Colajanni insists that there is wanting between alcoholism, crime, and suicide, constancy of relations, other equally as good authorities bear testimony to the vital connection between the consumption of alcohol and outbreaking lawlessness. Ferri notes that during the periods in France between 1843, which gave 479,680 hectolitres, to 1879, which gave 1,309,565, and 1887, 2,004,000 hectolitres, crimes and suicides increased, the latter from 1542 in 1829 to 8202 in 1887; and he traces a manifest corresponding increase and decrease between the number of homicides, assaults, and malicious woundings, and the more or less abundant vintages.

In 13 leading states in Europe, suicides increased from 104 per 1,000,000 in 1868, to 134 per 1,000,000 in 1882.[1] In the United States the same distressing facts prevail. In 1893 the total number of suicides was 4436, an increase of 576 in one year, and of 1255 over 1891, or one in every 15,000 of the inhabitants, estimating the population at 66,000,000. The supposed causes given were as follows: despondency, 1913; liquor, 297; unknown, 972; disappointed love, 220; insanity, 450; ill-health, 242; domestic infelicity, 245; business loss, 97. The government reports show that these three years represent in the aggregate the greatest corresponding increase in distilled, brewed, and domestic liquors in the United States since 1881, and the greatest quantity consumed of all liquors and wines between 1840 and 1896 inclusive.[2] It has been physiologically

[1] "Encyclopædia Britannica," Vol. XXII, p. 663.
[2] United States Bulletin, No. 17, July, 1898, pp. 510–518.

demonstrated, that, as the nerve tension of a people becomes more intense, the desire for stimulants and the susceptibility to the invasion of the drink habit become more acute; and what has not inaptly been termed the "nerve belt" is also the *drink belt* of the more highly civilized races, and imperceptibly, in conjunction with other agencies, paves the way for these nervous and mental disorders. It reacts upon the disordered nervous organization in the form of chronic irritability and distrust, ready to flame into precipitate attack upon the most trivial occasion. I have no doubt alcoholism is the direct as well as the indirect cause of much of the homicidal tendency in European countries, and that it has stamped Western civilization with an unenviable reputation.

TABLE X

CENSUS TABLE OF HOMICIDES (INTERNATIONAL), ACCORDING TO POPULATION

COUNTRIES	POPULATION	YEARS	TRIED		CONVICTED	
			Annual Average	Per 100,000 Inhabitants	Annual Average	Per 100,000 Inhabitants
Scotland . .	2,841,941	1882–6	60	2.11	21	0.74
England . .	19,898,053	1882–6	318	1.60	151	0.76
Holland . .	3,172,464	1882–6	35	1.10	28	0.88
Germany . .	35,278,742	1882–6	567	1.61	476	1.35
Ireland . .	3,854,588	1882–6	129	3.35	54	1.40
France . .	31,044,370	1882–6	847	2.73	580	1.87
Belgium . .	4,377,813	1881–5	132	3.02	101	2.31
Austria . .	17,199,237	1883–6	689	4.01	499	2.90
Hungary . .	10,821,558	1882–6			625	5.78
Spain . . .	13,300,889	1883–6	1584	11.91	1085	8.16
Italy . . .	23,408,277	1887	3606	15.40	2805	11.98
United States	61,908,906	1890			7386	11.93

In the Tenth Census, there were reported 4608 prisoners charged with homicide. In the Eleventh Census the number had increased to 7351 (single offence), an increase of 2743, representing 11 in 100,000 of the population. This is much larger than the tables of other countries, partly prepared by Dr. Bosco, will show by comparison, from which fact it will be seen we stand next the head in the sad competition, Italy alone outstripping us in the race.

Deducting from the total number of homicides in the United States (Table 13, pp. 38, 39, U. S. Census Bulletin, No. 182, Homicides in 1890) 7386 (double crimes), 973 whose habits are not given, the remaining 6378 are classed as follows: total abstainers, 1282; occasional or moderate drinkers, 3829; drunkards, 1267, or 19.87 per cent (35 women omitted), which latter is doubtless much below the real mark, as many of the occasional drinkers and perhaps total abstainers very properly might be included among the latter; moreover, homicides, being proverbially among the better class of offenders, are averse to adding to their crime the additional onus of being designated a drunkard, unlike the professional criminal in this respect who does not hesitate to cover his defection under the cloak of inebriety.

As a further local study in this respect, and fairly representative of sections, the two extreme Coast states and a leading Middle state offer a fair illustration of similar conditions. Take, for example, California's leading prison, San Quentin, for 1890. There the number of prisoners for that year set down as habitually intemperate at the time of commitment is given at 683 out of a total prison population of 1392, or 49 per cent of the whole. The Auburn Penitentiary, New York, 1897, out of 1005 prisoners shows 430 intemperates, or 42.78 per cent. Joliet, Ill., shows 271 out of 1319, or 20 per cent intemperates. From the California statistics we learn, as still more directly allied to the criminal propagation, that, in 437 instances out of the 1392 individual criminal transactions, liquor was put down as the direct cause of the deed, and in 271 instances the saloon was the actual place of the committal of the crime. The position which the saloon and the drink habit hold in the order of criminal causation is readily inferred from these figures.

The direct bearing of these facts upon the aggregate criminal problem is tremendous, while the indirect and moral influence is incalculable. The " Dictionaire des Sciences Medicales " has thought it of sufficient importance to institute the broad comparison between causal relations existing between intemperance and crime in the following figures, which it publishes upon this subject, and which would, perhaps, fairly state the real relation, if it could be definitely ascertained : England, 43 per cent of crimes as the result of alcohol; Belgium, 80 per cent; Sweden, 31 per cent; Germany, 44 per cent, and Denmark, 74 per cent. The saloon is the disturbing cause, the crime-breeding centre, and direct inspirational source where both young and old hatch their schemes and receive their common incentive ; and alcoholism as a disease is the condition par excellence that engenders the criminal habit and strengthens all its abnormal proclivities. Dr. Grenier, of Paris, considers it one of the most active agencies in race degeneracy; and Dr. Dujardin-Beaumetz looks upon it as a natural plague; while social and political economists as well as criminological experts everywhere are unanimous in designating it as the most prolific source of criminal contagion. Dr. Baer, of the Imperial Board of Health and Chief Prison Physician of Berlin, states that 50 per cent of all crime comes from alcohol, and asserts that between 1877 and 1884 (the latter a year prolific in the number of persons condemned, 1066 per 100,000 inhabitants), 11.71 per 100,000 inhabitants on an average entered the hospitals of Germany as chronic alcoholics and afflicted with delirium tremens. The following table from "Die Trunksucht," 1890, will serve to illustrate these figures more in detail:—

1877	.	10.0 per 100,000 pop.	1881	.	9.2 per 100,000 pop.
1878	.	9.5 per 100,000 pop.	1882	.	11.1 per 100,000 pop.
1879	.	10.6 per 100,000 pop.	1883	.	15.6 per 100,000 pop.
1880	.	9.3 per 100,000 pop.	1884	.	19.8 per 100,000 pop.

Dr. Carothers declares that 10 per cent of the estimated half million inebriates in the United States are yearly convicted of crime. Statistics will show 20 per cent of purely alcoholic homicides in the United States, and 70 per cent in other countries.

The editor of the *New Voice* addressed the jailers of the 3000 county jails in the United States with the inquiry, "In your opinion, what proportion of the prisoners in your jail were brought there directly through the use or abuse of intoxicating liquors?" Replies from 1017 sheriffs and under officers, representing 50 different states and territories, were elicited, out of which 257 placed the proportion of such causes at 90 per cent and above; 525 at 75 per cent and above; 73 at 50 per cent and above; while out of the entire 1017 jailers, only 181 could be found to place their estimate below 25 per cent — and 55 of these were from prohibition territories and reported empty jails. However superficial such "returns" as touching the real cause of crime, sufficient may be gathered therefrom as showing that the popular and sympathetic adjunct of criminal wrong-doing is drink.

Ignorance goes hand in hand with these vice-producing environments, and pervades its theoretical phase as the natural darkness favors it in its more concrete form. Aside from its essential value as a purely intellectual stimulus, the bearing of education upon the moral qualities is, of course, the essential to be considered in its purely criminological bearing. The mere acquisition of knowledge in its moral and intellectual aspect must be considered as a *potential*, rather than as an actual, power; *i.e.*, it holds the possibilities for good or evil, as impelled by underlying impulses and motives. Thus, quickening of the mental faculties might only fit the rogue for greater mischief, and but serve to put more dangerous instrumentalities for harm into the hands of the already evil-disposed. An educated professional criminal with his sharpened intellect would prove but the more dangerous enemy, being thus better qualified and equipped to perpetrate his nefarious schemes against society.

Upon theoretic grounds, much divergence of opinion exists relative to the effect of education upon crime.

For instance, Dr. Ogle, in a recent report, has shown that, in 1881–1884, as the result of the passage of the "Elementary Education Act" in Great Britain, 85 per cent of its population were able to read and write, representing an increase of 10 per cent since its passage, with presumably a still greater growth up to date; but he asserts, notwithstanding this progression in educational matters, crime was steadily on the increase. The assumption is hardly borne out by the facts as shown by the prison population of Great Britain. It steadily decreased in serious crimes from 1878 down to 1892, and this notwithstanding the increase of population in the same periods. Mulhall records a decline corresponding with the increase of schools in that country. Dr. MacDonald, in his valuable résumé on "Education and Crime," gives us, as the summary of his painstaking labor, his conclusions from the tables furnished, that in France (1830–1881) and Italy (1866–1887), there has been a relative increase of both education and crime; in Germany (1882–1887), there has been a general increase of both university education and crime; while in Austria, Norway and Sweden, Great Britain, Australia, Japan, Würtemberg, and Saxony, there have been an increase of education and also a decrease of crime. Numerous other concomitants, not taken into account here, also enter into these comparisons, that have their due weight in bringing about these results, and in consequence weaken any arbitrary conclusions with reference to the influence of education on crime; but on the whole, perhaps, it is as good a test as any, taken by itself.

These statistics cannot but fail to impress the fact that crime grows best under the shadow of ignorance. The criminal springs so universally from the illiterate classes as to force the conclusion that ignorance sustains a vital relation to criminality, as a whole. The report of the Eleventh Census gives us in this respect the following data: 13 per cent of those reporting out of prison population could neither read nor write; 1 per cent claimed to have been in college; 4 per cent in a high school or academy; 48 per cent in grammar grade of public school, and 20 per cent in private elementary school. Individual prison reports give us still lower percentage of illiteracy, as indicated by the three representative institutions already named; viz., Auburn, N. Y., San Quentin, Cal., and Joliet, Ill., each giving us a percentage of illiteracy as follows:—

TABLE XI

PERCENTAGE OF ILLITERACY. COMMON SCHOOL AND COLLEGIATE

YEAR	INSTITUTION	ILLITERATE	COMMON SCHOOL	COLLEGIATE
1897	Auburn, N.Y.	9.4	77.00	2.1
1897	San Quentin, Cal. . .	20.30	70.53	
1896	Joliet, Ill.	6.52	62.54	6.82

It must be remembered by those unfamiliar with the prison element, that what is here given as common school education is, in the great majority of cases, the most superficial possible and in many instances not much removed beyond the rudimentary. There are of course exceptions to this rule.

Lombroso's table as to education shows that 95 per cent out of 507 criminals were versed in elementary instructions, as against 69 per cent out of 100 normals; while analphabets and superior instruction claimed 12 per cent each of criminals, as against 6 per cent analphabets and 27 per cent superior instruction respectively among normals, showing the superiority of the higher education in its relation to crime.

A priori, it is not a difficult matter to establish a connection between crime and a low mentality and ignorance on the part of its personnel; or *vice versa*. The direct result of the educative process upon the individual is the strengthening of every faculty of mind (especially the memory), the reasoning powers, and proportionately the imagination and the will. The two latter factors enter vitally into the criminalistic activity (as has already been illustrated), whose cultivation and strengthening must have a strong reflexive influence upon the moral character, giving to it a clearness of perceptivity and mental forecast with which to weigh transgressional suggestion, thus aiding to hold the attention to morality and virtue. It moreover equips the would-be offender with direct moral safeguards, thus enabling him to play a better part in the social competition, especially when the educative processes take upon themselves a multiple character in the form of a practical, all-round training, — intellectually, morally, physically, hygienically, industrially and economically, as it should, in order to prove genuinely effective. It gives a larger outlook, imparts broader views, affords firmer grip upon the means and avenues of success, while it strengthens self-control, inspires self-respect, and the better equips the subject to fight life's battles. This especially applies in the matter of trades education, in respect of which the average criminal is lamentably deficient.

What has been said of illiteracy with reference to the native born criminal applies with greater force to our foreign population, among whom the percentage of illiteracy is 38 per cent greater than among the native born whites.

Among all the vicious crime-producing instrumentalities that converge about the central personality, none can be found more directly effective and virulent in the perversion of the moral and social instincts and the consequent hopeless inuring of the subject in crime, than the fact of imprisonment itself.

Ostensibly incarceral in scope and purpose, it is, in reality, the promulgative source of practical and theoretic crime, where all its nefarious methods and principles are thoroughly canvassed, new ways and means devised, old errors corrected by comparing notes, and where more systematic overtures are perfected for future exploitation. No small proportion of the concerted feints upon property and person is unquestionably planned in prison, where the prevailing congregate system offers such exceptional opportunities therefor. The penitentiary is the veritable finishing school of crime, where the apprentice-hand is readily trained under the tutelage of experts; and where every lingering instinct of good in the bosom of the novice is mercilessly crushed out in the pressure of an all-pervasive moral impact. A moment's reflection enables one to catch a glimpse of the intense retrogressiveness and moral enervation that must surcharge the atmosphere in a place where the legally elect of all nations and climes, all shades and degrees of depravity, are congregated in a festering mass; the semi-savage instinct and rudimentary proclivities all in bold collusion with the overthrown moral sense working together in suppressed ferment, all together presenting a picture hardly favorable to contemplate from an inspirational and educative standpoint.

The novice may enter such environment with a certain degree of moral upgirding, possibly with a sense of genuine repugnance at first; but no sooner there, than he rapidly adjusts himself to the situation, and, once familiar, soon becomes a sympathizer in its pervading spirit. One touch of nature makes the whole place kin. In the multitude of instances, he finds his ideals there; and is content, save as he chafes under temporary restraint.

A taste of prison life, its freedom from conventionalities and responsibility, the delightful paternalism and *bonhomie* prevailing there, render it fully as endurable (at least to the majority of recidivists) as the precarious vicissitudes of " outrageous fortune " that harass them upon the street.

It is not necessary to descend into particulars in order to afford a hint of the depths of depravity that tend to brutalize and harden the average prison habitué, while a discussion of institutional principles that nourish and make possible such a state properly belongs to another branch of criminology.

Sufficient to say, the prison from every point of view is the chief ostensible promoter of every ill it essays to cure, and offers the main incentive to crime in the objective and exemplary inducements it holds out thereto by virtue of its congregate system of indiscriminate herding together all classes of offenders. Hence, it is safe to say, it succeeds in turning out more direct results in the shape of confirmed criminals, hardened to the contemplation of theoretic vice in all its forms and degrees, ready to put their knowledge into practice, than any other accredited agency within the range of experience or devised by the folly of man, resting in the consent of the masses.

These environmental with further minor details that crowd both the instinctive and habitual offender on all sides, will be further noticed in connection with subsequent chapters on "The Single Offender" and "The Juvenile Offender," under which their discussion thus equally fall, together with the concluding chapter, in which latter they naturally group themselves under their several heads as conserving factors in the criminal interpretation.

With such faulty environment on all sides, it is not difficult to trace the rise, progression, and development of that numerous class of moral and social malcontents who have received their impress chiefly from without at the instance of a vicious social environment with which they stand associated, or possibly through pre-existent taint or inherent weakness (though ever less markedly distinct from the normal) than in the case of the congenital criminal.

The habitual criminal represents about one-fourth to one-third of all legal offenders; and together with the instinctive criminal element (about ten per cent) comprehends perhaps forty per cent of the total recalcitrant population.

Their diathesis is vitally allied to social degeneration in conjunction with low mental, moral, and physical standards, unmodified by the ordinary intermediary correctives, social and educational palliatives and prevenient methods, that usually operate as counteractants under normally constituted social, family, and institutional ideals.

CHAPTER IX

THE SINGLE OFFENDER — HIS PERSONALITY AND ORIGIN

Social Environment

THERE remains but little to be said as bearing distinctively upon the personal features of the classes mentioned in the categories as coming within the strict purview of the special criminologist. Under his scrutiny the rank and file of the host militant have successfully passed in review, thus far filling the foreground to the exclusion of still another portion, who, while excelling in numbers, fall beneath their compatriots in general interest and class distinction, coming, as they do, more particularly under the patronymic of those upon whom the law, rather than nature, has set her seal.

The so-called "occasional criminal" of the schools comprises, roughly speaking, about one-half of the total prison population, and may be said to compose the neutral tint against which the more pronounced delinquent stands out in bold relief. We have sought to sketch the latter without extenuation, and it has hardly proven a difficult task to describe him as he is, for the reason that he is not as other men. In saying this, we are not unmindful of the fact that, in many respects, the average recalcitrant is not so markedly different from the generality of mankind save in the tone and quality of his moral fibre and in his anti-social proclivities, in which respects he is distinctively unique in contra-distinction from his normal fellows.

Judging him from the strictly anthropological standpoint of normality, he presents a strange and incongruous anomaly, with contradictions so glaringly at variance as to render him largely inexplicable, and yet not, as we have seen, with sufficiently unifying forcefulness, physiologically, to set him apart distinctively by himself. To view him in his proper attitude as a true moral delinquent, his personality becomes more distinct and its composite details more homogeneous. In other words, the very incongruities of the real abnormal constitute the essential components and are the accredited indices of what he really is, and serve to explain him in detail even as the traits and characteristics of the good man fit in and harmonize with *his* character and illustrate *its* essential unity. We expect the latter to be consistent, and are shocked when he is not; we look only for ultra wrong-doing in the evil-disposed and criminal, and are surprised when we discover traces of good. The one we expect to find the synonym of all that is virtuous and upright, the other the personification of all that is diabolical, forgetting that the rudiments of each are to be found overlapping in both, and that there is none so good but he might be better, and few so bad they might not be worse. Man is a bundle of contradictions and incongruities, whose merits are chiefly accentuated in the essentially good and in the intrinsically bad, but lost sight of in the mediocre and the commonplace.

We here tread closely in the footprints of that large company of purely legal offenders whom Lombroso has not inaptly termed "criminaloids," and Tyndale and Ferri, with less felicity, "criminals by occasion," — a nomenclature that has already been characterized as vague and contradictory, covering indiscriminately, as pointed out, at once the perpetrator by a single act, and the author of unnumbered crimes. This class lies, properly speaking, outside the pale of true criminalism, while indubitably sharing in the common reprobation affixed by law and custom. Culpable by an isolated offence, possibly as the outcome of a train of antecedent circumstances and secondary causes that received their initiative from a state of affairs for which society itself is largely to blame, he has never in the past, doubtless will not again in the future, so challenge public sentiment and violate the letter of the law as to pillory him upon its bosses because of such transgressional shortcomings.

Thus, omitted from the criminal rôle (save by implication), he must unfortunately be given a *pseudonym* in the criminal classification, both perhaps in justice to himself, and partly in accord with the facts. To do otherwise would be to assign him to an arbitrary rôle not merited, since it follows from the above analysis that he is something *less* than a criminal, and something *more* than a non-criminal. It is for this reason Lombroso has well said, and Ferri and Benedikt bear out the assertion, that "there is, properly speaking, no such thing as an occasional criminal, in the sense of a normal individual casually launched into crime."

As in the case of the habitual, so here, the mere external nature of the offence is not of itself sufficient to assign him to any particular category, for the offence may be one of theft, or murder, or common assault committed under different psychological moods, or a mixture of several, as in the cases of ordinary habituals and instinctives. Again, his offence may be against property in its various forms, as forgery, embezzlement, burglary, or common theft; or, as against person, as homicide, murder, or simple assault with or without pretext; or, as is commonly the case, a purely impromptu affair under stress of passion, or at the instigation of a grievance, or as the result of alcoholism, all of which may leave him much as it found him, in every respect normal.

It is the pretext, motive (or want of it), in connection with predetermined character, the enormity of the act, or the fact of recidivation, that forms the usual criminal test. As in case of the habitual, an isolated act, whatever its nature, though apparently standing isolated and without apparent provocation or psychological antecedent, may nevertheless be associated with a long line of predisposing causes of which this single overt act is but the climax; it may be traceable directly to antenatal or otherwise criminalistic causal relations as clearly defined as in previously cited distinctively criminal cases.

As to his essential nature, be it said, this class generally presents all the salient characteristics of the normally sound. It is in this regard rather than with respect to the particular act with which he stands impugned, that a great gulf is fixed between the criminal by nature and the casual offender here delineated.

Abnormality is a deviation from commonly accepted standards. Humanity is sound at heart. One need but compare the untoward with the good, as we see it exemplified on the whole in everyday life, to be convinced that dishonesty or distrust in human affairs are the exceptions, not the rule, and that conduct in generality is founded upon this universal concept. All business and mutual intercourse, the amenities of society, the very fabric of civil and social institutions presuppose the inherent stability and integrity of human character. Without it, man's very existence would be imperilled, since it is evident upon but the slightest reflection that a state of society where the contrary prevails could not of necessity endure. This is what we mean when we speak of a normal state to which we unconsciously refer by way of comparison, and to which we make our common appeal in the fulsomeness of confidence from the veriest commonplace to the most momentous transactions in life. We here walk by faith, not by sight, as in the higher realms of experience.

The vast bulk of humanity respond to this characterization, and their aggregate conduct in this respect may be summarized as a type of universality, whether applied to man as an individual or as a member of organized society. Non-conformity to these essentials gives us the moral anomaly as exemplified in the criminal personality whose psychological likeness alone is cosmopolitan, morally recognized the world over.

Unique in many respects, the moral attitude of the

habitual offender is especially so viewed in the light of his persistent and unthinking antagonism against law and order, which is but another name for organized morality, and which answers for the conservatism of the race. As a lawbreaker, he stands isolated in the midst of an irresistible force. The exponent of a brutalizing and immoral retrogressiveness, he is ingulfed in the onward rush of the world torrent. As the enemy of peace and order, he is the cynosure of an argus-eyed legal guardianship, against all of which he is forever arrayed as an enemy of his kind and a foe to the social order.

Reasoning by analogy, it would indeed seem plain from the foregoing that a nature thus distorted verges closely upon the border-land of moral insanity.

Moral recoil is a criterion of normal functioning. Its absence in moral delinquents, as set forth in foregoing descriptions, is the mark of psychical degeneration. Remorse is the echo of the original moral protest. Its presence illustrates the difference between the permanent and the temporary delinquent, and in ninety-nine cases out of a hundred is the subjective factor that operates as an effective deterrent against criminal relapse in the case of the normal (legal) delinquent.

Consciousness, of course, can never be said to be impervious to criminal suggestibility. The soundest mind is subject sometimes to its insinuations. The will interposes in the normally conditioned and effectively plants itself to check the anti-social outbreak. Self-control is the habit of a sound mind. Its own self-sufficiency protects the susceptibilities from self-surrender to open compact with what might otherwise prove the door to self-entailed habit or to spontaneous wrong-doing, as in the case of the criminal by passion or impulse.

The criminal mind is such, not because it is open to suggestibility but by reason of this lack of inhibitory power in the right place and at the right time, hence falling away at the first onset of the criminal insinuation; while the normally sound, in spite of outward provocation and inward oscillation, maintains his moral equilibrium, undue pressure alone being able to subvert him, and that always in the face of moral protest.

As we have seen, the *first* personal factor to assert itself in the rise of the individual (and the race) is the self-preservative instinct; so the *last* to be acquired are the social instincts. In the psychopathic metamorphosis above described the reverse is true; the first to fall away are the social and the last to disappear the personal factors, the criminal and brutal instincts remaining long after he has ceased to be a man and become less than an animal.

Man in his normal capacity acts from motive. The difference between the strictly criminal and the non-criminal lies in the fact that, like the mentally unsound, the slightest provocation or suggestion may induce him to the perpetration of the gravest offence; while, as we have seen in the case of the normally constituted, the strongest incentives are seemingly necessary to push him into transgressional acts. In the one instance, the end to be gained is entirely incommensurate with the risk involved (which is the test of normal as well as of mental functioning), the true criminal ever acting without adequate provocation, in its broadest acceptation, at least without a proper sense of compensation, such as we find ordinarily actuating the generality of mankind. He functions mainly (as already premised under separate heads) from two general sources; viz., instinct, or as the result of acquired habit.

The single offender is impelled to crime by neither of these inciting causes, consequently the explanation of his active genetics must be sought elsewhere; viz., in line with ordinary motives and impulsions that usually move ordinary minds under given conditions. Motive must here, however, not be confounded with deliberation, in which latter sense the habitual is not always found wanting, and into which a certain shade of intelligence and cunning enters as the conserving element. As a rule, the more intelligent the perpetrator, the more deliberative the act. Intelligence and volition have not yet lost their power to discriminate and control, as is so frequently the case among chronics, with whom, as is well known, it is not uncommon to deliberate a given crime in order to attain the most trivial end, though the act be fraught with the most serious consequences. The records abound in these curious psychological studies, where singular inadequacy of ends are coupled with imminent risk, leading to the inference of mental unsoundness rather than moral instability as part explanation of such criminal psychosis. It points to lack of causality, however, as part of the mental equipment, a marked feature of degeneracy (arrested development) in the pronounced criminal. A certain deliberativeness may thus be not incompatible with a low (immature) mental state, and may be associated with or without intent, alike in the first or in the second offender. Deliberativeness has respect to the modality; motive, to the result. Intelligence conditions the latter, cunning corresponds to the former. Deliberativeness coupled with motive enters into all forms of semi-commercial criminalism, as forgery, embezzlement, attempt to defraud, etc.; deliberativeness without adequate motive constitutes the majority of instances that make up the descriptive criteria of an ordinary criminal, especially of the pettier order. This is not saying, however, that all crime must be premeditative in order to assign its perpetrator to a peculiarly distinctive rôle, for it is well known the most pronouncedly instinctive criminal may also be the most profoundly impromptu offender who may strike without either motive or deliberation. One class of offences primarily arises from the higher social motives, the other springs from mere animal cunning mingled with the self-preservative instinct. The distinction is a vital one. It is the difference between subverted functional activity and the moral sense aroused to do battle, thereby testifying to qualities altogether lacking in the true moral anomaly. The normally equipped demands an equivalent as the price of his non-instinctive self-surrender; the criminal degenerate's sole compensation lies paramountly in the seeming satisfaction afforded in the perpetration of the act itself.

It is akin to the joy of battle; the excitement of covert attack, survival of the primitive instinct, that unquestionably accounts for much of the peculiar criminal equipment above depicted, and that apparently has only emotional and nerve incitation to fall back upon for explanation. "Oh! I just love to steal, it is a joy," remarked an unfortunate, to the writer, upon a certain occasion, — a subject in whom the religious instinct was involved in fierce though unequal battle with the neuro-psychic taint.

There is no attempt in all this to palliate the normally equipped and otherwise sound legal derelict ; rather the greater reprobation, in proportion as his healthier equipoise the better qualifies him to resist encroachment, to obey the moral law, and thus yield to the demands society makes upon him.

Moral responsibility follows in the wake of motive and correspondingly testifies to freedom and consequent criminal culpability. It is not suggestibility, but *consent*, not temptation, but self-surrender, that constitutes the essence of the criminal act; the ability to accept or to reject forming both the moral and legal test. The divergence between the predestined criminal and the normally sound, is manifestly the difference between the scales of responsibility in equibalance, and the same with the sword of Brennus cast in. One is at liberty to accept or reject; the other, to act apparently alone (beyond a certain point) in the grooves of a predestined auto-activity cut by habit, or heredity, or both.

The single offender is the true responsible personality in the criminal categories, and must, therefore, be considered such in respect of both the ethical and legal acceptance, save and except always in so far as he gives unmistakable evidence of the presence of the instinctive criminal trait or of the character of the hardened habitué.

It is for this reason the law emphasizes motive as a concomitant in criminal conduct, thus proportionately enhancing the guilt. The more normal, the more fully motive is presumed to enter in as a moving principle with a tendency to force the subject over into the sphere of true legal accountability, from an ethical standpoint. Motive being the first to disappear in the wreck of the ethical faculty, its presence or absence relatively indicates the criminal, or the pseudo-criminal, in detail. The latter stands at the end of the anthropological criminal scale, as already outlined, with no distinguishing traits, intellectually or morally, to differentiate him from the rest of mankind with whom he may, therefore, be properly classified, by habit, by social and intellectual bias, by predisposition and bent, by anthropological and biological characterization, as well as by every test that ordinarily fathoms motive and sounds the will. This motive may be either good or bad ; i.e., it may be at the dictate of an exaggerated egoism, or it may arise out of any of the innumerable social, personal, or economic incitants, which, acting upon an impressionable nature already keyed to respond keenly to natural and material impressions, evoke the latent instincts that lie dormant in the breast. He is dominated by motives, swayed by passions, moved by impulses, as the generality of mankind, rather than by any direct criminal impulsion, or at the dictates of habit directly acquired at the instance of a vitiated environment, or through the prenatal taint. His dereliction usually stands associated with an environment that has upon its surface the stamp of social respectability, from the depths of whose conventionalities it receives its initiatives and draws its inspiration, without any further distinctively anti-social proclivities to account for him.

These associations and environments (though less pronounced than in the cases of the instinctive or acquired criminal disposition) are nevertheless fully as effective when brought to bear directly upon an otherwise impressionable and sympathetic organization readily susceptible to their insinuations and responsive to the calls of natural inclination or the cravings of artificial tastes and stimuli.

Society, though not so directly, is nevertheless as broadly responsible for the occasional offender as for the more pronounced criminal in so far as a false, if not vicious, environment may be so held accountable.

Bearing in mind the vital connection existing between the individual and the social whole, also the direct mutual reciprocity traceable between the two on the moral side, the casual delinquent has been not inaptly termed the "social offender." His anti-social proclivities are symptomatic, not organic. He is a social offender because he was first society's protégé. Social potentialities are unlimited either as to their good or as to their evil effects. The same resourcefulness that accounts for its charitological, educational, and religious amelioratives also precipitates its sins and crimes. The identical fountain sends forth at once both sweet and bitter waters, whose moral outcome unfortunately cannot always be prognosticated or labelled in advance as either amelioratives or irritants. We must take them as they come, and they are found not infrequently to partake of the natures of both. Like its protégé, society contains alike the seeds of progress and decay, of life and death. It holds no more than is put into it. The relation between society and its parts is mutual and vicarious.

If the individual member is accountable to the extent of yielding to the criminal insinuation, society is equally responsible to the extent of furnishing the incitants. Upon which is chiefly imputable the weight of reprobation becomes thereafter merely a question of casuistry which must remain unanswered so long as it remains undetermined as to whether crime in itself is largely the fruit of bad environment, or whether a bad environment is the result of the criminal propension. In a primitive state it might have been easier of solution. Civilization injects the unknown quantity that renders it enigmatical. As society progresses the criminal problem becomes more abstruse. The law is from simple to complex.

So distinctively socialistic and inter-communal is this particular phase of what we might properly term "modern criminality," that a critical analysis fails to disassociate the parasite from its host, the plant from the root to which it adheres and from which it derives its sustenance and life. The most brilliant and dogmatic of the empirical school have not hesitated to assign as the chief vehicle to criminal causation a defective social organism, cherishing at its heart and cultivating in its customs the spore of the criminal propagation to which it largely stands sponsor.

" As far as the investigation of criminals has gone," says Dr. MacDonald, the most eminent criminological expert in this country, "the indications are that the cause of most crime lies in the surroundings rather than in the criminal. . . . There can be no scientific sociology in the rigid sense of that term until a thorough study is made of the individual in society." [1] Büchner asserts that defect of intelligence, want of education, and poverty, are the three great factors of crime. " Nature," says Lombroso, "is responsible for the born criminal; society, in a great measure, for the criminal by occasion." Ferri, while he does not claim crime to be the exclusive product of the social environment, looks upon it as the centre of a network of causes of which organic and psychical anomalies of the criminal are co-related and interdependent as the "heart and lungs or stomach of the mammal are to the life of the animal." He gives social causal relations, next to psychical and organic, foremost place in the field of criminological research.[2] "Man acts, but society leads," says Laurent. Society is to the individual only the larger organism, in which, as in the physiological, all moral action and reaction are mutual and interdependent. Which is the initiative, is of less importance than which is the most readily amenable to amelioration and cure. Here, too, be it observed, the law of retroaction holds good; and whatever in-

[1] " Criminological Studies," U. S. Reports, p. 1675.
[2] " Criminal Sociology," p. 56.

fluences the parts affects the whole; and conversely, that which moves the whole influences the parts.

The tide of the criminal incursion is against person, against property, and against purity. The socio-criminal homology is indicated by the varied degrees of homicide, of theft, and of violation, each of which, arising in the vitiated personal centres, is fed by the communal streams, and, if permitted to exist at all, thus receives the stamp of public approbation and the acquiescence of the prevailing social conscience. "Every society has precisely the amount of crime it deserves,"—and it deserves precisely that which it allows. This permission is either tacit or implied. Whatever form of wrong is *permitted* to exist, be it potential or otherwise, thereby receiving the assent of public opinion, is impliedly legitimatized thereby; and the community cannot complain when such evil turns and rends it. Society stands sponsor to her own ills. Homicide, the primitive crime, as we have already pointed out, is perpetrated in many ways, and in no small degree under, the shield of municipal authority in the shape of legalized institutional patronage, the direct and indirect abettor of a large per cent of its aggregate crimes. Public sentiment is to this extent *particeps criminis*, the ally of past retrogressive movements plus its contemporaneous brutality. We help create our criminals for a consideration, who thus become a sort of politico-moral tax — "for revenue only."

Aside from these more serious defects, society moreover becomes the accredited patron, if not the responsible moral agent, of innumerable misdemeanors and casual offences that inhere in many of our accepted customs, which, like a social undertow, draw imperceptibly to vice, and which, because of their drain upon the moral forces of society can only be likened to broken-down nerve centres in a diseased physical organism to which they may be compared by analogy. The great bulk of minor offences and acts of violence, it may be said, result directly and indirectly from drink, gambling, fast living, and the jealousies and antagonisms incident to an expanding and complex social system in which the economic and industrial conditions are far from settled; while erotic offences (indecent assaults, etc.) are largely engendered by similar causes, incident, among other things, upon the close herding together and promiscuity of the sexes, which wait upon poverty, and are the bane of city life, as already illustrated.

All these temptations, it is to be observed, especially evoke the evil genius of youth and go to make up largely the bulk of offences among habitués; though among the special class here considered as falling away, the burden, as a rule, must perhaps be shifted upon the shoulders of the more mature, conservative, and well-to-do, who, as will be readily surmised, are better equipped to withstand relapse and the consequent abandonment to persistent crime so characteristic of the instinctive and habitual criminal. I am not aware of any statistics upon this interesting phase of the subject, but doubt not, as the drift of former deductions, that maturity is unfavorable to the formation of the criminal habit as such. The single offender's fall,

as a rule, is that of the impromptu offender; his rehabilitation is usually permanent.

Looseness of social affiliations and predilections, many
of them harmless in inception and perilous only in their
potentialities and abuse when brought into actual contact
with weak resistant powers, are the minor agencies that
pave the way for incipient moral instability. They premise every shade of self-indulgence and excess which
usually find shelter under the patronage of fashionable
resorts, and midnight clubs, and drinking bouts, whose
inevitable tendency is to weaken the family tie and
lessen the healthy influences of domiciliary restraint, for
which reasons these forms of self indulgence chiefly
prove dangerous. The inevitable consequences of such
recourse for nerve stimulus and excitement are conducive
neither to the strengthening of morals nor to the conser-
vation of the physical vitality (rather the reverse), besides
tending to create wrong social ideals and false notions
of pleasure. The gilded resort and the groggery present a distinction without a difference in this respect, the
matter of respectability being hardly worth considering.

While, of course, many of these social connectives
may be said to be *unmoral* rather than immoral (depending largely upon the subjectivity of the person
himself), it is the potentialities involved that imperil,
especially as they come in contact with weak, impressionable, and pleasure-loving natures, or those already
under the prenatal blight. From the standpoint of
environment alone, the distinction between the habitual
and the casual offender, it would seem, might be one
only of an advanced stage of the same malady, attack-

ing in the one instance an already impoverished vitality, and in the other undermining the healthier organism that has hitherto resisted assault. Much of the iniquity of our social system doubtless is due to the unnatural competition among social castes and between individuals. This tends to stimulate the above abnormal conditions to fever heat. The struggle among the lower classes is here shifted from a battle for existence under badly adjusted economic conditions, to the middle and higher planes, where it takes the form of a no less bitter though far more shameful form of a scramble over superfluities. The object of the strife is changed, metaphorically speaking, from the crumbs that fall from the rich man's table to the plate that glitters upon his board. This feverish and unrestful state thus harmfully infects chiefly the middle classes who strain to emulate the extravagance of those with whom they may not laudably compete. Both male and female share alike this folly, the wife not infrequently dragging down the husband in the desperate effort to "keep up" out of an insufficient salary; the head of the family being compelled to hedge upon his honesty in order to meet the imperious demands. This class, driven to desperation, usually resorts to forgery or embezzlement to supply the drain, or are brought to face defalcation by a shorter route. These comprise largely the more respectable classes, who, better educated and more intelligent, defy legal conventionalities to yield to the social demand. They constitute a large proportion of single offenders.

In the business world, many of the same inconsistencies prevail that we see in other departments of the social order when run at high pressure, having less regard to means than to ends. The inequalities of the law, as affecting rich and poor, are here oftentimes brought into glaring contrast. This perhaps has something to do with embittering certain classes of social outcasts, and too, with some show of reason. Thus the minor offender and the petty misdemeanant, it can but be observed, are uniformly visited with summary justice and swift retribution upon first offence; while, in strong contrast, the higher grade, who sin out of their abundance and therefore have not the excuses of the more impoverished classes, are not unusually treated to a retributory penalty lenient inversely to the gravity of their offence. The assault of the forehanded and well-to-do upon the common integrity, business sense, or official fidelity, is a far more serious shock to the social conscience and goes farther toward lowering public moral tone than all the petty misdemeanants that crowd the calendar. And the reason is plain. Society is warranted in imposing confidence in the intelligence and mature sense of responsibility of those whom fortune favors, and who, when they turn robber, usually rob those below them in the social and financial scale. In the conventional order, the poor rob the rich; here the rich rob the poor, perhaps under the guise of "trusts" and "corners" and "syndicates" — a systematic form of assault under color of business, usually as heartless as it is unjust, because at the instance of an exaggerated selfishness perpetrated under fiction of corporate rights which are artificially and arbitrarily set up above private rights. The war of commercialism is really only a change of front from primitive assault upon the person to one upon property. As the life of the "*villain*" was anciently in the hand of the feudal lord, so the material destiny of the present dependant rests as fully in that of the industrial baron and the financial princeling. The battle-ground has only shifted a stage higher, from the field of physical to that of socio-industrial competition, there to be fought out eventually to the betterment of all classes. This present unnatural condition, when pressed to extremes at the instance of super-self-interest as an exaggerated form of selfishness, verges closely upon criminalism, especially when pushed to ultra-aggressive and defensive attitudes, as it frequently is.

The spirit of gamble, under above inspirational sources, may be said to fairly pervade the fabric of competitive life in the modern, as in the ancient, world. To purchase for one dollar what is worth two, or to sell for two what is worth one, is the *ne plus ultra* of the business world. From the race-track and the poolroom it filters into the stock jobberies and exchanges; and thence the spirit of chance seeks every avenue of trade and occupation from the lowest to the highest. When Fortuna was introduced among the pagan deities, Plutarch tells us she folded her wings on entering, signifying she had found her abiding-place. She remains with us. The Legislative Committee of New York reported that in three years preceeding 1882, the optional cash sales of wheat at the New York Produce Exchange amounted to $244,737,000, while the total of optional sales of all kinds during the same period rated up to the enormous sum of $1,154,367,000. The United States Commission, sent to investigate the New Orleans cotton deal, in 1892, reported 52,000,000 bales as being disposed of on the New York Exchange, and 16,000,000 in the New Orleans, or 68,000,000 in all. As a matter of fact, *but seven and three-fourths millions bales all told were raised in the United States* during that period, and a little over 400,000 of these were sent to New York.

These all represented bogus sales upon fictitious basis, and really stood for gigantic swindles in the name of legitimate business. The same infects brain and brawn, charities and churches; has imperilled even the stability of one sovereign state, and threatened others. The absorbing fascination, linked to the insatiable greed for wealth (which is the crying evil of the times), renders this the most infectious of modern social evils. It bespeaks ill for the nation and the individual, and is undoubtedly the source, indirectly at least, of much of its crime and misery, especially in high places. The majority of defalcations in offices and in trusts, private and corporate, are largely traceable to these vices, which are essentially evil in their inception, criminal in their execution, and demoralizing in their effects. Gambling is but a polite way of robbing under enforced consent and false honor, whether in orthodox fashion or made palliative in the form of trade emulsion. Its effect, in many instances, upon the nervous system, is almost ineradicable; "some of the worst forms of such shock I have ever seen have sprung from this cause," being the verdict of a prominent medical authority upon this subject.

These are all morbid and degenerative states of the social organism, which, as we have seen, reflect a correspondingly deteriorating effect upon the individual member, making the whole social system responsive to every accent of its moral tone. It is for this reason that the periodicity in crime, already alluded to, varies on the side of the lesser offences with the corresponding fluctuation of social and economic conditions, while the graver offences that inhere in the anthropological features of human nature as the fixed result of past racial retrogression, are characterized by greater uniformity and stability.

It is not necessary to go further into detail for a general view of this feature of the subject; sufficient to say, the foregoing deductions serve to show the close and vital relation existing between social environment and crime, and the indirect character of its general influence upon public conduct.

This view of the subject does not in any wise relieve the individual offender from his share of personal responsibility as a member of the social order (the original source of accountability ever remaining in him as before); it only goes to strengthen that postulate of the criminalistic theory that makes environment the secondary non-individualistic patron of the criminal impulse, and calls upon society to assume its share in the joint responsibility both as to its origin and cure. If, in this latter respect, she cannot absolutely supply the remedy, she can at least lend her moral support and pledge her material aid toward the amelioration of these contributive sources to the social disease.

The female delinquent, who, of course, shares in the sad inheritance, for our purpose comes more particularly under the description of the single offender. Of course, the general underlying principles above discussed that thus far apply in the analysis of the instinctive, the habitual, and the single offender, apply with equal pertinency in the case of the female offender, except as related to certain physical idiosyncrasies, forms of crime, and the matter of numerical ratio, as to which latter fact more especially the disproportion between the sexes is, of course, very great. The percentage of indictable females as compared with males, in European countries, is as eighteen to eighty-two, or one woman to four and one-half men. In the United States the ratio is less.

International comparison gives us approximately the following table for the different countries, which represents the whole recalcitrant population, both misdemeanants and higher offenders : —

TABLE XII

COUNTRY	NUMBER OF EACH SEX CONVICTED PER 100 CONVICTIONS		
	Females	Males	Total
England and Wales	18	82	100
Germany	18	82	100
France.	17	83	100
Hungary	16	84	100
Austria	14	86	100
Belgium	11	89	100
Russia	9	91	100
United States	9	91	100
Italy	8	92	100

The United States census (1890) gives the total number of female delinquents at 6405 out of a total prison population of 82,329, or 7.78 per cent. Out of this number of offences in detail, 16 were against the government; 3833 were against society, including public morals, public peace, and public policy; 770 were against the person, and 1325 against property; while miscellaneous crimes (462) constituted the balance.

Physically, virility is the distinguishing characteristic of the female offender. Generally speaking, the lower jaw of the female offender is heavier than in the case of normals, and the orbital capacity is likewise larger, as a rule. The heads of fallen women are smaller; those of poisoners being the largest; and the minimum is found among thieves. The skull exceeds the male in the greater number of Wormian bones, as well as in the simplicity and anomalies of palate and atlas. The female criminal skull approximates more to male, especially as to the occipital region. The same may be said as to physiognomy, voice, etc. The brains of 42 Italian female criminals, examined by Varaglia and Silva, weighed 1178 grammes each. In 148 normal woman, Fleger and Wechsel found the average weight to be 1189 grammes.

Other data descriptive of the female delinquent have already been interspersed in the course of the preceding narrative, and need not here be further enlarged upon.

Lombroso, and all criminal anthropologists, note the rarity of the female criminal type, so called, as well as the lesser number of anomalies, as compared with the male offender. Congenitally, she is less inclined to wrong-doing than men, being atavistically less savage. Her primitive bent is negative, though when depraved, it is observable that her degeneration is more complete. When pressed to primitive conditions, she is more cruel and revengeful. She is frequently a single offender, though relapses among female prisoners are many. The female offender is longer lived than the male, and four to five times less addicted to suicide than the latter. She is less easily reclaimed than the male. Female criminality, on the whole, is on the wane.

CHAPTER X

I. *Recidivation.* II. *Increase.* III. *Decrease.*

THE statistics of crime have been so interwoven with the woof and texture of the criminal problem and form so large a portion of its recital, that they may, without violence, be termed the skeleton and framework of the same. Numerical data (to extend the figure) are the ligaments and tendons that bind together and connect the anthropological and social features, and give to the subject its proper structural and proportional bearing. Numbers trench upon the domain of every known science, from the study of the individual to that of the social economy, penetrating even the regions of the moral and the spiritual. "Man is an enigma as an individual, in the mass he is a mathematical problem."[1]

Demography—the science of statistics—is essentially modern. Its absence constitutes the chief defect in our knowledge of past events, whose recorded facts come down to us largely in fragmentary form, leaving it for us to reconstruct them inferentially into something like a consistent whole.

Its vital bearing upon criminological study is evident at a glance. The *technique* of crime as a social fact is largely based upon the sense of numbers. Its numeri-

[1] "Vestiges of Creation," p. 70.

cal ratio, as compared with the mother population whence it sprang, gives us the primary accepted standard of proportion with reference to the criminal status. Registration from one period to another affords the sole insight into criminal fluctuation; and when studied in conjunction with the moods and variations existing in industrial and economic realms, — the conditions of the harvest, climatic, and other fluctuations, all of which are largely determined by numerical data — it is noticeable that figures are determining values in the sphere of the criminal phenomenon, from whence the student draws conclusions, and casts his horoscope.

The subject has thus far associated itself inseparably with the narrative. Further elaboration in this respect may seem superfluous, save as bearing directly upon the broader subject of relative increase or decrease of the criminal population, local and international. The broadest statistical generalization of the criminal subject lies in the threefold division of: I. *Recidivation;* II. *Criminal Increase;* III. *Decrease.* An analysis along these lines is of the highest importance, not only in ascertaining the actual status of crime, but also in enabling us to forecast results with reasonable accuracy, and thus aid to shape legislative and prevenient measures to meet the constantly changing requirements of the criminal and penological problem intelligently.

I

Recidivation

Recidivation — criminal repetition — is the conventional form under which chronic criminalism manifests itself.

Relapse is the distinguishing peculiarity of the genuine criminal everywhere. The natural instincts and predisposing bent of the congenital and habitual offenders are instinctively toward repeated transgressional acts as the legitimate outcome of the criminal propensity. With him, as has been truly said, reformation is the exception, recidivation the rule. This applies with equal force to that larger number of delinquents who make up the brunt of the criminal classes and whose range of progressiveness, being more diversified, is open to crime from many sides, as well as to those more pronounced offenders whose primitive atavistic proclivities nevertheless incline them toward a less wide field of offensive operations, generally confined to the person, though under modern socialistic impulses also associated at times with crimes against society and property.

The burden of recidivation runs largely to offences against the social order, as of the property instinct, as commercial crimes, such as forgery, swindling, embezzlement, etc., which, in some form or other, are mainly invaded by the professionals, the former running largely along the line of larceny, petty thieving, burglary, and robbery, in their order. In Italy, the highest percentages of relapses are afforded by persons convicted of theft, petty larceny, forgery, rape, manslaughter, and conspiracy in their order; and the lowest are those convicted of assault, murder, and infanticide. In France, relapses against the person comprise 36 per cent; those against property, 58 per cent. Against person, the most frequent are assaults on officials, 86 per cent; bigamy, 59 per cent; rape, 44 per cent; murder, 42 per cent, and manslaughter, 39 per cent.[1] Against property their most frequent relapses occur in the cases of thieves, 72–74 per cent; vagabonds and drunkards, 71–78 per cent; and mendicants, 66 per cent. In France and Sweden, one-third of the recidivists are thieves and vagrants.[2] The tendency to petty thefts, of course, is the most frequently subject to repetition. Italy attributes 20 per cent of her crimes to that form; France, 24 per cent; Belgium, 23 per cent, and Prussia, 37 per cent.[3]

Thus, we find relapse among homicides, as compared with offences against property, much the rarer. In Italy and in the United States (in which respect these countries take the lead), the former, in 1887, for simple homicides gave us 224 who had been already condemned either for the same crime (63) or for a crime mentioned in the same section of the Penal Code; and of those condemned for qualified manslaughter, 78 had already been condemned previously, either for the same crime or one of like character. Of the 7386 cases in the United States in 1890, 534, or 7.22 per cent were recidivists (519 men and 15 women — 186 being negroes and 64 foreign born), and only 35 out of that number were guilty of double crime in connection therewith. The same general principle may be said to prevail with reference to criminals by passion proper, a given assault, whether one of indecency or simple violence, being rarely repeated in one and

[1] Ferri, " Criminal Sociology," p. 16.
[2] " Abnormal Man," MacDonald, p. 32.
[3] " Verbrechen und Verbrecher in Preussen," Starke, Berlin, 1884, p. 92.

the same person, as compared with those of a more mercenary origin. It is comparatively rare to find offenders of this class in our American prisons for a similar offence the second time, such as murder, homicide, indecency, or even simple assault with or without attempt to kill, except in cases of congenital criminals.

The tendency of crime, it is observable, is frequently along a given line, that of the habitual offender not infrequently tending toward specialization. Particularly is this true of the burglar, the pickpocket, and the petty thief. All those offences that have back of them an effort of the will seem more prone to expend themselves in isolated overt acts, such as forgery, embezzlement, etc., and are more rarely repeated, except in cases of mental defectives. Intelligence, the force of past prestige, together with a healthy volitional function here interposing, without doubt, tend to strengthen innate character, and thus check repetition. Perhaps, on the whole, the bulk of recidivation is along general lines, the paths travelled having a tendency to cross one another indiscriminately without much regard to the previous offence. English statistics are noteworthy with respect to the accuracy with which this interesting feature of criminalism may be analyzed, such results giving us about the following summary as to criminal repetition : viz., against property with violence, 66 per cent; without violence, 64 per cent; malicious injury to property, 42 per cent; offences against the person, 30 per cent. As to particular crimes, we have those of larceny set down at 78 per cent; burglary, 66 per cent;

robbery, 64 per cent; forgery, 20 per cent: bearing out my assertion that the tendency to recidivation decreases, first, in direct proportion as they become personal, and second, in the ratio in which they stand implicated with an act of the will — in other words, that instinct and impulsion are the psychical explanations and origin of, and play leading rôle in recidivation, as they do in instinctive criminalism.

The instinctive conduct of the true criminal attests itself in repeated relapses, especially when associated with some form of neurosis, as arson (pyromania), petty theft (kleptomania), and all that long line of functional derangements superinduced by the alcoholic habit (dipsomania), which latter may ever be depended upon manifesting itself in greater or lesser periodicity.

Precocious criminalism is not so subject to recidivism, at least as to its earlier stages. Precocity and relapse are both certainly more common to born criminals than to others; although Lombroso thinks not. Habitual wrong-doing in a penal sense can hardly be affirmed of the youthful offender until at the furthest the sixteenth year, the limit of incarceration prescribed by English law; when the juvenile merges from the chrysalis state into the adult criminal period, though presaged earlier in the embryonic offences already depicted, as: truancy, petty theft, lying, general waywardness, etc. Among first offenders of the "Star Class" in convict prisons in England, in 1879 up to September 30, out of 2183 male convicts, but 20, or 1.1 per cent of those discharged, were returned to penal servitude under fresh sentences; and only 11, or .6 per cent,

had their licenses revoked or forfeited.[1] Of the 747
received into penal institutions during 1897, above 18
years, 34 per cent had served a previous term.

Recidivism varies in different countries, owing largely,
no doubt, to the relative severity of the laws, strictness
of enforcement, vigilance of police, and brevity of
sentence, which latter, next to prison life itself, is the
most prolific cause of recidivation. So long as chronic
and hardened offenders are visited with short and
easily served sentences, so long will imprisonment have
its fascinations, and incarceration prove conducive to
the criminal habit. Statistics show that short sentences
are a bid upon habitual lawbreaking and an incentive
to the chronic repeater. Wherever this is a rule, recidivation is rife, though the number of first offenders
may not be thus affected. Length of imprisonment
is bound to affect materially this phase of criminality,
since it is apparent the longer the term of detention of
the professional, the more will his opportunity for mischief be curtailed and his purposes frustrated. The
tendencies to recidivation, on the whole, as between
males and females, vary in different countries; as, for
instance, in England, in 1897, it was 50.94 per cent for
males, and 73.62 per cent for females; in Scotland,
44.42 per cent for males, and 57.17 per cent for females;
in Italy, 26 per cent for males, and 13 per cent for
females; in Denmark, 26 per cent for males, and 24
per cent for females; in France, in 1867, it was 43 per
cent for men, and 31 per cent for women, and in

[1] Report of the Commissioners of Prisons and Directors of Convict Prisons, 1897, p. 13.

Austria, 59 per cent for males, and 51 per cent for females.[1] In the United States (1890), the percentage of recidivists among men (18,763) was 24.42 per cent, and among women (2991) 46.70 per cent.

In the United States, the total number of recidivists by the last census report (1890) was 26.42 per cent of all prisoners. Of this number, 16,975, or 20.61 per cent, were whites; 11,891, or 14.32 per cent were native whites; and 4907, or 5.96 per cent, were foreign born whites. The actual number doubtless is much larger than the figures here indicate, as the prisoner, frequently coming from another state, is able to hide his previous record and thus deceive the prison authorities as to his antecedents. Recidivation varies, of course, in the different states. Mr. Brockway, at the Fourth International Prison Congress (1890), estimated the total number in New York, inclusive of juvenile institutions, jails, and houses of correction, at 60 per cent. Sing Sing, in the Report for 1897, gave 56.27 per cent; Clinton, 37.33 per cent, and Auburn, 43.28 per cent. The number of recidivists in California, an extreme Western state, in 1897, was 26 per cent. The State Prison Report of Joliet, 1896, in a typical Middle Western state, was 20.77 per cent. The North Atlantic section (1890) reported the largest number of recidivists by geographical division, 11,148, or 39.45 per cent out of an aggregate of 28,258 prisoners, the Western, the smallest, 1140, or 16.95 per cent, out of an aggregate of 6724 prisoners. The negro recidivists numbered 4678, or 19.26 per cent, out of 24,277 colored criminals

[1] "La Recidiva," Giuseppe Orano, Roma, 1883, p. 298.

of their own race. Though they comprise 29.48 per cent of the total criminal population, they yield but 5.68 per cent of its recidivism.

TABLE XIII

PERCENTAGE OF RECIDIVATION IN EUROPE

COUNTRY	YEAR AND PERCENTAGE		YEAR AND PERCENTAGE		YEAR AND PERCENTAGE		YEAR AND PERCENTAGE	
England . .	*1871–77	40%	1877	44%	*1880–92	48%	‖1897	56%
Scotland . .					‖1893	52.38%	‖1897	61.65%
Germany . . (Imperial.)			²§1886	29%	²§1892	34%	²§1897	39.7%
France . .	†1872	41%	2*1876–80	48%	2*1886	56%	²‖1895	41%
Italy . . .	†1872	24%			*1888	36%		
Austria . .	‡1872–75	17%	‡1876–80	22%	‡1880–90	27%	‡1891–95	28%
Würtemberg	†1872	50%			²†1890	57%	1897	60%
Russia . .	†1872	7%						
Spain . . .	†1872	16%						
Denmark. .	†1872	25%						
Switzerland .	†1872	45%						
Belgium . .	†1872	46%			‖1890	33%	‖1898	39%
Holland . .	†1872	80%			¶1890	45%	¶1897	44%
Sweden . .	†1872	40%						
Norway . .							1895	50%
Prussia . .					²‡1890	79%	²‡1898	82%
Europe . . (Average.)								§50–60%

* *Fortnightly Review*, April, 1894.
† Mulhall, Ed. 1892, p. 163.
‡ *Oesterreische Statistik*, Jahrgang, 1895, Heft 3.
§ *Criminal Sociology* (Ferri), p. 14.
‖ Prison Commissioner's Report, 1897.
¶ *Statistiek Gevangeniswezen*, 1890, 1897, pp. 20, 26.
2* *Revue Scientifique*, 8 Mars, 1890.
2† State official (Minister of Justice).
2‡ State official (Minister of Interior, State Prison).
2§ *Kriminalstatistik*, für das Jahre 1897, p. 303.
3‖ De La Justice Criminelle Report, 1895.

The period between twenty-five and thirty is the age of recidivity. The maximum of relapses is usually reached at the first repetition. Thus, from the Commissioners' Report of English Prisons (1897), we find first relapses numbered 21,056; second numbered 10,866; third, 7371; fourth, 5526; fifth, 4365, etc., which is perhaps fairly representative of other countries and institutions. The preceding table will serve to show the recidivation list of European countries at different periods since 1871, as far as I have been able to gather from various sources.

Yvernes, "La Recidive en Europe" (Paris, 1874), gives the following statistics of relapses in Europe by periods : —

TABLE XIV

RELAPSE	ENGLAND, 1871 (Prisoners)	SWEDEN, 1871 (Thieves)	FRANCE, 1826–74 (Tried)	ITALY, 1870 (Tried)	SCOTLAND
Once	38 %	54 %	45 %	60 %	16 %
Twice . . .	18 %	28 %	20 %	30 %	13 %
Thrice . . .	44 %	18 %	35 %	10 %	

Old offenders sometimes attain high preëminence in criminal degrees, thus in Germany 32 men and 16 women had been imprisoned 31 or more terms; and 644 men and 163 women, from 11 to 30 times. The Scottish statistics (Report, 1897, p. 81) give instances of 119 persons who had been previously convicted from 150 to 200 times; 154 who had been previously convicted 101 to 150 times; and 1125 who had been so convicted 51 to 100 times.

Recidivation is unquestionably on the increase; the

conditions of civilization together with the prison system in vogue being conducive to the habit. Italy, from 13 per cent in 1878, rose to 22 per cent in 1882. France, according to the same authority, has shown a growth of from 10 per cent in 1826 to 42 per cent in 1867, and 50 per cent in 1879. Prussia, from 77 per cent in 1871, grew to 80 per cent in 1877 and 68 per cent at the present time.[1] In 1885, 80 per cent of the inmates of Prussian jails had been previously convicted.[2]

Recidivation is not necessarily an evidence either of the social retrogression or of increase in the personnel of crime. Rather the reverse. It must be remembered, in the first place, that society's peril lies not so much in the *fact* of criminal relapse itself as in its contaminating effect upon the healthier portion of the social organism. The mere fact of an habitual's repeating his offence is not nearly so grave an event as that of a novice for the first time embarking therein. *The creation of the offender, not the committal of an offence*, is the greater menace to society. *Recidivation is not an increase in individual criminalism.* It is safe to say that, were crime confined to this class alone, its repression were less difficult, and might be summed up in a single word — *elimination* — permanent detention. This form of the social disease could thus, as it were, be attacked in the lump, and the main source and bulk of the criminal current cut off at a blow. Under existing conditions, it may be safe to

[1] " Criminology," Dr. MacDonald, p. 158.
[2] " Handbuch des Gefangnessiwesens," Vol. I, p. 170, MM. Holtzendorff and Jugeman.

hazard as general conclusion that, wherever recidivism is rife, and in proportion as wrong-doing has been confined to this phase of the criminal phenomena in any given community, in the same proportion will the aggregate prison population on the whole fall off. Illustrations of this fact are numerous in the history of crime. References to the tables under head of "Decrease" will suffice to illustrate this fact.

England, in 1873, had a recidivation list of 39–40 per cent.[1] In 1897 it had grown to 56 per cent, an increase of about 17 per cent.[2] Her prison population, on the whole, has decreased, as is evidenced farther on. Of 146,952, the "total number committed on convictions to local prisons or direct to convict prisons" during the year ending March 31, 1897, a total of 84,071 out of that number had previously been in prison under sentence, leaving but 62,881 first offenders to be accounted for, this being at the rate of 56 per cent for second termers, as against 44 per cent for first offenders. Or, in other words, England has but 62,881 first offenders out of a total prison commitment of 146,952, while we possessed 60,575 such first offenders out of a total criminal population of 82,329. Sir Edmund du Cane, Chief Director of British Prisons, has shown by elaborate analysis, with reference to the subject of criminal decrease and recidivism in England, that during the decade between 1883 and 1892 the number of first offenders decreased from 100,422 to 77,857, while recidi-

[1] *Fortnightly Review,* April, 1894, pp. 461–463.
[2] Report of the Commissioners of Prisons and Directors of Convict Prisons, for year ending March 31, 1897, pp. 105–107.

vation for the same period increased from 44 per cent to 48 per cent. The average number, according to that eminent authority, confined in local prisons in 1876–1877, was 20,361 ; and in 1891–1892 it was 12,663 ; its indictable crimes fell from 52,397 to 35,335, and its summary offences from 192,440 to 159,534, while between the same periods her recidivism grew from 40 per cent in 1871–1877 to 48 per cent in 1892.[1] Crime in England is on the decline, and recidivism correspondingly on the increase.

The United States, as compared to this, presents an opposite tendency. More lax in judicial severity and methods, it presents a recidivism of 26.42 per cent out of her aggregate prison population, as against 56 per cent recidivation in England and in Wales. Our recidivistic prison population does not keep pace with the expansion of the mother prison population, as in Great Britain. With us, crime is making an inroad upon the hitherto sound portion of the social tissue — the danger line in criminal propagation ; while England, with a much larger misdemeanant class as a whole, compared to population, is restricting her criminal virus to her already contaminated portions. She is slowly reducing her criminal problem to a scientific proposition (as is the case generally throughout the leading European countries), as will be seen by a careful study and analysis of her methods and statistical reports.

France, according to Mulhall, gives us a somewhat similar history, as will be seen from the following table gathered from that source, with reference to her prison history from 1852 to 1884 : —

[1] *Nineteenth Century Review*, March, 1893.

TABLE XV

Year	Galleys	Prisons	Reforma-tories	Total	Per cent of all Recidivists
1852	6,800	47,000	6,400	60,200	1850, 28 per cent
1870	2,600	33,600	6,800	43,000	41 " "
1880	11,700	40,600	9,000	61,300	48 " "
1884	13,400	40,000	7,000	60,400	

It will be seen by the above table that, whereas the fluctuation of crime as a whole has been variable between the periods above given, the increase of recidivation was uniform, and noticeably where the decrease in general criminality was greatest (1870), viz. 45.18 per cent, recidivation was also greatest; and conversely, where the increase in general criminality was most marked (1880), viz. 42.55 per cent, the increase in recidivism was least.

It will be seen by reference to the table of Prussian criminalism of the more serious grades of offences,[1] a steady decrease in the total number of prisoners for penal offences is noticeable (except during two periods) from 1890 to 1898, while during the same period there is a gradual growth in recidivism, based upon daily averages. The total number of prisoners for serious offences has fallen over 22 per cent since 1881. Recidivism has risen from 79.89 per cent in 1890 to 82.21 per cent in 1898 in the line of all graver offences. Its criminals have become more pronouncedly professional,

[1] Table XXIX, p. 256.

and its type of criminalism, chronic. Out of 18,049 prisoners confined in prison in 1894, 5261 had been in prison before from 3 to 5 times; 7545 from 6 to 10 times; 4928 from 11 to 30 times, and 315 more than 30 times. Eleven hundred and fifty of those served their first term when less than 14 years old; 4936 when between 14 and 18 years of age; 4367 between 18 and 25 years of age. Of those discharged, the prison officials gave, as their opinion, that 17,045 would return as "incorrigibles," 563 "doubtful," while 441 were "considered cured."[1] Inclusive of misdemeanors and petty offences, the aggregate rate of percentage of recidivism is of course materially reduced, which is apparent in the criminal record of the Empire as a whole, where crime in general has apparently kept pace with the growth of recidivism, owing mainly to the multiplication of petty offences (elsewhere referred to), as will be seen by reference to the table of general criminalism in Germany.

The prison statistics of Austria reveal similar characteristics, as shown by her latest reports, under head of "Decrease."[2] It will be seen by reference thereto that in those years wherein her prison population has decreased (1891–1892), recidivism has correspondingly grown, and *vice versa*, where the prison population has advanced (1893), relapse has fallen off. Her quinquennial table of recidivism shows the following comparative ratio of growth as between recidivists and first offenders:[3] —

---

[1] Table XXIX, p. 256.   [2] Table XXXII, p. 258.
[3] *Oesterreichische Statistik*, Jahrgang, 1895, Heft 3, p. xli.

TABLE XVI

YEARS	Previously Convicted for Penal Offences	Per cent	Previously Convicted for Misdemeanors	Per cent	Total Per cent	FIRST OFFENDERS	Per cent
1866–70	33,129	27.4	21,126	17.5	44.9	66,680	55.1
1871–75	35,195	25.8	24,544	17.9	43.7	76,770	56.3
1876–80	40,041	25.5	35,003	22.2	47.7	82,096	52.3
1881–85	39,094	24.8	39,709	25.2	50.0	78,574	50.0
1886–90	34,314	23.8	40,226	27.9	51.7	69,629	48.3
1891–95	34,620	23.6	42,404	28.9	52.5	69,616	47.5

In the above it is observable that, in proportion as the percentage of recidivists has gone up, that of first offenders has gone down, the latter from 55.1 per cent to 47.5 per cent, and the former from 44.9 per cent to 52.5 per cent from 1866 to 1895.

Belgium, by her latest criminal and prison report, gives the total number of convictions in the Court of Assizes, and Tribunal of Corrections, for the year 1890, at 40,362. In 1896 it was 44,857, an increase of 11.11 per cent. Her actual prison population during these periods, in both "centrales" and "secondaries," were 4284 for the former and 4395 for the latter periods, a growth of only 2.59 per cent. Her recidivists during these same periods increased from 2362 in 1890, to 3582 in 1896, respectively, an increase of 51.65 per cent. Recidivism is on the increase, crime in general is on the decrease, in Belgium.

Japan, newly aroused from lethargy, attests to this

same principle in the law of criminal growth as the first fruit of her reconstructed penological system. She gives in a late published prison report[1] (1898) a total criminal *entrée* in 1890 of 208,420. Her recidivist list of *entrée* during the same period was 13,336, representing 6.4 per cent of population. In 1895 her *entrée* of recidivists numbered 23,476, an increase of 2.2 per cent compared with the *entrée* aggregate of 271,603 for the same year. Or, putting it in another way, comparing the ratio of prisoners with that of 100,000 of the population, we have first offenders in 1890 numbering in the ratio of 482.2 per 100,000, and in 1895 587.02 per 100,000, while her recidivist population rose from 32.9 per 100,000 in 1890, to 55.5 per 100,000 in 1895.

Russia possesses, perhaps, the largest aggregate prison population in Europe. In 1892 her total prison population was estimated, according to the " Statesman's Year Book," at 113,729; in 1893, at 116,376. A total of 734,196 entered, and 742,819 left, her prisons. Her recidivist population, in 1872, numbered but 7 per cent of the whole.

Spain, with the second largest homicidal record in Europe, giving an annual average of convictions of 1085, has a recidivist list during the above period of but 16 per cent. Out of 2249 criminals in Spain, 1569 were returned for similar offences, and 429 or 27.34 per cent of such repetitions were for murder.

Norway, with the lowest state prison population of any country in Europe, possesses also a high recidivist

[1] Résumé Statistique de L'Empire du Japon, 1898, p. 111.

record compared to the number of prisoners, 50 per cent in 1894 and 1895, as against 615 and 621 state prisoners respectively.[1]

Holland, as against but 517 state prisoners, in 1889–1890, reported 45.84 per cent recidivists; and in 1896–1897, 44.08 per cent recidivists out of 325 state prisoners.[2]

From the above facts, I think the general rule may be fairly deducible, that: the *larger* the recidivation the less the general criminal increase and the proportionate number of first offenders; and the *shorter* the recidivation list, the greater the aggregate prison population in a given community. Recidivation is the gauge of the prison population, as it is the relative test of the virulence of the criminal disease everywhere — the main stream upon which crime may rely for a steady supply, not so much in the way of accumulation of new material through infection, as in the direct line of criminal growth through repetition on the part of old offenders. While as to the steady numerical increase of recidivation in general, there can be no question, viewed thus; and face to face with wise and vigorous repressive measures, it need arouse no alarm. To diagnose a disease is half the battle, and to be able to ascertain correctly the main sources of the criminal contagion is to lay bare at once both cause and remedy so far, at least, as farther spread from contaminated individual nucleus is concerned. It is plain, from these observations, that an examination into the main question: What shall we do to curtail the criminal aggression? must

[1] " Beretning om Rigets Strafarbeidsanstalter," 1895 and 1896.
[2] *Statistiek Gevangeniswezen*, 1890, pp. 20, 21 ; 1897, pp. 20, 21.

fairly be prefaced by the antecedent inquiry: What shall we do with our recidivistic classes which constitute the backbone of crime and the criminal propaganda, and which give to them their chief virulency and force? Upon the answer to that form of the inquiry hangs largely the practical outcome of the criminal problem.

As to the relative causes of recidivation, as already indicated, they are, generically speaking, personal, environmental, and institutional; *i.e.* relapse is primarily inherent in the individual criminal, plus environment and the influence of the prison. Roughly stated, repetition is what constitutes the individual a professed criminal — the *outward* expression of the *inward* man. The state prison, with its present methods of incarceration and the absurd system of sentencing and punishments in vogue are the chief external ministerial agencies that go in aid of the recidivistic habit. Brevity of sentence in the case of the recidivist, and undue length of punishment in the instance of first offenders, tend unequivocally and irrevocably to create and infix the criminal temper, and encourage to almost certain repetition. This subject, however, comes more particularly under the head of " Punishment and Reformation," where it will be briefly discussed in connection with prevenient methods.

II

Increase

The transition from the subject of recidivation to that of general criminal increase is an easy one. Ordinary criminal increase, as we have studied it, may be organically considered as largely the result of infection from the former — as the cancerous growth in the physical organism which, radiating from a given centre and throwing out its roots and fibres, distributes its germs to the surrounding tissue until it gradually involves the whole. Contamination from the above (recidivistic) source is no doubt to a large degree accountable for the spread of crime, through the power of suggestion, and the force of example, as well as by more direct and indirect contact. The subject of the growth of crime, as a whole, is a difficult one, fraught with many subtle and complex ingredients.

The deductions and inferences obtained from statistical compilations alone are not always either satisfactory nor conclusive, as is evidenced by the testimony of experts themselves, many of whom pronounce their dictum one day only to reverse it the next. The components that enter in to influence criminal fluctuation are numerous, and have been already sufficiently indicated to obviate the necessity of more extended survey. In its purely numerical character, not one but many causes contribute thereto; and are not to be disposed of altogether by simple mathematical formula. All conclusions based upon individual statistical data must be received with caution, as being constantly amenable to new evidences and therefore liable to alteration, if not reversal. The increase of crime has been the prolific theme, alike on the part of optimist and pessimist, either of whom generally approach its oracular altars with prejudice "aforethought" and shape their conclusions in accordance therewith. A study from the basis of national or international statistics, offers the only tolerably safe ground from which to arrive at anything like satisfactory conclusions, and affords a fair insight into the actual criminal status. A brief analysis of its tables furnishes results which we can approach with some degree of confidence. Taking the year 1850, for instance, as a base line, the data furnished by the last census reports give us an approximate idea of the criminal progression in the United States during the last four completed decades of our national existence.

The existing criminal status of the United States may be summarized in the following tabulated form, as drawn from official sources (omitting 907 in 1890, nativity unknown) and fairly present the subject in succinct form : —

TABLE XVII

SUMMARY OF PRISONERS IN THE UNITED STATES FROM 1850 TO 1890

SEX, COLOR, NATIVITY	NUMBER OF PRISONERS					RATIOS TO 1,000,000 POPULATION				
	1850	1860	1870	1880	1890	1850	1860	1870	1880	1890
Total . .	6,737	19,086	32,901	58,609	82,329	290	607	853	1,169	1,315
Male				53,604	75,924				2,101	2,368
Female				5,005	6,405				203	210
Native born . .	4,326	10,143	24,173	45,802	65,070	207	371	733	1,054	1,233
Foreign born . .	2,411	8,943	8,728	12,807	15,932	1,074	2,161	1,568	1,917	1,788
White				24,845	41,861	57,310		740	964	1,042
Colored				8,056	16,748	25,019		1,621	2,480	3,275

The aggregate number confined in the United States by the last census (1890) was 82,329; 55 per cent out of which were confined in penitentiaries, 24 per cent in jails, 12 per cent in workhouses, and the remainder were scattering, of which 4 per cent were confined in city prisons; 3 per cent were leased out, and 1 per cent each were in military prisons and in insane hospitals.

The aggregate number of prisoners in penitentiaries alone, in the United States, 1895, was 54,244; 52,256 males, and 1988 females.[1]

The comparative ratio of criminal increase with population may be more particularly set forth in the following tables : —

TABLE XVIII

COMPARATIVE TABLE OF INCREASE OF CRIMINAL POPULATION WITH POPULATION OF UNITED STATES SINCE 1850

YEAR	UNITED STATES POPULATION	PER CENT OF INCREASE	CRIMINAL POPULATION	PER CENT OF INCREASE	CRIMINALS AS COMPARED TO POPULATION	CRIMINALS TO 100,000 POPULATION
1850	23,191,870	35.87	6,737		1 in 3,442	29.04
1860	31,443,321	35.58	19,086	183.30	1 in 1,647	60.69
1870	38,558,371	22.63	32,901	41.99	1 in 1,171	85.32
1880	50,155,783	30.07	58,609	78.14	1 in 885	116.85
1890	62,622,250	24.85	82,329	40.47	1 in 757	131.46

TABLE XIX

INCREASE OF CRIMINAL POPULATION AS COMPARED BY ITSELF

In 1860	.	.	.	2.83 times as large as in 1850
In 1870	.	.	.	1.19 times as large as in 1860
In 1880	.	.	.	1.77 times as large as in 1870
In 1890	.	.	.	1.40 times as large as in 1880
In 1890	.	.	.	12.22 times as large as in 1850

A study of the above tables is of interest as tending to show the twofold drift of the criminal comparison; (1) as related to the increase of the general population

[1] *United States Bulletin of the Department of Labor*, No. 5, July, 1896, p. 459.

during the past forty years, and (2) as illustrating its growth as compared with itself, decade by decade, or alternately. As elucidating the first observation, it will be noted that while the growth of population has maintained a comparatively steady increase since 1850 (averaging 28.27 per cent each decade), the criminal procession throughout the same period, though presenting a remarkable fluctuation every alternate decade, has averaged 85.97 per cent, being over three times as large an increase as that of the population per decade.

The second consideration, comparing the criminal growth by itself, makes it evident that it has fallen alternately every other decade to a marked degree; viz., in 1870 over 400 per cent as compared with that of 1860; and again, nearly 100 per cent in 1890 as compared with that of 1880, and this without any marked deviation during corresponding periods in the general growth of population.

Thus, while the last-named decade (1890) gives us the smallest rate of criminal increase (40.47 per cent) of any when compared with itself, it is equally true that it pre sents a certain steady ratio of increase throughout, when compared with 100,000 population, at the rate of 60.69 in 1860, 85.32 in 1870, 116.85 in 1880, and 131.46 in 1890.

From the above, we have a growth in the criminal population both relatively and absolutely (though in varying degrees), neither presenting any alarming evidence of increase, on the whole. We reach the same conclusion by a more direct application of the tables drawn from the United States census for 1890 by geographical divisions:—

TABLE XX

GEOGRAPHICAL DIVISIONS	RATIOS TO 1,000,000		INCREASE	DECREASE
	1880	1890		
The United States	709	722	13	
North Atlantic	768	832	64	
South Atlantic	704	730	26	
North Central	510	491		19
South Central	891	842		49
Western	1,268	1,341	73	

The above shows that the ratio for 1880, which gives the relative proportions upon the basis of total population at 1169 per 1,000,000 and that of 1890 at 1315 on the same ratio, exhibits but the slight increase of 146 per 1,000,000 in ten years. When we turn from these to other figures that indicate the lesser crimes punishable by jail sentences, we find the increase more marked, as the following table drawn from the same sources will indicate : —

TABLE XXI

GEOGRAPHICAL DIVISIONS	RATIOS TO 1,000,000		INCREASE	DECREASE
	1880	1890		
The United States	443	565	122	
North Atlantic	639	758	119	
South Atlantic	340	556	216	
North Central	327	359	32	
South Central	358	619	261	
Western	855	813		42

Crime, it must be remembered in this connection, is something not necessarily synonymous with imprisonment. Detention is one thing, conviction another. All criminals are not in prison, neither are all prisoners necessarily criminals. Many are simply "detained," awaiting trial, others as witnesses, etc. Thus, in 1880, half of those found in county jails and 9 per cent of all in detention, were awaiting trial at the time of the taking of the census. The Italian authorities recognize the distinction between arrest and conviction in making up their statistics. The English system, more discriminating than the American, gives the odds of conviction as against acquittal, those against property with violence being ascertained as 6 to 1 for conviction; for offences against property without violence, 6 to 1, against person, 2 to 1. The English census rests upon the fact of conviction. The American is calculated upon imprisonment, hence presumably in excess of the real facts. Thus, in 1890, 9715 of the total number of prisoners confined were awaiting trial; 48 were debtors, 291 were insane, and 66 were detained as witnesses, making a total of 10,120 who were thus detained in prison but not sentenced, at that date.

The grouping of misdemeanants with more serious offenders as partaking in the common opprobrium, must also be considered in a scientific analysis of the criminal enumeration as tending to give it a weightiness and seriousness of aspect hardly warranted, since the number of petty offences is usually far in excess of that of indictable crimes, implying in the majority of instances a violation of the letter of the law rather than any serious moral infringement. While there is no doubt that, in the matter of lesser offences, the bulk of criminality in the United States is on the increase, it is also true, as shown by the above tables, that the more serious crimes reveal neither material increase nor diminution, save that of homicide, which shows a marked steadiness both in the Old and in the New World, running as a base line through all criminosity, with a tendency to exaggeration in Italy, and more than maintaining its own in England. The vigilance of officers, and the efficiency of the police and constabulary system, are also matters of great importance in the matter of criminal fluctuation and summary, much necessarily resting with them as supplying the judiciary with the raw material.

The subject of criminal increase in the European countries is a mixed one, owing largely to the uncertainty of data and the lack of a general international distributing centre, or "intelligence office," to gather up and systematize the same for a more intelligent and practical comprehension of the criminal statistics of the world, and as a foundation for social investigation and future bearing.

While the tables of German criminalism, as already pointed out, set forth a uniform criminal increase from 1890 up to 1897 (date of last report), the bulk of such increase is in the due line of petty offences and misdemeanors, especially as against the person, notably for assaults, slander, for resisting officers, etc., while for graver offences, such as murder, assaults to murder, and against property, as larceny, etc., there has been a decrease.

The following table, drawn from the "Statesman's Year Book" and *Kriminalstatistik* (1897), serves to show the increase from 1890 to 1897, viz.: —

TABLE XXII

| YEAR | NUMBER OF CONVICTIONS | | | CONVICTIONS PER 10,000 INHABITANTS | PER CENT OF INCREASE AND DECREASE | RECIDIVISTS | | |
	Males	Females	Total			Total Number	Increase and Decrease	Comparative
1890	314,192	67,258	381,450	112.0		125,068		32.78%
1891	321,657	69,407	391,064	112.4	2.52	133,065	6.39	34.02%
1892	347,051	75,276	422,327	119.9	7.99	146,691	10.24	34.73%
1893	356,232	74,171	430,403	121.0	1.91	151,679	3.4	35.24%
1894	370,392	75,718	446,110	124.4	8.06	164,721	8.6	36.02%
1895	377,214	76,997	454,211	125.1	1.81	172,169	4.52	37.90%
1896	382,432	74,567	456,999	124.4	0.61	177,574	3.14	38.05%
1897	387,054	76,531	463,585	126.2	1.44	183,843	3.53	39.70%

From the latest report of the German Empire (1897), we gather that of the 463,585 persons convicted in the German Empire, 9765 were committed to the penitentiaries; 259,322 received jail sentences from one day and upward, and the balance, with the exception of 147 committed to fortresses, either paid a fine or were dismissed with a reprimand. Thirty-nine and seven-tenths per cent were recidivists out of the total, and 9.9 per cent were juveniles between the ages of 12 and 18 years.[1]

Switzerland, in 1892, had a total prison population of 2201 (50 per cent recidivists), 1005 being in penal institutions. The total number received during the year was 3142, 52 per cent being recidivists.[2]

The history of crime in France has been variable dur-

[1] *Kriminalstatistik*, für das Jahr 1897, pp. 166–167, 302–303.
[2] " Statistique pénitentiaire Suisse."

ing the last decade, as shown by the following table compiled from authentic sources : [1] —

TABLE XXIII

YEAR	ASSIZE COURTS	CORRECT TRIBUNAL	POLICE COURTS	TOTAL	PER 10,000 INHABITANTS
1884 . . .	3,082	195,725	470,904	669,711	175.2
1885 . . .	3,082	211,797	450,773	665,652	174.2
1886 . . .	3,128	210,805	451,369	665,302	174.1
1887 . . .	3,179	216,461	443,763	663,403	173.5
1888 . . .	3,034	215,993	429,988	649,015	169.8
1889 . . .	2,989	210,119	420,249	633.357	165.7
1890 . . .	2,918	211,731	447,273	661,922	173.2
1891 . . .	2,933	216,908	447,203	667,044	173.9
1892 . . .	2,945	230,060	436,601	669,606	174.6
1893 . . .					
1894 . . .	2,795	225,466	448,474	676,735	176.4
1895 . . .	2,372	221,234	398,723	622,329	162.1

Here, a decrease in all offences is noticeable from 1884 to 1889–1890, from which latter date there appears an increase in Courts of Correctionals, and general total, up to 1894, from which period it again began to show a decline.

In 1894, according to report (1895), the number sentenced to more than one year was 4032; to one year and less, 133,751 ; which with fines and conditional release, gives a total of 265,270. In 1895 (date of report), the former fell to 3795 and 122,615, respectively, a total of 256,430, being a decrease of 3.33 per cent in one year. The same may be said with reference to

[1] " Statesman's Year Book," 1899; " Compte General de l'administration de la justice criminelle en France et en Algerie," pendant l'année 1895, pp. vi, xi, xii, 102, 103.

recidivists, state prisons, houses of correction sentences, and petty offences. In Courts of Assizes, the number of recidivists for the first time decreased from 1590 in 1894 (1507 males, 83 females) to 1380 in 1895 (1309 males, and 71 females). The number of recidivists previously also had undergone a remarkable reduction; from 104,644 (95,115 males, 9529 females) in 1894, to 99,434 (89,548 males and 9886 females), or a total decrease in recidivism from 106,234 in the former to 100,814 in the latter period, a falling off of 5.11 per cent.[1]

The actual prison population in France, including Algeria, from last official report (1898) for the years 1895 and 1896, for the more serious offences, shows a perceptible falling off in penal and reformatory population and inmates of jails over three months' detention, on the 31st of December of each year, as indicated by the table below : —

TABLE XXIV

Year.	Penal Institutions	Jails for over Three Months	Reformatories and Houses of Correction	Solitary	Banishment	Total	Per cent of Decrease
1895	12,101	24,960	63,81	46	206	43,694	
1896	11,372	23,698	6,118	44	121	41,353	5.36

European Russia, at the Fourth International Prison Congress, assembled June, 1890, at St. Petersburg, reported a prison population in 1888, as follows : —

[1] "Statesman's Year Book," 1899; "Compte General de l'administration de la justice criminelle en France et en Algerie," pendant l'année 1895, pp. vi, xi, xii, 102, 103.

3 Central prisons	.	858
29 Reformatories for men	.	10,645
Prisons for short term	.	79,462
Preventive prisons for men and women	.	1,050
Depots of transfers	.	3,295

Establishments for Young Boys and Girls

Girls — agricultural colonies	.	428
Industrial asylums	.	372
Young girls — industrial asylum	.	52

Siberia

FORCED LABOR PRISONS: —

Men	.	8,446
Women	.	900
Hospitals for convicts and exiles, men and women	.	275
Correctional prisons, men	.	512
Prisons for short term, men and women	.	8,745
Depots of transfers	.	1,814

The annual admissions for short term prisons was 590,714. January 1, 1883, there were received 593,514 men and 88,236 women. There were that year 832 places of detention, with a population of 101,518, three establishments not reported. There were 13,003 exiles received in Siberia.[1]

III

Decrease

The conditions that make for the growth of the criminal phenomenon are the same which, when modified or altered, will, substitutionally or otherwise, likewise tend to the diminution of crime and the decrease of its numerical proportions. Increase in crime is not unusually the cry of the special pleader who comes to substantiate a theory. Crime is as frequently the mark of a vitiated vitality as of direct degeneration. If the social organ-

[1] Report of Fourth International Prison Congress, 1891, p. 27.

ism nourishes the germs of crime, and civilization fructifies it, that superabundant vitality that carries both successfully forward is likewise sufficient to cope with the evils thus engendered in the course of growth. As in the physiological, so in the moral and social spheres, the social system presumably possesses that fulness of recuperative energy that enables it to successfully cope with its own maladies. Like the physical organism, she has the power, under given conditions, to build up her own broken down nerve centres, and conserve her wasted energies in the direction of health and growth. Let such injury but once take place, and these reserve forces rally to supply the waste and repair the injury. It is so with reference to the problem of crime, wherever the march of civilization has caught the subject in its onward current. Civilization is as effectually the *discoverer* of crime as she is the sympathetic and indirect *source* of crime. She uncovers crime as well as breeds it, which is half the remedy. The secret of criminal growth is quite as much attributable to the more intelligent effort and effective machinery which enlightened society puts forth toward ferreting out wrong-doing and bringing the perpetrator to justice, as in lending her indirect influences toward criminal propagation. The defensive measures of society gather strength in proportion to the exigencies that call them forth. Wherever and in whatever countries these means and methods are employed, whether in the line of preventives as conditions precedent, or as subsequent modifiers in the shape of reformatory and institutional agencies, the effects of such appliances are felt in the curtailment

of the criminal animus as well as in appreciable reduction in its numerical ratio. As an evidence of the
diminishing prison population in a given community,
under the stimulus of wisely organized and consistently
applied preventive measures and prison and reformative
methods, we have but to point to the countries that have
adopted such appliances as part of their laws.

The country that stands first and foremost, as presenting the most encouraging features in respect of the
steady and systematic reduction of her criminal population, especially in the line of the graver offences (unless perhaps that of homicide), is England, where a
gradual diminution is recorded (as already pointed out)
during the past twenty years and more, both in matters of imprisonment on indictments and on summary
convictions. Before 1877, it deviated alternately every
three years, as with ourselves at every alternate decade.
From that period to the present, the fall has been
gradual in both daily and annual diminutions, as
shown by the Commissioners Report for the year
ending March 31, 1897. The latter shows a decrease
from 1880, when the daily averages in local and convict prisons (the former answering to our jails, and
the latter to state prisons) were respectively 19,835 and
10,299, making a total of 30,134. In 1897, the same
reported respectively, 13,987 and 3089, total 17,076, or
an average yearly reduction from the former period to
the latter of 2.55 per cent.

The table shows for the corresponding periods the
population of England and Wales, with the number
of prisoners sentenced to death ; to penal servitude for

life; to penal servitude for a term of years; to imprisonment on indictment, and on summary conviction, or want of sureties, in each year from 1880. It presents interesting and important information as illustrating the history of crime in that country, and which, together with table of general increase or decrease of crime at intervals of longer periods than one year, are herewith appended for the purpose of more accurate information.

As regards the general increase and decrease of crime at intervals of longer periods than one year, the same report furnishes us also with the following table of relative increase and decrease by 100,000 population, since 1885 : —

TABLE XXV

YEARLY AVERAGE NUMBER OF PERSONS IMPRISONED IN ENGLAND AND WALES	ON INDICTMENT		ON SUMMARY CONVICTION	
	Actual Number	Number per 100,000 of Population of England and Wales	Actual Number	Number per 100,000 of Population of England and Wales
During five years ended March 31, 1885 . . .	9,962	37.8	149,046	566.4
During five years ended March 31, 1890 . . .	9,126	32.7	140,722	505.6
During five years ended March 31, 1895 . . .	8,253	28.0	137,291	467.1
During year ended March 31, 1896	7,933	26.1	146,019	480.4
During year ended March 31, 1897	7,386	24.0	140,727	458.1
Decrease per cent . .	25.8	36.5	5.5	19.0

Report of the Commissioners of Prisons and Directors of Convict Prisons, for the year ending March 31, 1897, p. 6.

TABLE XXVI

TABLE SHOWING POPULATION OF ENGLAND AND WALES, WITH
THE NUMBER OF PRISONERS SENTENCED TO DEATH, FOR LIFE,
TERM OF YEARS, INDICTMENT, SUMMARY, ETC., FROM 1880

YEAR.	POPULATION OF ENGLAND AND WALES.	NUMBER OF PRISONERS SENTENCED TO					
		DEATH	PENAL SERVITUDE FOR LIFE	PENAL SERVITUDE FOR A TERM OF YEARS		IMPRISONMENT ON INDICTMENT	IMPRISONMENT ON SUMMARY CONVICTION OR WANT OF SURETY
				By Ordinary Courts	Courts Martial		
1880	25,708,666	28	8	1,515	13	9,663	152,347
1881	25,974,439	23	17	1,508	9	9,266	141,913
1882	26,334,776	22	7	1,357	50	9,715	153,267
1883	26,626,639	23	10	1,368	31	9,455	156,215
1884	26,921,737	38	13	1,336	2	9,135	152,628
1885	27,220,105	25	8	1,019		8,891	140,213
1886	27,521,780	35	8	902	2	9,199	147,068
1887	27,826,798	35	10	938		9,355	140,717
1888	28,135,197	36	4	920	2	9,014	146,925
1889	28,447,014	20	3	915	3	7,857	139,214
1890	28,762,287	24	3	726	1	7,775	134,722
1891	29,002,525	19	4	747		7,548	130,803
1892	29,403,346	22	1	893	2	7,780	138,931
1893	29,731,100	28		960		7,775	149,763
1894	30,060,763	29		956		7,671	141,673
1895	30,394,078	19	1	803	3	7,448	148,010
1896	30,717,355	33	6	750	4	7,057	142,397
INCREASE IN 17 YEARS.	5,008,689	5					
DECREASE IN 17 YEARS			2	765	9	2,606	9,950

Ibid., p. 104.

Here we see the average increase of population during the period of 17 years, between 1880 and 1896,[1] is 1.14 per cent per annum, while the decrease of indictable offences is 1.78 per cent, and that of summary convictions is 0.39 per cent. As compared with the United States, while the latter's population has increased 24.85 per cent in the decade mentioned, between 1880 and 1890, the English population in the same period has increased but 11.48 per cent, but her criminal roll has gone down 12.40 per cent as against an increase of 40.47 per cent in the States. Also, while the number of serious offences in the latter country has appreciably increased, that of England has decreased materially.

Australia has followed the example of the mother country in respect to the above favorable showing. In 1896 the prison population of New South Wales numbered 17,012. In 1897 it had decreased to 14,737 showing a falling off of 13.3 per cent in one year. The jails' entries in that country decreased during that period 20 per cent. The general population increased the same year from 1,297,640 to 1,323,460. In 1880 the proportion of entries to prison to the general population was 2.32 per cent. In 1867 it was 1.11 per cent.

In Scotland the number summarily convicted annually since 1893 has been variable, with an increase on the whole, while those convicted on full committal have decreased, on the whole. The following table, gathered from its latest report (1899),[2] illustrates its criminal history during that period: —

[1] Table XXVI.
[2] Report of the Judicial Statistics for the years 1877–1899.

TABLE XXVII

YEAR	NUMBER CONVICTED			AVERAGE YEARLY NUMBER OF CRIMINAL PRISONERS FOR PERIODS OF 5 YEARS			
	Summarily	FULL COMMITTAL		5 Years to Dec. 31, 1886	5 Years to Dec. 31, 1891	5 Years to Dec. 31, 1896	Annual Number in Year Ending Dec. 31, 1897
			Recidivists				
1893	105,045	1903	997 — 52.38 %	48,143	47,543	50,956	51,327
1894	112,092	1937	1050 — 54.21 %				
1895	107,212	1652	944 — 51.14 %	Recidivists			
1896	115,275	1704	994 — 58.33 %	27,299	18,871	16,733	17,974
1897	110,783	1796	1112 — 61.91 %				
Average	110,081	1799	1019 — 56.65 %	56.81 %	39.69 %	32.84 %	36.02%

Ireland shows the following record of local and convict prisons from 1890 to 1897 :[1] —

TABLE XXVIII

YEAR	LOCAL PRISONS			CONVICT PRISONS			
	Committals	Daily Average. Prisoners	Daily Average. Per 10,000	Convicted	Discharged	In Custody, January 1	Total
1890	40,783	2,605	55	88	116	454	40,871
1891	37,568	2,497	53	125	117	463	37,693
1892	34,583	2,315	50	86	113	480	34,669
1893	34,387	2,428	53	106	103	471	34,493
1894	31,474	2,317	50	115	157	485	31,589
1895	30,270	2,155	47	102	154	464	30,372
1896	32,956	2,325	51	81	140	429	33,037
1897	34,911	2,332	51	68	144	397	34,979

[1] Twentieth Report of the General Prison Board, Ireland, 1897–1898, pp. 7, 11.

Prussia reports a decrease in criminalism, as shown by its latest official prison report,[1] as indicated by the following table of the more serious grade of offences during the last two decades : —

TABLE XXIX

YEAR	TOTAL NUMBER PRISONERS	PER 10,000 INHABI- TANTS	PER CENT		PER CENT RECIDI- VISM	COMPARATIVE	
			Increase	Decrease		Increase	Decrease
1890	18,056	4.13			78.89		
1891	18,050	4.09		.033	81.24	1.35	
1892	17,983	4.14		.36	81.55	.31	
1893	18,128	4.25	.8		81.60	.05	
1894	18,058	4.06		.38	81.87	.27	
1895	17,880	3.98		.98	81.03		.84
1896	17,556	3.77		1.81	80.74		.29
1897	17,057	3.69		2.84	80.76	.02	
1898	16,394	3.08		3.88	82.21	1.45	

Italian criminal statistics drawn from official sources [2] give us the following table of convictions from 1881 to 1896, inclusive : —

TABLE XXX

YEARS	PRETORS	CORRECTIONAL TRIBUNAL	ASSIZES	TOTAL	
				Total Number	Per 10,000
1881–86	251,545	57,682	5,718	314,945	109.21
1887–89	278,025	52,294	4,989	335,308	113.31
1890–92	286,194	66,057	3,180	355,431	117.85
1893–95	272,727	75,331	3,590	351,648	114.45
1896	293,106	80,997	3,345	377,448	121.36

[1] *Statistik Preussischen Strafanstalten und Gefängisse*, 1897–1898, p. xii, xiii.　　　[2] *Statistica Giudiziaria Penale*, per l' anno 1896, p. lii.

From the above it will be seen that, although the number of convictions before the Pretors and Correctional Tribunals has increased, the number before the Court of Assizes has gradually decreased. Specific crimes, on the basis of 10,000 estimated population, show, on the whole, a falling off in the more serious crime of murder; likewise a fluctuation in the more serious grades of offences against property; but a decided gain in all pettier offences, ranging from 404.53 per 10,000 inhabitants in the period between 1880 and 1886, to 784.21 per 10,000 in 1896, a gain of 379.68 per 10,000 in ten years, or nearly double.

The number and places of detention, from the same sources,[1] from 1891 to 1896, present the following:—

TABLE XXXI

YEARS	PENAL DETENTION				FINES	
	Galleys	In Solitary Imprisonment and Jail			Fines up to 5 f.	Fines over 5 f.
		Over 10 years	Under 10 years and over 1 year	Jail, over 5 days		
1881–86	416	109,308		174,660		29,016
1887–89	321	867	108,583	208,590		20,201
1890–92	110	936	158,707	23,086	130,003	42,415
1893–95	125	1,239	165,309	25,006	114,009	42,277
1896	124	1,376	174,276	25,282	132,732	43,598

[1] *Statistica Giudiziaria Penale*, per l' anno 1896, p. x.

Crime in Austria and Hungary, from published reports,[1] has decreased, while the aggregate has fluctuated during these periods:—

TABLE XXXII

YEAR	AUSTRIA			HUNGARY			
	In State Prison	Recidivists	Total Number Committed	Number of Prisoners in State Prison, Dec. 31	Discharged During Year	Received During Year	Average Number in Jails and Police Jails
1890	10,755	2,821	430,015				
1891	10,560	2,948	432,982				
1892	10,320	3,194	438,831	4,909	1,473	1,529	9,671
1893	10,467	3,020	422,328	4,841	1,645	1,700	9,179
1894	10,301	3,064	418,431	4,835	1,690	1,863	8,756
1895				4,892	1,687	1,838	8,967
1896				4,796	1,743	1,853	8,895
1897				4,680	1,593	1,660	8,945

Serious offences are gradually on the decrease in Sweden, as indicated by the table given below compiled from the latest published official report (1896). The total number of convicted felons serving time in the prisons during the last three decades are as follows:—

TABLE XXXIII

YEARS.	MALES.	FEMALES.	TOTAL.	PER CENT OF DECREASE.	PER 100,000 INHABITANTS.
1865	2,713	621	3,334		
1875	2,567	547	3,114	6.59	
1885	1,994	435	2,429	21.99	
1895	1,462	221	1,683	30.71	
1896	1,408	232	1,640	2.55	33.3

[1] *Oesterreichische Statistik*, etc. Jahrgang 1890, 1891, 1892, 1893, 1894, 1895. *Magyar Kiralyi Igazsdgügyministerium Müköaëse*, 1895–1898, pp. 480 and 553.

The total decrease in felonies between the years 1890 and 1896 has been from 2090 to 1640, or 21.53 per cent; jail offences, etc., 1652 to 1595, a decline of 3.4 per cent; while the total number of convictions for all classes of crimes and misdemeanors at those two dates has risen from 20,458 to 23,131 respectively, an increase of 13.06 per cent.[1]

In Norway, the total number of convictions for the more serious offences during the quinquennial between 1890 and 1894 inclusive, as gathered from the "Statesman's Year Book," is as follows: —

TABLE XXXIV

Year 1890.	Year 1891.	Year 1892.	Year 1893.	Year 1894.	Per Cent Increase.
2,603	2,548	3,026	2,949	2,948	13.25

The prison population has decreased from 679 to 615 in 1894, a decrease of 9.29 per cent, while the total number of convictions for crimes and petty offences has risen from 26,505 in 1890, to 29,885 in 1895.[2]

Crime in Denmark has increased but slightly. In 1890 there were for the more serious offences 3897 convictions and 2224 imprisonments. In 1896 there were 4002 convictions and 2391 imprisonments, but a slight increase per 10,000 inhabitants during six years. For the same period, fines by judgment fell from 1454 to

<hr />

[1] *Fångvårds-Styrelsens*, Underdåniga Berättelse för Ar 1890, 1896.
[2] *Norges Krininalstatistik*, for Aaret, 1894, p. 108.

1411; and those without judgment grew from 31,233 to 34,569, respectively.[1]

The past decade of criminal history of the Netherlands, from 1887 to 1897 (1891 and 1892 omitted), furnishes the following table : —

TABLE XXXV

Year	Number in State Prison	Number in Jails	Total	Total Number Convictions	Per 10,000 Inhabitants
1887 . .			2,263	19,774	44.4 [*1]
1888 . .			2,268	19,420	43.1
1889 . .	425	1,942	2,367	20,506	45.0
1890 . .	363	1,971	2,334	19,960	43.7
1893 . .			2,471	20,147	42.5 [*2]
1894 . .			2,577	20,411	42.5
1895 . .			2,547	19,317	39.7
1896 . .	245	2,340	2,585	19,021	38.6
1897 . .	224	2,297	2,521	19,031	38.0

Here the graver crimes (state prison offences) between 1889 and 1897 numbered a total of 517 (425 prisoners on hand December 31, 1889, and 92 received during 1890), while in 1897 there were 325 (245 on hand December 31, 1896, and 80 received during 1897), a decrease in seven years of 35.2 per cent in serious offences. The total number of convictions per 10,000 inhabitants has decreased.[2]

Japan shows a decrease in serious crime since 1885, somewhat in the following ratio : in 1881 the total num-

[1] Bureau of Statistics, Copenhagen, 1899.

[2] *Statistiek Van Het Gevangeniswezen*, over Het Jaar, 1890 and 1897, pp. 2, 3.　　　[*1] *Ibid.*, p. xiii, 1890.　　　[*2] *Ibid.*, p. xiii, 1897.

ber of criminals was 107,120; in 1885, 109,367; in 1886, 102,414; in 1887, 84,120; in 1888, 76,453, and in 1895, 77,551.[1]

Of course, the conditions that inspire the criminal problem in the Old World and in the New are somewhat dissimilar. The existence of penal colonies and the practice of transportion for grave offences, and the readiness with which existent conditions lend themselves to facilitate emigration afford a ready means of getting rid of the more undesirable and contagious elements of Old World criminalism, conditions that are non-existent and do not give themselves so readily in the New. Indeed, the unloading upon these shores of those already inoculated with the criminal virus, as already illustrated, while operating as a safety-valve to the former countries, is hardly conducive to criminal amelioration here where the gateway has usually swung but one way. Notwithstanding these disadvantages, and taking into consideration the large annual growth of population in the United States, the increase of her prison population in the ratio of 131.46 per 100,000 in 1890, as compared with 116.85 per 100,000 in 1880, certainly presents no alarming features in the social problem of the New World. The latter feature, immigration, as the chief source of supply to the Western criminal problem, is, however, of a local civil character, and may be remedied through proper legislation that closes the door to this source of criminal accretion, and therefore need hardly be further discussed in the list of prevenient measures.

There is no way of estimating the fluctuation of par-

[1] " Statesman's Year Book."

ticular classes of crimes in the United States, year by year, as is possible from the annual compilations of many of the European reports, owing to the custom of taking the census decennially in the United States. As to leading crimes, and their relative proportions in the ten years intervening between 1880 and 1890, the following tables compiled by myself may suffice to indicate the variational moods in the six leading crimes in groups of states under geographical subdivisions (as adopted by the United States census reports), by five principal states from east to west, and from north to south respectively, giving an interesting study and offering a fair indication of the prevailing criminal status in these several divisions as they exist both against person and against property, in the various portions of the Union : —

TABLE XXXVI

DIAGRAM SHOWING FLUCTUATION IN SIX LEADING CRIMES (MALE), BY GEOGRAPHICAL DIVISIONS IN THE UNITED STATES, PER 100,000 POPULATION

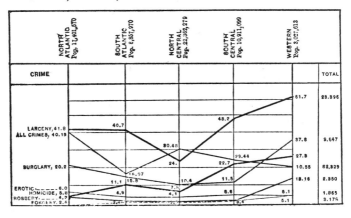

An analysis of the above shows that in the United States, as elsewhere, larceny as the leading crime is also the most fluctuating locally and periodically, depending upon climatic as well as upon industrial and economic conditions for support. Thus, its lowest ratio (24 per 100,000) is found in the North Central (agricultural) group of states, doubling as it merges into the South Central, and reaching its climax in the Western cluster of states where property and custom are perhaps less strongly protected than in the older and steadier communities. Burglary, as the more aggressive form of crime, is very nearly even in the North and South Central divisions, but pushes abruptly from 11.5 per 100,000 in the latter, up to 37.6 in the Western division. Robbery is quite uniform, asserting itself in the Western division with similar forcefulness; while sexual offences, usually attributed to warmer climates, appear to be most pronounced in the North Atlantic and the South Central states. Forgery keeps well apace with, and merges into, its twin brother, robbery, in the North and South Central divisions, to double in the Western. Homicide reaches its minimum in the North Atlantic (5.8 per 100,000), doubles (11.1) in the South Atlantic, again doubles (22.7) in the South Central, and reaches its highest (27.3) in the Western division.

Again, analyzing the sections by states and constructing a sort of isothermal criminal belt extending due east and west, and north and south, we have presented about the following chart of the criminal tidal wave in its westerly swell from the Atlantic until it breaks at the Golden Gate, and from the Inland Seas to the Gulf of Mexico.

TABLE XXXVII

DIAGRAMS SHOWING FLUCTUATIONS IN SIX LEADING CRIMES IN FIVE PRINCIPAL STATES FROM EAST TO WEST, PER 100,000 OF POPULATION

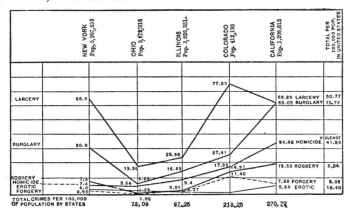

TABLE XXXVIII

SIX LEADING CRIMES IN FIVE PRINCIPAL STATES FROM NORTH TO SOUTH, PER 100,000 OF POPULATION

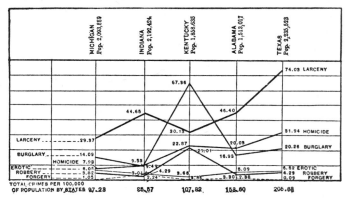

Here (Table XXXVII) larceny, burglary, and robbery start respectively at 65.6, 30.8, and 7.5 per 100,000 in the Empire State, burdened not only with its own domestic criminalism, but also receiving the floodtide of the Old World inundation, which according to the Tenth Census (1880) numbered 20.75 per cent, and by the Eleventh Census (1890) 19.35 per cent, of the total criminal population of the Union. In Ohio the above representative criminal offences drop respectively to 19.36, 6.69, and 2.23 per 100,000 (their lowest), rising perceptibly in Illinois, to reach their climax in the same order in the extreme westerly and mining sections. Homicide and robbery follow substantially the same general trend, though in lessening degree. In its southerly sweep (Table XXXVIII) larceny reaches its highest point in Texas, burglary in Kentucky, with homicide and robbery as in above cases following in lessening order.

It will readily be seen from a careful analysis of the foregoing tables that, while any accurate or satisfactory conclusion as to the actual relative increase or decrease of crime is quite impossible, enough may be gleaned to warrant the presumption that, while petty offenders and general misdemeanants are on the whole on the increase, perhaps somewhat in advance of the growth of population, serious crimes do not share in any appreciable degree in this onward movement.

Aside from the distinctions drawn between misdemeanants and the graver class of offenders mentioned above, it would be well to bear in mind the fact of the constant additions being made to the body of criminal law in the continual creation of new minor statutory offences not before existing, which appreciably affect the main criminal current and number of aggregate convictions in all civilized countries. With reference to English criminal history in these respects, the observations of the eminent British prison authority already cited[1] deserve attention, relative to the seemingly large proportion that go to help swell aggregate British crime, as, for instance, those of 1869–1870, viz., 578,841, and 1890, 70,392, are, as Mr. Du Cane has shown, not crimes at all, but simply violations of " Educational Acts," as already noted (as those of 1870–1896, 96,601); " Burroughs Laws " (35,681 to 59,108); " Begging and Vagrant Acts " (41,780 to 46,019); " Offences against Highways " (29,837 to 32,889), etc.[2]

The same authority has conclusively shown in tabulated form that the average number of sentences of penal servitude in England and Wales decreased as follows:[3] —

During the five years ending 1864	2,800
During the five years ending 1869	1,978
During the five years ending 1874	1,622
During the five years ending 1879	1,633
During the five years ending 1884	1,428

He has shown that the average number in local prisons from 1876 to 1877, was 20,361; 1891–1892, 12,663; the number sentenced to penal servitude in 1869 was 2006, and in 1891, 751 such sentences. Indictable offences from 1867 to 1868 numbered 57,812; 1877–1878, 52,397;

[1] Sir Edmund Du Cane.

[2] *Nineteenth Century Review*, March, 1893, pp. 492, 480, 490.

[3] " Punishment and Prevention of Crime," p. 92.

and 1890–1891 they numbered 35,335. Summary offences, 1873–1874, numbered 192,440, and 1890–1891,
159,534.[1]

.The increase of average convictions cited by another
authority (W. D. Morrison), and covering nearly the
same periods, illustrates the principles of increase in
minor offences as above, viz. : —

1873–77	513,162
1888–92	587,669
Increase	74,507

The same authority acknowledges, however, that the
"percentage of apprehensions for serious crimes has, on
the whole, been decreasing within the last thirty years."[2]

The same general principle undoubtedly holds true
with reference to German criminalism, where the
statutory enactments that relate to pettier offences
constitute the bulk of aggregate criminality, while the
graver offences fall away, even the crime of murder
yielding before new methods in her criminal curriculum.
France, Italy, Austria, Sweden, Norway, Belgium, and
the Netherlands present much the same leading characteristics with reference to comparative criminal increase
and decrease, as will be seen by referring to the tables
heretofore given.

In our own country, numerous subdivisions and refinements of the penal code are constantly going on, and
petty misdemeanors to-day become penal offences to-
morrow. In some of the states of the Union, the penal

[1] *Nineteenth Century Review*, March, 1893, pp. 480–490.
[2] *Fortnightly Review*, April, 1894, pp. 462–464.

codes reach four and five hundred statutory provisions where but a few years ago they were limited to one-half or one-third that number. The German code enumerates about 203 crimes and offences; the Italian, 180, and the new code, 200; and the French code, about 150. All this materially enlarges the scope and current of contemporary criminality, and gives it a weightiness and meaning hardly warranted by the real facts of the case. The increase in crime in the United States, as elsewhere, has been largest along the line of petty offences and misdemeanors, as is evidenced by a comparative study of the relative population of the penitentiaries and jails of the country at the time of taking the censuses of 1880 and 1890 respectively. In 1880 the number of penitentiary inmates was 30,659. In 1890 it was 45,233, an increase of 47.53 per cent. The inmates of city and county jails in 1880 numbered 14,357, and in 1890 23,125, a growth of 61.07 per cent or an increase of more than 13 per cent in petty misdemeanants over graver offenders in the period named. An eminent authority[1] estimated the total number of convictions for crime of every grade annually in the United States at 720,000, the number of committals to prison at 260,000. The number of prisoners in all jails (including the jails and juvenile prisons) is 85,000. A rough estimate of the cost of crime in the United States, including the expense of police and constabulary courts, trials, witnesses, etc., prison maintenance, and interests and investments for prison establishments, excluding from the calculation the amount of loss from crimes

[1] Mr. Brockway.

themselves, and the footing would exceed fifty millions of annual expenditures; one authority estimating it at sixty millions. More than 90 per cent are misdemeanors, not felonies, that is, punishable by imprisonment for periods less than one year in jails, workhouses, etc.[1] The convictions per million inhabitants of the various countries of Europe, on the whole, have been estimated as follows: England and Wales, 450; France, 612; Austria, 526; Prussia, 952; Italy, 1010.[2]

A question as to whether crime is on the increase or on the decrease is, on the whole, about as unsatisfactory as that other form of the inquiry: Is the world growing better or worse? The natures of the inquiries are not necessarily one and the same. It is possible to conceive of crime as on the increase or decrease, while the moral status of a community remains practically unchanged. The former is the phenomenon of the socio-judicial arm in more effective operation at one period of its corporative history than at another, while prevailing moral conditions are unmoved. The foundation principles of human nature remain practically unalterable. Men function from the same impulsions to-day, yesterday, and forever. The sources of all responsible conduct are inseparably interwoven with the personality. Crime is its social culmination. The moral cause of the catastrophe goes further back than any mere social or judicial remedies can reach. We do not expect crime to cease in this sense; it only changes expression. We can mitigate, we cannot cure.

[1] *Journal of Prison Discipline and Philanthropy*, January, 1898 and 1899, pp. 55, 56.　　　[2] *Bulletin Statistique*.

CHAPTER XI

THE JUVENILE OFFENDER AND THE REFORMATORIES

A CONSIDERATION of the field of special anthropological criminality would be incomplete without at least a cursory survey of the Juvenile Offender as a concomitant of the larger theme, and as having a direct relation to the question at large as well as a significant bearing upon the subject of prevention and cure.

If it be true, as the very constitution of the mind seems to imply, that the educative forces and postnatal influences are all essential formative agencies in human character, sometimes even to the extent of alteration in special predisposing tendencies, the juvenile offender, as a person amenable to correctives and with a corresponding view to ultimate rehabilitation, becomes at once a subject of transcendent interest and importance for consideration and study on the part of the scientific penologist, the political economist, and the philanthropist.

Logically, as well as bio-genetically, the youth stands at the inception of the criminological problem, both objectively and subjectively.

Morally, his age of responsibility under the common law commences with his ability to discriminate between right and wrong. Legally, the limit as fixed by canon law is 7 years. The Italian period is the 9th ; Holland,

Austria, and Sweden the 10th; and Germany the 12th year. In England, 16 years is the limit of committal fixed by law, and 18 years has been recently recommended. In the United States, the age is usually discretionary with the court.

In its moral and economic aspect, especially as touching the prevenient phases, the subject-matter deserves more than passing attention, however minimized by the comparatively meagre interest manifested by the public in the treatment of the same. Hitherto, the personality of the juvenile recalcitrant has been merged in that of the mass of incarcerates, it being not uncommon to find children of tender years confined in the state prisons and penitentiaries of the land, there to imbibe the concentrated criminousness they are expected to eschew without. On the other hand, be it said, that the theory of the law is theoretically lenient with this class of offenders, aiming to mitigate punishment by the intervention (at least upon first offence) of fines and admonitions, or detention in the public jails or houses of correction, thence to emerge, as it usually happens, more deeply imbued in crime than ever.

Society has had little heart in the matter of moral appliances, or of institutional supervisorial care of those unfortunates who, in the vast majority of instances, have attained their criminal status through entailment, or environment, into which they are cast by circumstances over which they had no control save that of open revolt, which of course is hardly to be expected.

Public interest in this youthful Ishmaelite is of recent origin, at first through private enterprise rather than public concern; though latterly it has deservedly attained its true significance and proper place in the popular mind as a matter of transcendent importance out of sheer self-defence.

Juvenile criminality has assumed an independent department in the subject at large through the impetus given it by the reformatory wave that is lifting it out of the rut of mere sentiment, and transferring it to the sphere of the tentative and experimental. As a distinctive problem by itself, and in the concrete, it may be said that the apparent increase of precocious criminality is due rather to the fact of this more systematic attention given it, and in the added fact that these junior partners in crime are now more definitely segregated and labelled from their senior malcontents, and regularly assigned to distinctively correctional institutions by themselves, especially adapted to their care and treatment.

The whole subject of youthful criminality is increasing in magnitude and importance as the growth of crime fosters its necessity in the public mind as one of the possible open doors for relief. Juvenile criminalism is on the increase. Ferri reports a continuous growth of precocious criminalism in Italy. In Holland, those under 16 years have doubled in numbers within the last ten years. In Russia, those between 14 and 21 have augmented much faster than the comparative growth of her population; while those of Austria and Hungary have decreased. In the German Empire, while her adult population has grown within the last ten years, her juvenile criminals have increased during the same time 50 per cent of the number convicted in the Empire in 1892, when 46,496 were reported under 18 years of age.[1] Forty per cent of the convictions in England every year are against young persons under 21 years of age.[2] In 1886 the number convicted between 18 and 21 years was 16 per cent of her prison population; 6 per cent between 15 and 18; and 3 per cent between 12 and 15 years of age. The number of persons convicted of indictable offences between the ages of 16 to 21 was 9298 in 1893, 9568 in 1894, 8634 in 1895, and 7834 in 1896. For children between 12 and 16 the figures are 6595, 6604, 5339, and 5773 respectively for the years above given.[3] Mr. Du Cane thinks that 58 per cent practised dishonesty when under 15 years of age; 14 per cent between 15 and 16; 8 per cent under 17, 18, 19; and 20 per cent under 20.[4] Juvenile criminals sent to prison were on the decrease from 1869 to 1881, according to one authority, at the rate of 53 per cent; according to another, amounting to one-third of the number annually committed thirty years ago, though he correctly states that the decrease of juvenile imprisonment does not imply any real diminution of juvenile criminality. This marked difference is attributed to the development of the reformatory and industrial movement throughout the United Kingdom. The children under fourteen formerly committed to prison direct have been sent since 1893 to these insti-

[1] " Statesman's Year Book," 1895.

[2] The *London Times*, June 13, 1865.

[3] Forty-first Report Inspector Reformatory and Industrial Schools, Great Britain, 1897, p. 15.

[4] " Punishment and Prevention of Crime," p. 198.

tutions. The Judicial Statistics for England and Wales for the year 1896 quoted in the Report of Inspectors of Reformatory and Industrial Schools of Great Britain for the year 1897 (pp. 19, 20, 21), give the following number of juvenile commitments to prison of those under 16 years of age: males, 1395; females, 103; total, 1498. For 1895: males, 1789; females, 179; total, 1968. For 1894: males, 2024; females, 228; total, 2252. The total number of juvenile commitments since 1861 to 1896 has fallen respectively from 8801 juveniles in the former period to 1408 in the latter period, a decrease of 80.70 per cent. For Scotland they have fallen from 1062 in 1860, to 618 in 1896, a decrease of 41.86 per cent. The figures for the year 1878 are in both instances for 6 months only.

The total number of schools under inspection in Great Britain on the 31st of December, 1897–98 (date of last report), was 229, viz.: 48 reformatories; 144 industrial schools; 14 truant schools; 23 day industrial schools. Of these 3 were reformatory and 8 industrial school-ships. The certified auxiliary homes in connection with industrial schools were 9. Seven of the industrial schools are managed by county authorities; 9 are managed by school boards; and one by corporation; the remainder under voluntary management. The truant schools and all the day industrial schools except 3 are under the management of school boards. The total number of juveniles under sentence of detention in reformatories and industrial schools at the close of 1897 was 30,246, viz., 24,849 boys, including 4423 on license from and 1211 in truant schools, and

5397 girls; an increase of 142 over last year. In addition to the above there were at the end of the year 2804 children, 340 fewer than in 1896, attending day industrial schools, and 405 children on license from these schools. There were 7870 admissions during the year 1897, exclusive of children sent to day industrial schools, an increase of 51 committals over the previous year. The total committals in 1897 for England were 1170, and for Scotland, 242. The details are as follows : [1] —

TABLE XXXIX

	Boys	Girls	Total
To Reformatory Schools			
England	1,016	153	1,169
Scotland	215	25	240
To Industrial Schools			
England	2,608	723	3,331
Scotland	756	241	997
To Truant Schools			
England	2,133		2,133
Total	6,728	1,142	7,870

The total admission to reformatory schools to December 31, 1897, amounted to 62,331, viz., 51,536 boys and 10,795 girls. The total discharges to the same date, exclusive of transfers, were 56,786, viz., 46,723 boys and 10,063 girls.[2]

The total admission to industrial schools, excluding

[1] Forty-first Report, for year 1897, of Inspector of Reformatory and Industrial Schools of Great Britain, 1898, pp. 7, 8, 9.

[2] *Ibid.*, p. 18.

transfers, up to December 31, 1897, was 91,360 boys and 24,636 girls; total, 115,996.[1] The total number admitted to truant schools up to the same date was 27,248.[2]

The number of juvenile offenders for various crimes in the German Empire, for the year 1897,[3] shows the aggregate of youth from 12 to 18 years numbered 45,329, 17.65 per cent of which were females. By states, Prussia claims 26,280; Bavaria, 6764; Saxony, 3278; Würtemberg, 1588; Baden, 1520; and the lesser states and free cities, including Alsace-Lorraine, 5947.[4]

In Prussia, on the 31st of March, 1898, there were 10,687 juveniles, divided among the following institutions: for lighter offences and when parents were at fault, there were given to families to board, etc., 5145; in reformatories (7) under district supervision,[5] 1349; in private reformatories (16) under inspection of government, 4180; and in prison on account of graver offences, 13. There have been sent to the reformatories since 1878 to 1897, 27,645 juveniles, and to 1898, 29,263 juveniles.[6]

France and Algeria, in 1887, numbered 6099 juvenile inmates in her reformatories, of which she possessed 11 for boys; also 21 for boys and 9 for girls on the

[1] Forty-first Report, for year 1897, of Inspector of Reformatory and Industrial Schools of Great Britain, 1898, p. 25.

[2] *Ibid.*, p. 29.

[3] Report, 1899.

[4] *Kriminalstatistick*, für das Jahr 1897, 1899, pp. 302, 303.

[5] "Regierungsbezirk."

[6] "Statistik der zum Ressort des Königlich Preussischen Ministeriums des Inner gehörenden Strafanstalten und Gëfänguisse," für den 1sten April, 1897, 1898, 1899, pp. 160, 161.

rental plan. In 1895 (December 31) she had 5235 boys and 1152 girls in her reformatories. In 1896 (same date) there were 6 public and 12 private reformatories and industrial schools for boys in France and Algeria, and 4 public and 7 private ones for girls in France, making 31 in all. France and Algeria had, on the 31st of December, 1896, 6118 reformatory inmates — 5023 boys and 1095 girls, France having 4838 boys and 1095 girls, leaving 183 boys for Algeria. The latter has one reformatory for boys.[1]

In Italy, in 1887, there were 5477 juveniles in her reformatories, 3633 boys and 1844 girls; and in 1891 they numbered 4343 — 2343 boys and 2000 girls.[2] In 1895, her total juvenile population in reformatories numbered 6147 — 3753 boys and 2394 girls; in 1896 (January 1) 6315 — 3775 boys and 2540 girls; and in 1897 (same date) 6522 — 3890 boys and 2632 girls. Fifteen hundred and eighty-two were confined in government, and 4940 were inmates of private institutions.[3]

Austria, in 1890, had 2 reformatories with but 66 inmates. In 1891, they numbered 105; in 1892, 129; in 1893, 131, and in 1894, 149. The number of juvenile offenders from 11 to 14 years of age from 1885 to 1895, averaged 673 annually; and those from 14 to 20 years of age averaged 5729 annually. Of each 100 persons convicted during that period the annual percentage of juvenile offenders averaged 21.82 per cent.[4]

---

[1] *Statistique Penitentiaire*, pour l'année 1896, pp. cclxxx, cclxxxi.

[2] "Statesman's Year Book," 1895.

[3] *Statistica delle Carceri*, 1897, pp. 282, 283, 286; 1898, pp. 258, 259; 1899, pp. 366, 367.

[4] *Oesterreichische Statistik*, 1895, Heft 3., p. xl.

In Hungary, between 1892 and 1897, the number of juvenile prisoners averaged but 164 per annum; and the average number committed annually was 236.[1]

Belgium, in 1890, had a total juvenile population in the reformatories of 905 — 803 boys and 102 girls; 1894, 317 boys; from which latter period there was such a small number of juvenile female offenders that the reformatory for that class was abolished, and the eligibles thereafter were sent to the prisons. In 1895 there were 258 boys; and in 1896 (date of last report), there were 249 boys in her reformatories.

In the Netherlands, juvenile delinquents under 10 years of age are sent to reformatories, of which there are 4, containing, in 1890, 703 juvenile inmates. In 1896 they contained 772 inmates, and in 1897, 806 inmates. The total number, including those over 16 (confined in prisons), were 1841 — 1690 males and 151 females.

In Switzerland, in 1892, the number of juvenile offenders between the ages of 12 to 20 years in prison numbered but 108; one being 13 years of age; four 14 years of age, and the rest over 16 years of age.[2]

Russia, in 1891, had 5 institutions for boys, with an average population of 82; and 7 for girls, with an average population of 56. Her agricultural colonies for juveniles numbered 428 inmates; industrial asylums, 372 inmates, and young girls' industrial asylums, 52 inmates.[3]

---

[1] *A Magyar Kirdlyi Igazsdgügyministerium Müködése*, 1895, 1898, p. 480.

[2] *Statistique Penitentiaire Suisse*, pour l'année 1892.

[3] Fourth International Prison Congress Report, St. Petersburg, Russia, 1891, pp. 25, 26.

In the United States the number of juvenile delinquents has been steadily on the increase, owing, no doubt, to much the same general causes that have aided to swell her bulk of aggregate criminalism, in addition to such as help to account for similar growths in the English records. The numerical tables published by the Census Bureau upon "Juvenile Reformatories" (1890), give a total of 14,846 inmates of reformatories — 12,903 white, 1930 negroes, and 12 Indians. Of this number, 1405 were foreign born, a percentage of 19.88 as compared to the total number of white inmates, viz., 12,903. As to parentage, 3965 of the parents of these inmates were foreign, and but 3245 were natives. In 1870 it numbered less than 8000. In the year 1880 it numbered 11,468, the ratio of juvenile offenders to the whole population being 229 to each million; in 1890 it was 237 to the million, an absolute increase of 3378, and a relative increase of eight to the million, or a total increase of 29.46 per cent in 1890 over the year 1880, being at the average rate of 337 annually. In respect of sex among these minors, 11,535 (9998 whites) of the total were males, and 3311 (2905 whites) were females, or 22.3 per cent of the latter as against 77.7 per cent of the former, which gives us a much larger female percentage as compared with adult criminals. As compared with English statistics, with reference to age at time of admission to her reformatories, in 1897, 19 were under 10 years of age ; 140 from 10 to 12; 516 from 12 to 14 ; and 734 from 14 to 16 years of age.[1]

[1] Forty-first Report of Inspector of Reformatory and Industrial Schools, for 1897, p. 17.

As to age, 21 were under 5 years of age; 707 were between 5 and 9 years of age; 6763 between 10 and 14; 6750 between 15 and 19; 240 between 20 and 24, and 54 were between 25 and 29 years of age, at the time of commitment. The average age of all juveniles confined in reformatories in 1890 was 14.23 years; boys averaging 14.09, and girls, 14.71 years.

Of the nature of the offences, 18 were against the government; 6930 were offences against society; 308 against person, of which 16 were homicides; 4515 were against property, prevailing in the order of petty larceny, 2544, larceny, 973, and burglary, 546; while the balance (2867) were of a miscellaneous kind. Offences against property (30.4 per cent) were the predominating forms of crime; those against person being but 2.1 per cent. In the New York reformatory, 94 per cent were of those against property. Of those received in the English reformatories as per above report, 87 per cent were against property; and 2.83 per cent against person. The prevailing specific crime was larceny, 79 per cent; next in order comes housebreaking, 2.97 per cent; then felonies, 2.33 per cent, and vagrancy, 5.59 per cent.[1]

The figures, as above stated, it must be remembered, bear no reference to the numbers still amalgamated with the regular state prison and jail incarcerates, which yet remain to be reckoned with in all countries, and which would help swell the aggregate of juvenile offenders materially. The more audacious as well as

[1] Forty-first Report of Inspector of Reformatory and Industrial Schools, p. 654.

unmanageable, otherwise eligible to the reformatories, are still assigned to these institutions under provision of law. Thus, as per the last United States census, there remained a residue yet to be added to the above : viz., 711 under 15 ; 8984 between 15 and 19 ; and 19,705 between 20 and 24 years of age ; while in England, March 31, 1897, there were left in her prisons 551 males and 53 females not more than 18 years of age. As to the juveniles actually received into reformatories annually, England receives between 7000 and 8000, inclusive of industrial and day industrial schools. Prussia averages about 2000 per annum ; Belgium, 176 ; Holland, 161 ; and the United States between 2400 and 3000, and is rapidly increasing.

International statistics of leading countries furnish us the following percentages of prisoners under 20 years of age, which may be of interest as illustrating this phase of criminal pathognomonics.

TABLE XL

PERCENTAGE OF CRIMINALS OF DIFFERENT COUNTRIES UNDER TWENTY YEARS OF AGE

COUNTRIES	MALE	FEMALE	COUNTRIES	MALE	FEMALE
England	27.4	14.5	France	10.	7.6
Holland	22.8	3.7	Denmark	9.9	9.6
Belgium	20.8		Austria	9.6	10.6
Scotland	20.	7.8	Ireland	9.	3.2
Sweden	19.7	17.	Italy	8.8	6.8
United States	10.71	1.06	Prussia	2.8	2.6

The criminal evolution, numerically, when summarized as to age, grows apace from an indefinite period until it reaches its climax between the ages of 20 and 25, thereafter gradually receding, as in the 25 and 29 years' period (Census of 1890), 16,348; 30 and 34 years' period, 11,678; and 35 and 39 years' period, when it reaches 8,329, thence down to the finale.

Biological conditions, and those in particular which are associated with the periods of maturity and pubescence, have unquestionably a great influence upon the mental and emotional natures of the growing youth. This fact is also noticeable in the moral sphere, the effects not infrequently manifesting themselves in crises, oftentimes culminating in decisive transformation periods. Studies along these lines have demonstrated, for instance, that moral and religious awakenings most frequently occur at this period of life contemporaneously as to age with superassertiveness of the lower propensities, extending from the time of puberty to the age of 24 and 25. It is the budding season of the sexual and functional activities, that carries along with it those subtler forces stirring at the heart of the mental and emotional natures, vitalizing its cross purposes, and quickening dormant principles into life.

From recent tables drawn from the reports of teachers in the examination of 7953 boys and 8520 girls, it appears that certain peculiarities or defectiveness in relation to age in children more usually show themselves at the age of puberty than at any other period. This especially holds true with reference to unruliness, which has been shown in such tables to reach its climax at the age of 14 years in the case of boys, with a per cent of 8.16; and in that of girls at the age of 15 years, with a per cent of .61; while sickness reaches its highest ratio among boys (6.61 per cent) at the age of 11 years; and in girls (6.94 per cent) at 13 years of age; nervousness shows its extreme ratio in the latter (.72 per cent) at 13, and in the former (1.62 per cent) at the age of 12 years.[1]

The period between 18 and 24 is the criminal age, the highest point being reached between 16 and 21, in English criminal records. The average age in the United States is but $2\frac{2}{5}$ years above the former figure, reaching its climax at the period between 20 and 24, showing inferentially that the bulk of criminousness is on the immature side of the table of vital statistics. This is significant as relating to the consideration of preventive measures, presenting the criminal problem, as it does, at the point of least resistance and consequently on its most responsive side.

The earliest recognized formative agency in the juvenile experience is, of course, the home life, which exerts the strongest direct influence and leaves the most enduring impressions upon the pliant character. It stands first and foremost in the list of personal forces directly concerned in the evolution of his moral character. Childhood shows remarkable aptitude for receiving early impressions and assimilating the good and evil that come to it from the objective teaching of home life and parental example. All experience distinctly shows that such, taken on in early life, become second nature.

[1] *Medical Times and Register* for June, 1899.

There is no such thing as escaping the predominating influences of these vital effective life forces.

A glance at the home environment of our city poor is sufficient to indicate the origin and trend of most of the deleterious influences that create the material that fills our reformatories and industrial schools. Urban centres, as in the creation of adult criminals, remain the most prolific sources of child contamination. Among four million dwellers in four leading cities of the Union, 14 persons in every 100 were bred in the slums, one-fourth to one-half of which could neither read nor write, and only 6.6 per cent of whom labored.[1] This authentic estimate, no doubt, fairly presents the social and domiciliary condition of our great cities everywhere, where the slum child is born, bred, and reared in dwellings that rent from $1 to $3 per month. There are no *homes* here, properly speaking, only places for temporary shelter and promiscuous herding, the sole conditions under which thousands of our cities' lowest classes subsist, and where they raise their progeny in utter disregard of the decencies and moralities of life, oftentimes glad to be rid of the responsibilities by means fair or foul. These are the raw material that make roughs, and desperadoes, and city toughs, cast in the moulds of an implacable environment as cruel as the grasp of necessitarian law. Ninety per cent of the acquired criminalism of the land is thus begotten and raised in, and receives the initial stamp of, the social environment in which it is engendered and which holds it ever after true to its ideal.

[1] Report of the Commissioner of Education, 1896–1897, Vol. I, p. 621, etc.

With or without these precise conditions actually present, the impaired family relation constitutes an equally perilous antecedent in the creation both of the juvenile delinquent, and in the accentuation of his more mature prototype, the instinctive and the habitual criminal, its bearing applying to all these classes equally. Fifty per cent of the population of the industrial schools are either orphans or the children of divorced parents. It is usual to find the ruptured parental relation as part of the moral inheritance and life histories of youthful prisoners. The increased business of the divorce courts helps swell the growth of youthful criminalism and the work of the criminal courts. Between 1867 and 1886, there were 328,716 divorces in the United States, 122,121 of which number took place in the first half, and 206,595 in the second half, of that decade, or 69 per cent more than in the former half. In the year 1886 divorces were more than $2\frac{1}{2}$ times what they were in 1867. Divorce and crime go hand in hand, and juvenile crime is sheltered beneath its wings. While illegitimacy itself has been shown to be perhaps less prophetic of future profligacy than the circumstance above named, the latter must be indirectly a strong aid toward juvenile criminalism. Of the 4838 juvenile male population in the reformatories of France in 1896, only 517 were of legitimate birth, and 4321, or 89.34 per cent, were illegitimate and born out of wedlock. Of the 1095 girls, 246 were legitimate, and 849, or 77.53 per cent, were illegitimate.[1]

In the cases of the 4328 inmates admitted into the

[1] *Statistique Penitentiaire*, pour l'année 1896, p. cclxxxv, Tableau VI.

industrial schools of Great Britain, deducting transfers in 1897, 391 were of illegitimate birth; in 183 cases both parents were dead; in 235 cases one or both parents were either destitute or criminals. Only 1754 cases were reported where both parents were able to take care of their children.[1]   Of the reformatory inmates (1409) 43 had lost both parents; 38 had been deserted; the parents of 11 were in prison; and 40 were illegitimate, as far as known.[2]   The economic and the social status of the ancestral stock in these instances are usually of the lowest.   In the Elmira Institute (1897) 3.2 per cent of the parents of inmates were pauperized; 80.8 per cent showed no accumulations; and but 16.6 per cent were forehanded.   The character of the home, as shown by the same report, in 46.7 per cent of instances was positively bad, and in only 12.2 per cent was given as "good."   In the United States (1890) 69 per cent of the parents of prisoners were poor; 8 per cent comfortable; and but 6 per cent were set down as "well-to-do."   It may be safe to say that fully 75 per cent of the parentage of professional criminals either was bad, or wholly unknown to them.   By reference to Table VI, Report of French Juvenile Criminalism,[3] out of the 6118 total juvenile protégés of France and Algeria, 1896, or 11.43 per cent, knew no parents.   The home is very apt to furnish the standard and inspiration for subsequent conduct and pattern in the offspring.   This

---

[1] Forty-first Report, for the year 1897, of the Inspector of Reformatory and Industrial Schools of Great Britain," 1898, pp. 17, 24.

[2] *Ibid.*, p. 17.

[3] *Statistique Penitentiaire*, pour l'année 1896, pp. cclxxxv, ccxcii.

state of things is actually responsible for the 3140, or 27.22 per cent, of the juvenile incorrigibles out of the 11,535 male delinquents in the United States reported from the official sources.

It would be a miracle, indeed, if the overcrowded tenement in the congested districts, with its promiscuity and squalor, ever upon the border of lawlessness, did not become the noxious hotbed of every form of youthful depravity, and eventuate in matured criminality.

Our provincial habitué is bred upon the street with idleness for his patron and the rum-bottle for his nursing-mother. It is the natural recruiting ground of the recalcitrant classes and the direct road to the penitentiary. Of the aggregate male juveniles in reformatories in the United States (1890), 9.56 per cent were set down as vagrants.

In the United States, destitution is assigned by 1111 inmates as the cause of crime among the 11,535 male members of reformatories, 128 being given as "without homes," and 62 per cent reported as living with their parents until 10 years of age. Among the males, 27.23 per cent were considered incorrigibles; among females, 27.73 per cent. The duration of home life, in a leading institution, records that 3.7 per cent of its inmates left home under 10 years of age, 6.3 per cent between 10 and 14, and 34.2 per cent soon after 14 years of age, 3677 out of 8319 being practically homeless at the time of admission to the institution.

The use of intoxicants at an early age, incident upon their unrestrained course of life, in numerous instances under the encouragement of parental example and undoubtedly without any corresponding attempt toward inculcating counter habits of self-restraint in its use, plays a foremost part here, as in the case of adults, in laying the foundation in permanently broken-down nerve-centres, as conditions precedent for subsequent physical and moral degeneration. Juvenile precociousness as to the drink habit in the United States doubtless exceeds that of the older countries, family surveillance and habits of self-restraint being here proverbially more lax, thus presenting more favorable facilities for overriding statutory provisions enacted for the protection of minors. Out of 11,535 male juvenile reformatory inmates, 525, or 6.87 per cent, were moderate or occasional drinkers; 211, or 2.76 per cent, were drunkards; 3888, habits "not stated," and 6911, or 59.91 per cent, were total abstainers — the percentage being calculated on the total basis of 7647 reported, omitting the 3888 "not stated."[1] One hundred thirty-one, or 1.13 per cent, were committed for reasons of intoxication. These figures doubtless fall far below the actual facts. Parental example is the greatest contributory cause in this respect; 25 per cent of the parents (one or both) of such unfortunates being set down as usually addicted to drink. This is especially the case with reference to city life, where the facilities and incentives for the abuse of intoxicating liquors are so great.

The want of industrial training and economic habits together with general mental culture, next to lack of proper parental care and defective home influences,

[1] Report on Crime, Pauperism, and Benevolence in the United States, Eleventh Census, Juvenile Offenders, p. 249.

are the chief sources of juvenile depravity. They indirectly invite to the first steps in the youthful criminal career. Elementary teaching is non-compulsory in the United States; the regulations and customs governing apprenticeship being equally light. The children of even the well-disposed poor are forced into unskilled labor (if at all) as a matter of necessity, while specific knowledge of handicraft is comparatively little known among them. With reference to the matter of skilled labor, 13,149, or 97 per cent of the total number in reformatories, had no actual trade at the time of commitment; but 399, or 2.94 per cent, were apprenticed, and but 8, or .06 per cent of the number, were skilled mechanics. As to employment of juvenile offenders at time of arrest, out of the total number of male juvenile offenders in such reformatories, the employment of 936 was not stated; 2128 were employed; and 8471, or 73.49 per cent, were idle at the time of such commitment. In the report of the Pennsylvania prison for 1886, a table of all the prisoners for the past ten years shows that out of 1069 male youths, 993 were unapprenticed and but 864 had attended school. Of the 8786 inmates in the New York reformatory from its inception (report of 1897), 23.9 per cent were put down as servants and clerks; 56.3 per cent as common laborers; 4.9 per cent as idlers, while but 14.9 per cent were employed in any sort of mechanical work at the time of their reception at the institution. Of 100 male prisoners at Wandsworth prison, London, aged 16, 17, and 18 years, 23 per cent were skilled and 77 per cent unskilled laborers. The increased use of machinery, the specialization of work and the necessarily high grade of skill required, and in many instances the interference of "labor unions," no doubt operate strongly to discourage any inclination toward the betterment of these conditions; and the burden of such responsibility in the future for this class must be thrown largely upon institutions under governmental paternalism. As to comparative illiteracy, 473, or 3.19 per cent of the total number of inmates of reformatories in the United States, were practically unable to read or write.[1] As in the case of the adult, so among juvenile delinquents, alien importation here helps largely to swell the ranks of the latter. In tables compiled from an analysis of the New York reformatory, the data, distributed according to national provenance, give us the following : —

TABLE XLI

PROVENANCE FOREIGN		PROVENANCE NATIVE		PROVENANCE UNKNOWN	
Foreign born,	1,163	American parentage,	2,274	One parent foreign,	361
Native born,		Negroes and Mulattoes,	179	Nationality un-	
Foreign parentage,	1,803	American Indians,	2	known,	83
Chinese,	4			Nativity unknown,	27
				Born at sea,	3
Total,	2,970	Total,	2,455	Total,	474

From the Census Bulletin Report, we gather that the foreign population of this country contributes, directly or indirectly, in the persons of the foreign born

[1] *Journal of Prison Discipline and Philanthropy*, January, 1898 and 1899.

or of their immediate juvenile descendants, 5851.5 to the aggregate population of these juvenile reformatories; while the entire native population contributes only 3726.5 to similar institutions. The difference, according to this statement, is 2125, or more than twice as great as in the penitentiary population, where it is only 1009.

Mr. Tallack, in his work entitled " Penological and Preventative Principles," discussing the various projects of advantageously disposing of the young persons who have been in reformatories in Great Britain, or those of a pauper or neglected stock in that country, calls attention to the fact that "thousands have been sent to Canada and the United States, through the efforts of various benevolent persons and societies"; a consummation more to be desired in the breach than in the observance, on the American side of the Atlantic.

The place of pernicious literature in the list of formative agencies in the genesis of precocious criminalism is incidental, applicable to a limited class, and by no means to be taken in the conventional sense usually attributed to it by theorists. The criminal mind is not responsive to literary ideals, its imaginative grasp being feeble, and, since the heroic rarely incarnates itself in minor offences, it follows that, if reached at all, it is by way of the more serious offences, as highway robbery, vendetta, etc. As these are the latter stages of criminalism, it suggests that flashy literature at the most only aggravates, rarely originates, the latent criminal propensity. But few respond thereto, and these chiefly as an advanced symptom of the malady. I have met but few such instances.

It requires but a glance to perceive the importance this feature of juvenile criminalism sustains to the general problem. The original material that composes it is unmistakable when taken in conjunction with its origin and environment and traced to bio-genetic and organic sources. These moral anomalies, it must be remembered, are the legitimate and logical outcome of preconditions over which the juvenile subjects themselves have but little control, and to which they are subject with all the pertinacity of an inviolable law. As it is natural for a normally constituted and well-balanced youth, springing from a sound stock with an unbiassed heredity and nourished by a favorable environment, to develop naturally into right-doing, and to grow up under favorable surroundings into a healthy, law-abiding manhood; so is it equally in accord with the irrevocable logic of things that the illy equipped and abnormally engendered youth, reënforced by vicious environment, should result in a distinctive moral anomaly and psychical degenerate. No being is responsible for the inborn weight of heredity attached to him, or for the untoward social conditions under which he was ushered into existence.

Whatever may be thought of the adult misdemeanant capable of mature judgment and subject to the reënforcement and guidance of past experience and good influences, who, nevertheless, deliberately embarks in crime, the youthful pervert, cast in a congenital mould and held in the grasp of implacable bio-genetic forces by which he is incited to crime, must be considered rather an object of commiseration than of condemnation, and should be a proper subject for public charity and just prevenient measures wisely administered, not in a spirit of vindictiveness or of retaliation, but with just ideas of proper amelioration and possible cure. This pursued from the high inspirational standpoint of wise social utilitarianism makes for the welfare of both the individual and the State. Construed as above, he is a *defective* rather than a delinquent, and should be treated as such. As Mr. Maudsley has well said in this connection, "Society, having manufactured its criminals, has scarcely the right, even if it were wise for its own sake, to treat them in any angry spirit of vengeance."[1]

Public sentiment should certainly be as profoundly imbued with, and as deeply interested in, the educational and regenerative welfare of these, its unfortunates, as in the ultra education of its better and more highly favored protégés in whose cultivation public interest is deservedly centred to the extent of the expenditure of vast outlays of money and talent. To be sure, such measures must of necessity have the mandatory force of law, sanctioned by an enlightened public sentiment, to sustain the additional financial burdens imposed upon the taxpayers, who, in their municipal and corporate capacity, must largely assume the task which nature laid upon the parent. This may seem not only a burden, but an evil, in the encouragement it affords to irresponsible parents to neglect their duties toward their offspring and shift the burden of responsibility upon the State, which undoubtedly has been the case in numerous instances, thus compelling honest and law-

[1] "Responsibility in Mental Disease," p. 29.

abiding citizens to bear the burdens and responsibilities of the shiftless and the unworthy.

To obviate this difficulty, laws should be enacted providing for the proper legal assessment of the heads of families for all those recalcitrant members of their households thus forcibly committed to reformatories and industrial homes at the expense of the State, the same to be estimated upon the basis of their respective property valuations, and operate as a lien thereon, as in the case of ordinary taxation, with the proviso of a minimum fine in lieu of property, the same to be worked out upon public works in cases of default. Bonds should be exacted from parents (who, in many instances, are morally incriminated with their offspring) in cases of incorrigibles left under parental care, the same to run to the age of majority. The Gladstone Committee, in Great Britain, in 1891, formulated and recommended some such a law, with provisions placing liability for juvenile offences in certain cases upon parents. A Court of Summary Jurisdiction was enabled (*a*) to fine a parent up to £1; (*b*) to order the parent to pay a compensation up to £5; (*c*) to give security for the child's good behavior. Such provisions, with the alternative of additional fines in case of failure to comply, and ultimate imprisonment, or compulsory labor, or both, would greatly simplify the financial part and materially facilitate the future of institutional work of this character, as well as enhance the sense of responsibility in the case of derelict and irresponsible parents.

As has already been noticed, the brunt of juvenile

offence is fifteen to one against property — 94 per cent
as given in one institution. The percentage of crimes
against the person increases with the age of the offender; of crimes against property, it reaches its
maximum during the period between 20 and 30. Of
crimes against society, it reaches its minimum about
the same period, so that those against property may
be said to be distinctively the crimes of youth. In
other words, he is distinctively a social offender as
against the atavistic order, and as such, his criminousness has its rise largely in external environment as an
acquired characteristic rather than as an inborn tendency. It follows, therefore, whatever may be said of
the adult, that the juvenile offender, as already pointed
out, is largely the victim of outward circumstances,
the indirect product of defective social organization,
much of which is set in operation and maintained
by direct operation of political and municipal authori-
zation from which the State or municipality derive
special revenues. The total government receipts, for
instance, from the liquor business, by states and territories, for the year ending June 30, 1896 (as per Government Bulletin No. 17, issued July, 1898), footed up in
license fees, or special taxes received by the general
government, at $165,020,175, while taxes on the prop-
erty invested therein amounted to $18,192,949.51 more,
out of which sum the states received $10,490,315.16, or
6.36 per cent; the counties received $5,389,782.81, or
3.27 per cent; and the municipalities, $34,689,215.26,
or 21.02 per cent. Is it not reasonable, if municipalities, counties, and states can afford to wring their sup-

port from creatures of the corporation that go directly to debauch its youth and manufacture criminalism, that these governmental departments should with equal open-handedness contribute toward undoing in part the mischief they themselves have inaugurated and from which they draw their chief revenues? If society makes the youthful criminal, it is obligatory upon her also to *unmake* him.

One of the leading reformatories of the United States, for the fiscal year 1897, received an appropriation of $210,251.92 to maintain 1525 inmates for that year; being at an annual cost, one year with another, of about $150.00 per capita. The same state (New York) in a single year (1872) licensed 267,744 retail and 1156 wholesale liquor establishments, which retailed $133,720,000 worth of intoxicants. The value of products converted into liquor[1] amounted to $36,780,377. That commonwealth can well afford to appropriate less than two per cent from such earnings off the liquor traffic for educational and reformatory purposes in order to neutralize the evils she herself has set in operation. Large allowances are made for liberal education. The same state in 1897 collected an annual revenue of $27,133,347 for public school purposes, or $16.12 raised for each child from 5 to 18 years of age; while the cost, per capita, for the single institution named for the reformation of 1525 youthful incorrigibles, is a little over three-fourths of one per cent of her total school receipts. New York is perhaps one of the best equipped states in the Union, both as to her common

[1] United States Report of 1898.

schools and as to her reformatory facilities, and what here applies to her, holds proportionately true in principle, if not literally, for every state in the Union.

If the State, in its corporate capacity, has an interest in the welfare of its normal protégé, such interest should extend to and be still more profoundly moved when applied to its recalcitrant youth, who, if uncontrolled, are sure to develop into mature and dangerous charges that must ultimately prove the source of far greater expense to the State at large when they reach the prison stage of their career. Taking for granted the State's equal concern in both these classes, the latter may be said to pay a double dividend on the amount thus invested, as compared with her more fortunate protégés, in the twofold fact both of the latter's acquired mental training and of his *social redemption* from a nonproductive and vicious social factor to a useful and law-abiding citizen. This, in face of all the facts, surely is as much a public duty as the ultra education of already sound and healthy stock.

Aside from any question of mere financial and economic reciprocity, the growth of the institutional idea is in full accord with the spirit of the age as it unfolds itself in practical philanthropy and scientific progression in all departments of the moral, material, and intellectual life. The application of the proper regeneratives as far up the current of the incipient criminal life as possible, is the true scientific theory in accord with all the facts. At any rate, it presents the only hopeful side of the criminal problem, and is society's main channel through which it may stem the criminal tide by taking it at the flood.

The inauguration of the reformatory theory at the prison end of the problem is to enter the field handicapped — when the battle is already lost. The point of vantage lies at the plastic period, at the inceptional stage, where the personal inlets and outlets of power are at command. There the possibilities lie spread out like a virgin spiritual empire inviting occupation. The modus operandi, it is true, is a total revolt from the old penitentiary theory, which is simply intimidatory, brutal in inception, and illusory in results. All conventional methods that are only retaliatory in their character, as applied in the case of the youthful offender, are but delusive and contain nothing regenerative in their efforts or results. Admonition, fining, suspended sentence, temporary imprisonments, etc., are mere legal makeshifts without pith or point in comparison as reformative agencies, when applied to this class. They only serve to harden; they rarely cure. The case in point demands incentives, not intimidations; example, not coercion; training, not punishment; to incite to action; to inculcate habit through proper motive, and thus by the training of hand, heart, and head, through the agencies of intellectual, manual, moral, and religious inculcation, lay the foundation of a reconstructed manhood in habits of self-respecting industry, which is the surest alterative of the individual criminal propension. These steps once entered upon, it will be found that habit and character reënforce each other, and that which was at first a coercion, becomes in time a necessity, and at last associates itself inseparably with the individual's conception of happiness and duty. "We acquire the virtue by doing the act," is the Aristotelian maxim, that is true to nature and offers sufficient guarantee for possible youthful rehabilitation. Success is mainly a question as to how early can the process be inaugurated and applied. In short, all methods and appliances for the reinstatement of these youths that fail to go to the bottom of the matter in combined training, to the crowding out of all ulterior objects, are superficial and worse than useless. A colt is not inclined to labor until broken and trained, when its perilous strength, joined to its task, becomes to it a source of pleasure (let us believe); and there is no reasonable ground to suppose that the human animal would do otherwise, unless its vitality were already depleted in the stock, in which case nature would set her limitations.

Seizing upon these central points, popular opinion is rapidly enlarging its ideas commensurately with the requirements of the case. The past two decades have witnessed great advancement, both in Europe and in America, with reference to practical reformative and prevenient methods, as applied to both old and young, upon broader theories and firmer basis in conjunction with public and legislative coöperation.

Cellular confinement for juvenile offenders was begun as early as 1667. San Michael, Rome, was opened in 1704 for that purpose. Improved ways of dealing with this class of offenders by special institutional methods existed in Holland and Germany in the sixteenth century.

It was then largely under private patronage. Legislative enactments with reference thereto commenced in France in 1850, and in England in 1854, rapidly spreading throughout Europe and the United States within the past twenty-five years.

Great Britain, especially, has made great advancement in these commendable enterprises, as indicated by the figures already given. It is well, in this connection, to keep in mind the fact that the Industrial school (which is the favorite in the British estimate) is more particularly intended for children, who, while not yet launched into crime, are in immediate danger thereof; while the Reformatory proper combines the principles of the penal and reformatory ideas and corresponds in a mild sense to a prison.

In the United States, New York passed the first House of Refuge Laws in 1824. In 1876, under the patronage of the New York Prison Association, the Elmira reformatory was completed, with its eminent founder, Z. R. Brockway, as its first superintendent. It is planned upon advanced methods in educational and corrective principles. Its inmates are committed under the indeterminate sentence (unfortunately at present with a maximum limit attached), with its corollary, the parole law, or conditional release, and a system of credits on the basis of good conduct and improvement. Proper segregation and cellular isolation by night are practised, with an excellent system of trades-schools, and industrial and mental training, together with physical culture and military exercise. It has become the ideal institution, from which others in the United States have taken their model until the number of such institutions has increased with their popularity and usefulness, attaining a reformatory population of nearly 15,000 in 1890, which has largely increased since then.

The real practical effect of such institutional agencies can hardly be determined from the mere array of figures of such institutions themselves. Their influences are chiefly perceptible in their effects upon the main stream of criminalism in course of time. It is an unwarranted optimism that would prematurely anticipate sudden transformations as the immediate outcome of these newly inaugurated institutional appliances. The counteracting influences (like those direct) are of slow growth. The gradual diminution of crime on the whole, in England, through her reformatories and industrial schools, year by year, may properly be credited in no small degree to these instrumentalities, which good results will doubtless continue, though periodicity must always be expected in the criminal flow. The total number of juvenile offenders recognized in British prisons during the year 1897, as having previously served a term in reformatories, was 1001 — 752 in England and Wales, and 249 in Scottish prisons.[1]

The direct result, as actually noticeable in and from the institutional life itself, may be fairly gathered from the yearly reports of these individual reformatories. Thus, the New York reformatory (1897) gives us an estimate of " Presumptive Reformation among its Discharged Inmates " for the year, of 86.5 per cent. " Re-

[1] Forty-first Report, for year 1897, of Inspector of Reformatory and Industrial Schools, Great Britain, 1898.

turned to the institution," 4.01 per cent. "Probably returned to crime," one-half of those who ceased correspondence while on parole, twenty-seven. "Sent to prison while on parole," or, "Known to have resumed Criminal Practice," one. Total, twenty-eight, or 9 per cent. The total summary of those "presumptively reformed" since its inception is 82.9 per cent. "Probably returned to crime," 15.2 per cent. The reports of other similar institutions are doubtless much in the same tenor. By the latest British report (1897), out of a total of 14,432 male ex-inmates of schools, 1687 were found in the army and navy, 1137 were employed in farm service, 959 at sea, 682 in factories, 1043 were mechanics and iron workers, 132 on railways, 4536 in other regular employment, 994 casual employment, 1503 unknown, dead, or emigrated, and but 1319, or 9.14 per cent of the whole convicted. The female record is equally satisfactory.[1] In an analysis of the report of Rev. Marshall Vine, Warden, comprehending the ten years beginning with 1888, after a thorough examination as to the subsequent history of such ex-inmates, it is found that out of 811 boys discharged during that time, just 100 had been re-convicted, making a percentage of 12.33 only for re-convictions, and 87.66 per cent not relapsed. The relapses were but temporary, as a rule mainly for drunkenness and minor misdemeanors.[2] Of the 604 inmates in prisons in Great Britain in 1897, under 18 years, 267 had been previously convicted. Sixty-four

[1] Forty-first Report, for year 1897, of Inspector of Reformatory and Industrial Schools, Great Britain, 1898, pp. 45, 46, 47.

[2] *Ibid.*, pp. 48, 49.

per cent in English reformatories commit crimes more than once. By the last report, it was estimated that out of the total number admitted to reformatory schools in the year 1897 (1409), 448 had not been known to have been previously convicted, and 961 had been previously convicted one or more times.[1]

The chief obstacle to reformation in all these institutions, it will readily be perceived, lies in the matured age and consequently greater degree of susceptibility to the criminal habit on the part of the subject; and, on the other hand, in the consequent brief period of their detention in these institutions from the time of commitment to their majority, or ultimate discharge. The age of admission, at Elmira, for instance, is between 16 and 30 years. In Illinois, the period is from 16 to 21; in Ohio, between 10 and 16; in Indiana, 8 to 17; in Pennsylvania, 15 to 25; in California, 8 to 21; in Nebraska, under 16, etc. These ages border perilously near the period when character and habit are beginning to take permanent shape. This period, of course, is different in different temperaments, the children of the poor maturing earlier than those of the well-to-do, poverty and hardship, as well as crime, having a tendency to prematurely age the subject. The time during which they are detained usually varies from two to four years; and in some industrial schools, from two to six and seven years — periods of time hardly sufficient to undo the mischief which a bad environment or the heavy hand of heredity has laid upon them.

[1] Forty-first Report, for year 1897, of Inspector of Reformatory and Industrial Schools, Great Britain, 1898, p. 17.

Much might be added with reference to the equipment and general management of these institutions, hardly admissible in a work of this nature. No cast-iron rules can be devised. Method is not so much an augury of success in these institutions as natural qualifications, the general adaptiveness of the authoritative heads and the wisdom of its advisory board. Petty regulations and strict surveillance have little necessary virtue. The genius that is associated with wise discretion and wholesome enthusiasm can alone win success in fields so exacting and that require such outlay of patience, devotion and peculiar talent. The ability to " walk alone " without arbitrary stay is, of course, the end to be desired in the juvenile inmate, both before and after liberty. In general, be it said as to occupation, those industrial pursuits and trades manual that savor of outdoor employment, as agriculture, carpentry, building, etc., are more conducive than any other as reformatory aids both as to juveniles and as to adults.

The system based upon the " open," or family plan, is represented as being the most efficient, as it is certainly the most natural in this respect. That at Lancaster, Ohio, organized in 1858, was the first founded upon this theory in the United States, following that of the " Rauhe Haus," Germany, conducted upon the "cottage plan." These have met with signal success, and are in vogue (with modifications) in Ohio, Connecticut, Massachusetts, Wisconsin, New Jersey, Indiana, Minnesota, Iowa, Michigan, Pennsylvania, and District of Columbia; and it doubtless presents the highest conception of the industrial and domiciliary ideal, and promises more toward the practical solution of the vexed problem of crime as a whole than any other purely institutional theory. There are at present about thirty reformatories in the United States upon the cottage plan.

The method in the treatment of juvenile offenders committed only for the brief period of a month or more, or for temporary detention, or awaiting trial, in places suitable for them, as in England, might be adopted in this country with advantage to themselves and with credit to our sense of humanity.

The "Summary Jurisdiction Act" of 1879 and the "Probation of First Offenders Act," 1887, in Great Britain, with reference to this important feature of practical criminology, are based upon the idea of summary hearing for first offences, and dismissal upon payment of costs, with admonition; or suspension of sentence dependent upon subsequent good behavior, and in graver cases with the alternative of the substitution of fines. The chief provisions of the latter Act might well serve as a model in the treatment of youthful recalcitrants in whose case incarceration is usually fatal to both character and morals. "In any case in which a person is convicted of larceny, or false pretences, or any other offence punishable with not more than two years' imprisonment, before any court, and no previous conviction is proved against him, if it appears to the court before whom he is so convicted, that, regard being had to the youth, character, and antecedents of the offender, to the trivial nature of the offence, and to any extenuating circumstances under which the same was committed, it is expedient that the offender be released on probation of good conduct, the court may, instead of sentencing him at once to any punishment, direct that he be released on his entering into a recognizance, with or without sureties, and during such period as the court may direct, to appear and receive judgment when called upon, and in the meantime to keep the peace and be of good behaviour. The court may, if it thinks fit, direct that the offender shall pay the costs of the prosecution, or some portion of the same, within such period and by such instalments as may be directed by the court."

Reformatories exist in Maine, New Hampshire, Vermont, New York, Massachusetts, Pennsylvania, Delaware, Connecticut, Ohio, Iowa, Minnesota, Missouri, Nebraska, Indiana, Illinois, Wisconsin, Kansas, Maryland, Kentucky, Louisiana, Montana, Michigan, California, Colorado, New Jersey, and the District of Columbia.

Reformatories for females are as yet but few in numbers, the leading ones being at Sherborne, Mass., and at Meriden, Conn.; Industrial Home Schools for District of Columbia; State Home for Girl Offenders, at Geneva, Ill.; the Women's Prison and Girls' Reformatory, at Indianapolis, Ind.; Mitchellville, Iowa; Industrial School for Girls, Beloit, Wis.; one each at Louisville, Ky.; Hallowell, Me.; Melville, Md.; Lancaster, Mass.; with two Houses of Reformation; Adrian, Mich.; Chillicothe, Mo.; with two Houses of Refuge, St. Louis; Trenton, N.J., with City Home at Verona; Delaware, Ohio; Rochester, N.Y.; Industrial School for Boys and Girls, at Milwaukee, Wis.; Golden, Colo.; Beloit, Kan.; Reformatory for Boys and Girls at Whittier, Cal.; Houses of Refuge for Girls, Baltimore, Md.; Deer Island, Mass.; St. Paul, Minn.; Manchester, N.H.; Westchester (Catholic), N.Y.; Cincinnati, Ohio; Philadelphia (with Reform School), Penn.; Howard, R.I.; and Vergennes, Vt. Reformatories splendidly equipped and managed are rapidly increasing in the Northern, Eastern, Middle, and extreme Western states of the Union, and much interest is being manifested in this matter of rational and scientific method of dealing with the problem of the rehabilitation of the youthful recalcitrant.

Perhaps nowhere in the world has the reformatory movement for youth, and liberal sentiment that prompts to adequate and even lavish expenditure in the erection and equipment of model institutions with these laudable ends in view, taken so great hold as in the United States, where, during the past few years they have sprung up as moral safeguards carved out by the civil arm and backed by public sentiment to help counteract the evils itself has so largely engendered. It is only another proof of the practical Christian philanthropy that characterizes the civilization of the present over the past, and that so signally distances the latter in practical utilitarianism and all true progress.

CHAPTER XII

HYPNOTISM AND CRIME

A DUE examination of the power of suggestion from the standpoint of ordinary experience has been sufficiently interwoven in the preceding narrative as to require no further consideration in these pages. Its position as a factor in abnormal psychological phenomena commonly designated under the name of "hypnotism," and its presumptive relation to accredited criminal obsession, is entitled to a more extended notice, since it plays an important rôle in psychic phenomena in general, and in the criminal activity in particular.

The subject, moreover, is worthy of a place by itself, in view of its tentative bearing upon the psycho-judicial phase of the criminal problem, as well as for the potentialities involved on the side of its purely individual manifestations as the *responsible* source of *irresponsible* conduct in the subtle functioning of the moral and intellectual faculties. Both the medical and legal sciences have given it place in their curriculum as a new arrival worthy of present consideration and prophetic of future possibilities.

Hypnotism, as it will be known in these pages, may be designated as that power of the human mind by which it arrives at conclusions otherwise than through the media of ordinary experience, but as acted upon subjectively, at the incitation of external (*hetero*), or internal (*auto*) suggestion. That suggestion may be visual (the usual manner), auditory, olfactory, or tactile, through any of which channels of sensory communication the subject may be approachable according to his varying degrees of susceptibility.

The cataleptic trance was known to the ancients, the people of Chaldea, Babylonia, Persia, Egypt, Greece, and Rome, being early familiar with its occult manifestations through " oracles " and soothsaying; their priests taking advantage of these means to enhance their particular calling, and thus obtain influence over the masses. Mesmer, during the latter half of the seventeenth century, brought the subject within the purview of mundane experimentation, though in the spirit and with the purpose of the charlatan, until the ascendency of the more scientific schools took it in hand and reduced it to its present *rationale*. M. Cloquet, an eminent physician of Paris, employed it successfully in cases of surgical operations, although Liébault was the first to use it in therapeutics.

Dr. Braid, in 1859, found the cataleptic sleep could be induced by simply concentrating the gaze upon a fixed object; and subsequent developments further attested the fact of the equal effectiveness of mere objective suggestion as a sufficient agency to invite the trance condition, which may be characterized as a semiconscious automatism, not *all* the sense channels being closed, but some remaining preternaturally impressionable, as in the case of the somnambulist who *acts* his dreams; the sense of smell by which individuals have been identified with unerring accuracy among large numbers (Carpenter), etc. The ordinary hypnotic sensitive is induced to follow implicitly the actions and suggestions of the successful operator. The trance may continue for hours, depending somewhat upon the completeness of the sleep, the subject being usually released at the will of the operator, or at the instance of a well-known sound.

The exact physiological and neuro-mechanical explanation of the hypnotic condition has not yet been satisfactorily ascertained, more than upon the theory of an inhibition of the ganglion cells of the cerebral cortex induced by weak stimulation of certain nerves (Heidenhain); or partial paralysis of certain central nerves, thus implying perverted nerve action, and not caused by objective or occult forces, as, "magnetic fluid," "odic force," etc., as at first claimed by Mr. Bertrand; or other certain "imponderable fluid," as suggested by Von Reichenbach. Dr. Hammond thinks that, in case of profound somnambulism, the whole brain is probably in a state of complete syncope, the spinal cord alone being awake. In this imperfect or partial state certain of the cerebral ganglia are not entirely inactive, and hence the individual responds to ideas as suggested by others.[1]

To this state Dr. Braid gave the name of "neuro-hypnotism" (νευρο, nerve; and ὕπνος, sleep), subsequently to be designated by the single term "hypnotism." The scientific investigations of Heidenhain, Weinheld,

1 " Spiritualism and Nerve Derangement," 1876, Hammond, p. 215.

Drs. Carpenter, Hammond, and the philosophic inductive studies of Mr. Moll, Mr. Hudson, Professor Sidis, and others, have placed the whole subject upon a more rational basis as a legitimate scientific study to which, latterly, much attention is being directed as both an effective therapeutic agency and as an aid in surgical operations, as well as a rational subject of inquiry in the study of mental and moral psychology.

The summary of all practical results thus far has been to reduce all hynoptic experimentations to the simple formula that: certain persons are susceptible to the power of suggestion, primarily, from without; and secondarily, from within (objectively and subjectively), a process to which the individual becomes gradually more susceptible in proportion to the increased number of successful experiments, until eventually a state of supersensitiveness is attained, by which a glance, a trick of the memory, or even auto-suggestion, will suffice to throw him into the lethargic state. Numerous instances have been well attested where the sensitive, returning to the spot where he had been previously hypnotized, was instantly thrown into a trance condition, so thoroughly had he become the passive instrument of such auto-suggestion.

In elucidation of the totality of the phenomena of hypnotism, has been brought forward the fact of the duality of the human mind. Two distinct psychic entities are premised of the mental nature, each governed by its own distinctive laws, and acting in a measure independently of each other; viz., the *objective* and the *subjective* mind. The former, operating through the ordinary sensory channels of communication with its threefold functional powers of reason, sensation, and volition, constitutes the rational entity that thinks, feels, and wills, the basis of all ordinary experience. The subjective mind, the internal world of spiritual forces, focussed primarily upon the intuitive faculties of the soul, and dealing with subjects not based upon, or the resultants of, external experience, may be best described by John Jay Hudson, whose interesting volume upon this subject claims foremost attention on account of its lucidity and range, and from whose work we shall take the liberty of freely quoting in this connection. The subjective mind may be defined, upon the words of this eminent authority, as, a " distinct entity possessing independent powers and functions, having a mental organization of its own, and being capable of sustaining an existence independently of the body." This subjective entity acts subconsciously, *i.e.* practically independent of the ordinary avenues of knowledge, at the instance of either objective or *auto* suggestion, manifesting itself automatically under the varied forms of somnambulism (sleep-walking, though Dr. Hammond does not think the phenomena of hypnotism are wholly those of somnambulism, but that three other conditions are present in more or less degree, hysteria, catalepsy, and ecstasy)[1]; clairvoyance (second sight), or spiritism, as it is commonly called (supposed communication with the spirits of the dead); telepathy (mind reading); mental therapeutics (Christian science, Mental healing, faith, and allied cures, etc.); all springing more or less from the

[1] " Spiritualism and Nervous Derangement," p. 197.

same root, and being but concrete manifestations of similar ground principle; viz., *suggestion*. Under its inspiration, it has long been well known that latent mental powers, not before suspected, are frequently discovered; as for instance, extra powers of memory, called "Mental latency," by Sir William Hamilton, to distinguish it from simple recollection (the subjective memory now being well known to be practically perfect), that suddenly, under the preternatural stimulus of hypnotic influence, call forth facts and recollections that have long lain dormant, as evidenced in the case of the ignorant servant girl mentioned by Dr. Abercrombie, in his "The Intellectual Powers," who, in the trance state superinduced by severe illness, was able to recite whole pages of Greek and Hebrew which it was afterward ascertained she had heard her previous master repeat years before, but of the meaning of which she was utterly ignorant. Dr. Carpenter gives a similar instance of the supernatural operation of the subjective mind, in the case of another, equally ignorant, who was able to accurately imitate in different languages the singing of Jennie Lind, and with precisely similar effect, though in her waking moments she was but an ordinary singer and familiar with but a single tongue.[1]

Suggestion plays the leading rôle in this psychic phenomena. Indeed, it might properly be considered the first term and potential factor in the hypnotic state, the relative passivity of the subject being at all times the gauge of success and fundamental to successful hypnotization. Passivity depends in no small degree upon

[1] "Mesmerism, Spiritualism, etc.," W. B. Carpenter, 1877, p. 20.

the nervous state and mental attitude of the subject at the time. Neurotic persons, or those said to possess weak wills, are not always the most susceptible, since the power of concentration (which implies volition) is more or less necessary to success. A certain degree of intelligence and consciousness is necessary, as the subject must be able to comprehend what is desired. Idiots and feeble-minded persons are not susceptible to hypnotism. Liébault considered it hereditary.

A discussion upon general merits would take too wide a range for a work like this; and, as the case is thus sufficiently stated, we would confine ourselves for our present purpose solely to the application of the phenomenon of hypnotism to the criminal psychosis, and inquire to this end: How and to what extent do these psychic conditions stand related to practical criminality? Does the hypnotic state, in itself, stand open to the criminal insinuation? Can the power of suggestion override innate impulses of the prehypnotic state to such a degree as to break down moral safeguards, override the will, and induce the subject to commit crime which he could, and perhaps otherwise would, repudiate in his normal condition? Can criminal suggestion arouse irresistibly latent instincts dormant in the already criminally inclined? Is the reflexive tendency of such hypnotic trance, especially where frequently indulged in, conducive to a criminalistic tendency on the part of its passive instrument, and will such repeated trances tend to weaken the inhibitory power of the will, destroy the mental balance, and thus ultimately tend to render the subject an easy prey to hallucination, insanity, and to the insinuation of auto-criminal suggestion? These are important problems left over after a thorough analysis of the subject in its general scope, and might well be deemed worthy of at least a passing consideration at the conclusion of our present task.

It might here be well to premise that the whole problem is not as yet out of the hands of the theorist, who, owing to the peculiar nature of the subject, is in this respect largely compelled to reason deductively from phenomena to causes, thus increasing the difficulties surrounding a problem so largely amenable to the inductive process.

Dr. Charcot, who looks upon hypnotism rather in the light of a neurosis, well sums up the problem of criminal susceptibility in connection with the somnambulistic state (a phase of hypnotism) into the question: " Given the suggestibility of a somnambule, can one use him to do a criminal act to which he would never have consented outside of the hypnotic sleep?" He reaches the conclusion that this can be done in the laboratory, with the additional reservation of " exceptional cases " who " refuse to obey," and insists upon the necessity of " training," in order to induce the subject to thus act. Dr. Laurent is undecided. He relegates the issue largely to force of circumstance, and to the comparative subjectivity or relative passivity of the individual. He testifies to the possibility of some somnambulists resisting successfully all post-hypnotic suggestions, and others who were unable to resist doing acts repugnant to themselves. Bernheim, in attempting to account for the motive principle in the Tropman murder, comes to the conclusion that in whatever way the idea may have entered the murderer's mind, it finally culminated in an "irresistible auto-suggestion, just as a fixed idea of suicide may culminate fatally." Dr. Voisin, physician of La Salpêtrière, in his address before the third International Congress for Criminal Anthropology, at Brussels, 1893, laid great stress upon the power of criminal suggestibility in the waking, or hypnotic state. Dr. Bérillon, editor of the *Revue de l'Hypnotism*, at the same congress, expressed the opinion that certain individuals present in the waking state such suggestibility that it would be possible to make them execute automatically, when under the influence of verbal suggestion, misdemeanors or crimes. Dr. Houzé, Professor of Anthropology, at Brussels, expressed his belief in the reality of such criminal suggestion. Brouardel is quoted as holding that the somnambulist realizes only agreeable and indifferent suggestions. Delboef is reported as saying that the hypnotized person knows that he is playing a comedy. Boris Sidis agrees with the Nancy School that: suggestion is all-powerful; the hypnotic trance is, in fact, a state of heightened suggestibility, or rather of pure reflexive consciousness.[1] Ribot thinks: " The hypnotic subject is an automaton which is made to move according to the nature of its organization. There is an absolute annihilation of the will, the conscious personality being reduced to one single and unique state, which is neither chosen nor repudiated, but undergone, imposed." [2]

[1] "The Psychology of Suggestion," 1899, p. 170.
[2] "The Diseases of the Will," Humboldt Library, p. 105.

The above citations fairly illustrate the position of the Nancy School of hypnotists upon the subject of hypnotic suggestion in relation to crime.

Their opponents hold equally strenuous views on the affirmative side of the proposition, claiming with much show of reason the rarity, if not impossibility, of such successful criminal or post-criminal suggestion, outside the laboratory. Such views in general are entertained by the " Salpêtrière School," which is able to rally to its support many eminent savants. The latter position is based upon now well-ascertained facts of the pertinacity of long-continued habit and settled principle on the part of the individual in his normal state, these retaining their legitimate mental sway both in the hypnotic and post-hypnotic state in spite of contra-suggestions on the part of the hypnotizer. " Habit and education play a large part here," says Moll, in discussing this feature of the subject; "it is generally very difficult successfully to suggest anything that is opposed to the confirmed habits of the subject. Expressions of the will which spring from the individual character of the patient are of the deepest psychological interest. The more an action is repulsive to his disposition, the stronger his resistance." That this phase of the psychological study is true both in natural as well as artificial sleep, is readily apparent to the careful observer. The will, in the former case, may even be trained during the waking hours to successfully combat desultory and unwelcome suggestions that have come to habitually insinuate themselves during the natural sleep. The hypnotic trance is but artificial sleep. May not the same underlying principles that control the subject in one case equally hold true in the other? The above author believes that, on theoretic grounds, it is possible with some subjects that crime be committed under the spell of hypnotic suggestion, but that there is much exaggeration in this respect, that few people are so susceptible as to accept the suggestion of a criminal act without *repeated* hypnotization, and that it is equally true that many would thus refuse even after long hypnotic training. " A hypnotic subject is not a suitable instrument for the commission of crime." " However," he adds, by way of reservation, " criminal suggestion is not impossible." [1] He also cites Liégeois, as holding that " hypnotism might be employed to obtain possession of property illegally," etc. The eminent authority, Dr. MacDonald, in his valuable contribution to this subject, considers it impossible, during a state of somnambulism (which he considers only an hypnotic sleep differing in degree), to compel certain persons contrary to their will to commit immoral or criminal acts, and to " otherwise violate their consciences and divulge their deepest secrets." He, however, cites the case of a person described by Liégeois, who, upon his suggestion, was induced after repeated efforts to sign a false note, on the pretence that she owed him a certain sum. For reasons hereafter made clear, he, however, expresses a doubt as to the success of such experiments outside the laboratory.[2] The attitude thus assumed toward this phase of the subject in controversy may be

[1] " Hypnotism," Moll, 1894, p. 319.
[2] " Abnormal Man," MacDonald, 1893, pp. 94–99.

best summarized in the words of Mr. Moll, the eminent authority above named.

"There are important differences of opinion about the offences which hypnotic subjects may be caused to commit. Liégeois, who has discussed the legal side of the question of hypnotism in a scientific manner, thinks this danger very great, while Gilles de la Tourette, Pierre Janet, Benedikt, and others deny it altogether.

"There is no doubt that subjects may be induced to commit all sorts of imaginary crimes in one's study. I have made hardly any such suggestions, and have small experience on the point. In any case a repetition of them is superfluous. If the conditions of the experiment are not changed, it is useless to repeat it merely to confirm what we already know. And these criminal suggestions are not altogether pleasant. I certainly do not believe that they injure the moral state of the subject, for the suggestion may be negatived and forgotten. But these laboratory experiments prove nothing, because some trace of consciousness always remains to tell the subject he is playing a comedy (Franck, Delboef), consequently he will offer a slighter resistance. He will more readily try to commit a murder with a piece of paper than with a real dagger, because, as we have seen, he almost always dimly realizes his real situation. These experiments, carried out by Liégeois, Foureaux, and others, in their studies, do not, therefore, prove the danger." [1]

John Jay Hudson, in his interesting work on the same subject, already quoted, takes substantially similar

[1] "Hypnotism," pp. 337, 338.

grounds, emphasizing the impossibility of making the law of suggestion the pliant tool of crime in the hands of a vicious control. He regards it, indeed, to use his own language, as one of the strongest demonstrations of the universality of the law that hypnotism cannot be so employed, and thousands of experiments daily being made demonstrate the impossibility of controlling the hypnotic subject so far as to cause him to do what he believes or knows to be wrong.[1] In corroboration of this position, the author makes much of the self-preservative instinct as a saving factor to nullify any criminal suggestion that insinuates itself into the otherwise passive mind of the semi-unconscious subject, to the subversion of those moral ideas that have hitherto held autocratic sway in the waking subject. This fundamental instinct of the subjective mind, independent of all other considerations, it is held, being sufficient to safeguard the otherwise passive mind from yielding peremptorily to immoral suasion, such a consideration, to quote his own words: "tending to operate as potently in the hypnotic condition as it would in the normal state. It would be an instinctive auto-suggestion, just the same as in the case of suicide, although it would operate indirectly in one case, and directly in the other. The deductive reasoning of the subjective mind, as we have seen in preceding chapters, is perfect; and in the case supposed, the subject would instantaneously reason from the supposed crime to its consequences to himself. The same law would operate in preventing the commission of crimes of less magnitude with a resistance decreased in pro-

[1] "The Law of Psychic Phenomena," Hudson, 1898, pp. 127, 129.

portion to the nature of the offence.   But it would, in all cases, be a factor of great importance in the prevention of crime; for the subjective mind is ever alert where the safety and well-being of the individual are concerned.   This law is universal, and has often been manifested in the most striking manner."[1]   Maudsley, in discussing this theme in its somnambulistic phase, ventures the assertion that: but few persons can call to mind an instance in which an act of homicide or incendiarism has been perpetrated during trance-sleep. "Having regard, however," he adds, "to the complicated acts which somnambulists unquestionably do perform in their sleep, there is certainly no reason, in the nature of things, why they should not set fire to the house, or commit suicide or homicide."[2]

Of course, all matters of post-hypnotic crimes come practically under the same general category, possibly in an aggravated sense, as Forel is quoted as properly saying: a person who would commit a crime by post-hypnotic suggestion would, generally speaking, not be a person of the most honorable character, some morally defective being easier to affect in this way than those with stronger principles.   Such examples, however, are known, and Sonde cites a case of post-hypnotic illusion that lasted two years.

The possibility of employing deception, or specious reasoning, or of persuasion, as inducement to criminal conduct, is of a somewhat similar nature, and is affirmed by some and denied by others.   Thus, Liégeois induced

---

[1] "The Law of Psychic Phenomena," p. 136.

[2] "Responsibility in Mental Disease," Maudsley, 1897, p. 269.

a subject to steal a watch, which he at first refused to do. When it was represented to him that the watch was his own and that he had a right to it, he readily assented.

It will be seen at a glance that between these two contending opinions lies an issue of very grave significance, both as applied to the subject in its individual bearing as a moral agent and also as a factor in medical jurisprudence as affecting, not only the matter of the credibility of witnesses, but as touching upon the crucial test of legal responsibility in overt acts, as well as members of organized society. If it be true that the sensitive, placed under the influence of the hypnotic spell, enters into a state of suspended consciousness so profound that he becomes temporarily the pliant tool of an unscrupulous superior will-power, it follows, not only that all moral and legal responsibility ceases with it, so far as the subject is concerned, but the whole matter becomes one about which not only our judiciary, but the moral philosopher, may well recast their theories and readjust their legal notions. Standing midway between a compromise between these two theories, the unprejudiced censor is at a loss to know where to begin or where to end amid the bewildering entanglements of a subject whose foundation pillars are lost amid the subtleties and profundities of the subjective man.

A correct conclusion, in view of the difficulties presented in the above views, it will be readily seen, lies in the difficulty of submitting to deductive processes a matter so largely subjective in its nature. This very characteristic of necessity surrounds it with an air of metaphysical speculation, and at the same instant presents an inviting field for charlatanry and fraud. The consensus of opinion as to the relative merits of the views above presented and the conclusions drawn may be said, on the whole, to favor the theory of the practical impossibility of employing hypnotism as a successful media, through the power of suggestion, of inducing a normal person to the commission of an overt criminal act. At the same time, the impossibility of such successful induction at the instance of *repeated* experiments, or through the *employment of deception* while under such hypnotic trance, is not quite so clear. Whether the resistant force of the subjective intuitive faculties already referred to in all such cases, are, in and of themselves, sufficient to successfully resist such encroachments, must remain a question. Also, as to whether this suggestive attribute operates *equally at all stages* of the hypnotic trance from profound syncope to where it verges upon, and is hardly distinguishable from, the normal waking state, must also remain doubtful. If it be true (as is claimed) that the more complete the hypnotization the more autocratic the supremacy of the moral and instinctive attributes, or where (as has been still more strongly put) " he believes, because he *must* believe, suggestions made to him "[1] (the italic is my own), the reverse must then hold equally true, and the more *imperfect* such lethargic state, the *weaker* the power of these intuitions and hence the more susceptible to the inroads of immoral suggestions. It is a rule that cannot work both ways,

[1] Hudson.

and anything in the way of a provisional hypothesis will certainly fail to meet the requirements.

The chief danger of hypnotism as an actual crime-producing agency doubtless lies in cases of a sexual character, where the natural propensities of the sensitive are unduly inflamed through contact with a stronger control possessed with perverted sexual appetites. Dr. MacDonald holds to the same opinion, and says that in the lethargic or cataleptic state, in this respect, the subject is easily influenced.[1] It is readily conceivable that the above circumstances, taken in connection with the helpless condition of the victim as well as the confused state of mind that supervenes hypnotization, would naturally tend to break the force of the criminating testimony on the part of the subject. Some authorities, however, think that, owing to the reasons already given and the fact of the superior strength of the victim when under the hypnotic state, these facts would render such acts, against the will of the individual, all but impossible. Numerous illustrations, however, attest to the possibility of such a fact. The desire for revenge, anger, in short, any of the germinal passions, are fair fields for the display of the hypnotic test, the subject here doubtless more readily responding to criminal suggestion than where the stronger self-preservative instincts prevail, as in cases of homicide, suicide, etc.

However, we conceive that the chief force of hypnotic phenomena as crime-producing agencies, lie rather (as in the case of the growth of crime from recidivistic germs, discussed in a preceding chapter) in the fact of

[1] "Criminology," p. 136.

the contagion arising out of the contact of a latent criminal impulse already residing in the subject with an active criminal principle in the control. Let us suppose, for example, A has hitherto shown no marked criminal inclination; nevertheless, his propensities are such as to lead us to believe he would present a more or less ready susceptibility to criminal suggestion. A comes into contact with B, a control of pronouncedly criminal proclivities who readily induces A into the cataleptic state. Suppose B, through such objective influences, succeeds in so impressing A with criminal suggestion that he readily assents to wrong-doing. Then, if the axiom holds true that "in the hypnotic state of two contrary suggestions the stronger must prevail," it follows that the pronounced inherent tendency to crime in the passive subject, B, must prevail over all those feebler counter-resistant impulsions that ordinarily dominate the waking state of A, thus finding a willing victim in the latter under *abnormal* conditions where, in the normal state, he would not so readily (if at all) have yielded to criminal suggestion, but presumably have remained a law-abiding person. Now suppose (to extend the illustration to cover the whole case) the subject resists successfully the initial experiment described above. The same is repeated, again and again, under the inspiration of the dominant influence at the instance of the anti-social proclivity. However strong may have been the original intuitive powers of the subject along lines heretofore laid down, is it not highly presumable that, after repeated attempts to break down such inhibitory powers, they must finally succumb to such repeated assaults, until at last the recipient surrenders to the suggestion of the superior will and thus falls a victim to the criminal aggression? Mr. Moll has already been quoted as committing himself to the affirmative of this proposition. Indeed, the inevitable result must be the weakening of nerve centres, the breaking down of the will and the final superinducing of a state of nervous apprehension and chronic suggestibility. This would prove to be the case under ordinary circumstances, to say nothing of abnormal conditions, which latter would carry with it the added fact of the absolute subversion of the will and the consequent irresponsibility of the hapless victim who has ceased for the time being to be master over himself.

Bernheim, in enumerating the dangers of hypnotism under irresponsible and unskilful hands, warns against these incursive effects of repeated hypnotization, and adds that, "after having been hypnotized a certain number of times, some subjects present a disposition to go to sleep spontaneously"; and that, "after being delivered over to the mercy of any one deprived of psychical and moral resistance, certain somnambulists thus become weak and are moulded by the will of the suggestionists." He then adds, by way of seasonable warning: "The moralists who are careful of human dignity, and who are preoccupied with the thought of such great responsibilities of danger, are in the right. They are right to condemn a practice which may rob a man of his free will without the possibility of resistance on his part; they would be a thousand times right, if the remedy were not side by side with the evil." [1]

[1] "Suggestive Therapeutics," p. 413.

It can hardly be questioned that repeated return to the hypnotic state must inevitably result in ultimate moral and mental, as well as nervous, instability; and the unnatural subordination of the subjective to the objective state can but demoralize the whole man, since it is a practical reversal of the phenomena of sentient life, and a misdirection of its potential forces, and hence can but prove destructive in the end by an inexorable law that visits the violation of natural laws with penalties alike upon the just and upon the unjust. "All immorality, all vice, all crime, and all insanity arise from one and the same cause; viz., the dominance of the subjective faculties, and have a tendency, unless for good purpose, to arouse to abnormal activity those emotions and propensities which, uncontrolled by reason, lead to immorality, vice, crime, and insanity." [1]

It is at least presumable, from the above hypothetical cases, that the claim of the deductive process of reasoning from the proposed crime to its consequence, as a sufficient guarantee against yielding to wrong-doing under hypnotic influences, would be thrown away, and the individual would succumb, notwithstanding, to dormant criminal proclivities at the incitation of abnormal trance conditions. This must be presumed to be the case, unless it is primarily assumed that there is a reserve of latent moral force stored up (so to speak) in the subjective mind upon which it may draw in such emergencies, and thus present a moral front it could hardly maintain in the waking state. Such assumption would smack strongly of the *a priori*, and needs further proof in verification.

[1] "Scientific Demonstrations of a Future Life," Hudson, p. 316.

Here, then, if anywhere, rests the chief danger of hypnotism as a factor in the criminal psychosis, a position that, it seems to me, is worthy of careful consideration in all cases where the receptivities of the subject are sensitive to the approachment of criminal suggestion at the instance of the stronger, and where the inflammable material of an already perverted moral predisposition lies ready to catch fire upon the occasion of the first contact with sympathetic initiatives. Hypnotism might thus prove in this sense, if in none other, a serious adjunct to the many crime-producing agencies that appeal to it from the numerous other sources heretofore mentioned.

The above position is as much as conceded by advocates of the Nancy School, as reflected in the opinion of an eminent advocate (Hudson) heretofore quoted: " If the subject is a criminal character, he might follow the suggestions of a criminal hypnotist and actually perpetrate a crime. But in such a case, a resort to hypnotism for criminal purposes would be unnecessary, and no possible advantage could be gained by its employment," a position that, considered on the whole, can neither add to, nor subtract from, our attitude above assumed with reference to the propagative character of criminal suggestion in connection with sympathetic subjects, a position which, if at all tenable, must certainly be held responsible for a multiplication of crimes, if not for the multiplication of criminals.

As to the legal features involved in the phenomena of hypnotism, with reference to its essential merits in a given case, either as entering into the *res gesta*, or as pertaining to its evidential value, little need be said at this time, and this largely by reason of the paucity of material which legal science in this country has been able to collate upon the subject-matter, though Continental authorities have written more largely upon it. We are not aware of any criminal cases in which the subject of hypnotism has materially figured. Its value, in testimony, either as going to sound the credibility of witnesses, or as to the guilt or innocence of the accused, must of necessity be reduced to a minimum, owing to the comparative ease with which the hypnotic state might be simulated, though Moll and other writers dwell upon the difficulties of such deception.

The only case that comes to the knowledge of the author, is that of "The People vs. Ebanks," [1] wherein the defendant, a mulatto, was convicted in the Superior Court of San Diego County, California, for the crime of murder; found guilty, and sentenced to be hanged. Defendant appealed from judgment and order denying his motion for a new trial. Among other facts in the case it appeared that defendant called a witness and offered to prove by him that witness was an expert hypnotist; that he had hypnotized defendant, and that, when hypnotized, defendant had made a statement to him in regard to his knowledge of the affair, from which statement witness was ready to testify that defendant was not guilty, and that defendant denied his guilt while in that condition.

The court sustained an objection to the testimony, saying: "The law of the United States does not rec-

[1] 117 California Reports, p. 652.

ognize hypnotism. It would be an illegal defence, and I cannot admit it." The court then repeated in substance what it had said to the jury, and ordered them to disregard the offer.

The comment of the Supreme Court on this proposition is brief.[1] It says: "We shall not stop to argue the point, and only add the court was right."

In a concurring opinion, Judge McFarland says, among other matters, "It will not be necessary to determine whether or not testimony tending to show that a defendant committed the act charged while in a hypnotic condition is admissible until a case involving that precise question shall be presented."

This is the only case known to the author in the judicial history of the United States, in which reference is made to the subject of hypnotism, or to the hypnotic condition, as a defence to a charge of crime; and since the court cites no other authority in its opinion, it is presumable there is none other.

[1] 117 California Reports, p. 666.

CHAPTER XIII

CONCLUSION

I. *Punishment.* II. *Reformation.* III. *Prevention*

THE aim of all systematic penological effort lies in the directions of (*a*) the punishment of the offender; (*b*) the reduction of the criminal problem as a social evil through the interposition of the civil arm and the intermediary of reformatory and ameliorative agencies. As a logical proposition, it may safely be said the correctional idea is necessarily implied in that of rational punishment. Aside from purely retaliatory principles, this must ever have floated dimly as substance and shadow through all rational conception of punishment, the effect of every such visitation of necessity presupposing this.

Theoretically, punishment is one thing, prevention another. Prevention is in the character of an anterior solvent to the end of rendering crime impossible; the other is in the nature of a subsequent event, repressive in character, and for the purpose of preventing a repetition of the offence. Incarceration is the prevailing mode of punishment; the application of proper correctional methods is the underlying principle in the reformative idea; and the readjustment and substitution of environmental and social conditions is the soul of the prevenient remedy.

In conclusion, a study of crime and the criminal would be incomplete without at least a cursory survey of these underlying principles.

I

Punishment

The first notion of punishment was, of course, that of direct retaliation for the offence upon the person of the offender. The purely expiatory nature of retribution has already been sufficiently examined in connection with historical outlines. The earliest social ideal no doubt readily conceived of crime as an injury to the solidarity, and quickly organized its defensive resources in the organized forms of guilds and hundreds, upon which devolved the sole political responsibility with which to meet the criminal aggression. These quasi-legal organizations stood practically as sureties for the public peace, and in connection with the ecclesiastical system together formed the earliest constabulary, usually expressing their authority in summary torture and sanguinary reprisal. Detention, if employed at all, it may readily be surmised, was but a temporary make-shift to pave the way for the severer ordeal. Carceral punishment, as such, was unknown to the ancients, save as the unhindered instrument of practical intermural burial, to which the chambers and subterranean dungeons of the ancients, as well as of the mediæval ages, bear ample testimony. Torture, among all nations, was the prevailing rule, and in the latter ages Roman citizens and the soldiery alone were exempt therefrom. The recital is the most pathetic in human history. It bears its own testimony to the severity of the primitive retributive arm, whether balanced on equity or resting on caprice. Its spirit and methods descended into modern times. As late as the reign of Henry VIII., no less than 70,000 executions, under color of authority, took place in England.

But a comparatively brief period has elapsed since the prison was looked upon as a place of detention alone for convicted felons. The ideal conception hitherto had been that of a place of torture, to be employed without much reference to the guilt or the innocence of either the convicted or the unconvicted, the capacity for usefulness of which was estimated by its approximation to the barbarous. The earliest revelation as to the actual condition of the inmates of jails and penitentiaries came as a shock to the civilized world. Death, branding, burning at the stake, mutilation, crucifixion, selling into slavery, drowning, and all manner of cruelties were the favorite modes of expiation that were compelled to give way imperceptibly to the no less barbarous custom that thus revealed itself in all its horrors to the gaze of these first philanthropists and prison agitators, whose hearts were stirred by what they saw.

Incarceration grew into favor during the Middle Ages. The feudal lords and bishops usually possessed private dungeons built into their castles. Prisons, more latterly, became the places of detention chiefly of petty offenders, debtors, and those intended for the scaffold or the stake, the same quite as frequently becoming their permanent abodes. No mention is made in ancient Anglo-Saxon law of incarceration, though prisons existed from time immemorial.

The first movement toward the betterment of these places of detention has been attributed to Clement XI., 1700. If so, its circle was limited, circumscribed practically to a single institution — St. Michael's, at Rome. The real innovators with a fixed purpose were the English, under the leadership of John Howard (1773), Blackstone (1765); Beccaria, in Italy; Montesquieu, in France; and Mrs. Frey and her company of Friends, who began their labors about that time. Transportation, with its many abuses, ceased in 1867. Guided by these philanthropic torches, parliamentary eyes at the beginning peered incredulously into the darkness of these living tombs; while public interest, ever apathetic, at first stood aghast, then gradually became accustomed to the spectacle there revealed. The great bulk of incarcerates were awaiting trial, generally for debt, and the balance — death. Crowded together promiscuously, reeking in filth, deprived of proper food and clothing, and usually chained, they were allowed to fester unnoticed. Out of the agitation that followed rose by slow degrees a more clearly defined punitive system and humane incarceral treatment. The initial legislative enactment was passed by Parliament in 1779, which gave to the new movement its first authoritative force. Ideals, as the famous "Panoptican" of Benham's, originally planned for Russia, eventually gave place to more material realizations, like that of the first large structure at Gloucester, in 1791, and the earliest stone penitentiary of Pentonville, England, in 1840, both built with separate cells. These were quickly followed by the consolidation of minor affairs, and the rapid construction of fifty-four larger prisons under central control (1877) and a properly organized prison commission composed of intelligent and humane persons, subject to governmental inspection and open supervision.

Prison reform in the United States was the legitimate offshoot of the movement thus begun in the mother country. It was the indirect reaction from colonial apathy and early physical severity. To a certain extent, its progress ran parallel with that of the innovators. The old Colonial penal system was without form and void. Disused buildings and abandoned mines formed the usual places of detention, as in Connecticut from 1773 to 1827; pits entered by ladders, as in Maine; in which places the immured were usually fastened by chains to bars overhead. In 1790, the Pennsylvania legislature made suitable provision for a rational penitentiary system, and laid the foundation for the first separate cellular prison in the United States. Model penitentiaries were immediately erected, one in Philadelphia, and one in Pittsburgh, the " Eastern Penitentiary " being modelled after the radiating prison at Ghent (1773), fitted up with suitable cells next the outer walls. In 1816 the Auburn penitentiary, in New York, followed, thus inaugurating throughout the Union a series of new prisons based upon advanced ideas.

The Quakers (1786) had abolished capital punishment in Pennsylvania for robbery and burglary, and introduced Solitary Confinement accompanied by labor in the cells. Other states rapidly followed. The error

of this form of imprisonment, however, was soon noticeable in impaired health of body and mind, following the
wake of the unnatural restraint thus imposed.   Out of
its necessities soon sprang the second great theory.
The Silent System is less rigorous than the Solitary, in
that, while insisting upon separation by night in single
cells, the inmates are allowed to labor in companies
during the daytime, though ostensibly under the rule of
silence.   Both systems consecutively found favor in
America and in England, and for a time each in its
order claimed precedence.   In 1839 the cellular system
was introduced into the latter country, and in 1843 the
great prison at Pentonville was erected, with 520 cells,
and the theory of separating prisoners was permanently
begun, 54 prisons in England alone having adopted
the practice to a greater or less extent.   Practical and
theoretic penology now began to work out their joint
salvation along parallel lines, not only in these two
great English speaking countries, but throughout the
civilized world.

Belgium was among the first of the Continental
states to improve its prison system upon the lines thus
laid down.   The great prison at Ghent, that had earlier
set the example, now became the model of cellular
prisons on the separate plan.   Briefly stated, its prevailing theory is isolation, though prisoners are allowed
to be visited frequently by Wardens, Trade Instructors,
Chaplains, Doctors, etc.   The labor is industrial (useful
handicraft), and the general treatment is correctional.
Part of their earnings go to the prisoners.   School and
religious instructions are for all, and the prison admin-

istration, as well as equipment, are practically perfect. A marked diminution in crime has usually followed these reforms.

The general prison régime of the German states is more or less uniform. Cellular imprisonment is the rule, and educational and religious instructions prevail, while useful trades are universally taught, and in some states, as in Baden, special prisons exist for thieves, robbers, etc. The credit system in curtailment of sentence, and the progressive gradation of prisoners on the basis of good behavior and general improvement are practised. Both cellular and associated imprisonment exist in Prussia. A portion of the earnings go to the prisoners. First offenders and juveniles are kept apart from the hardened criminals. Provisional release is granted after three-fourths of the sentence has been served.

Austria organized the cellular system in 1867, with classification based upon the ages, crimes, and mental conditions of the prisoners. Religious care is exercised over them. Trades, with the contract system prevail, with substantial wages of which the prisoner receives half. Their care and régime is excellent.

France possesses a mixed prison system, divided for a time with transportation, and a partial cellular plan, with classification. Juvenile reformatories are on the increase, though prison progression has been slow.

The prison system of Italy is generally congregate, the cellular or separate plan to some extent prevailing. There are different prisons, as for simple detention,

hard labor, long periods, and life detention. Penal
Colonies have also been established on islands.

In the Netherlands, the cellular and congregate plan
exist side by side, with simple detention or hard labor,
the latter being industrial with partial appropriation
of wages by the prisoner. Provisional release is granted
after serving half the term.

The Russian prisons have greatly improved since
1819. They are generally based upon the associated
plan, with cellular accommodations to a limited extent.
The fortresses are employed for political offenders, and
they are usually severe. They are generally under
military supervision. Deportations are largely for political reasons, and the systems are congregate in form.
Little attention is paid to the intellectual or spiritual
welfare of the prisoners, and there are no attempts to
teach trades or to make provisions for the general
welfare or betterment of inmates. The whole prison
régime is behind most of the other Continental countries.

The same may be said of Spain and Portugal, the
bulk of prisoners being detained in presidios, or convict
establishments.

The prisons of Norway and Sweden are divided between
fortress-prisons and cellular appointments. They practice the separation of incorrigibles, have industrial labor,
enjoy the privileges of schools and of religious services.

In Switzerland, the cantons have independent prison
systems. They are usually supplied with cellular accommodations, and have a progressive system of credits,
making toward comparative freedom, with ultimate
provisional liberty. The labor is chiefly industrial.

Canada shares the British advanced idea in penology. Six prisons exist, with cellular appointments, and labor in association for long-termers. The rolling stock for the government railways, and clothes, boots, and shoes, are produced by them.

The prison system of Denmark was organized in 1840, resulting in four principal prisons, with cellular privileges for about three-fourths of first offenders and for youth. Religious and secular instructions are administered in the cells.

This brief summary will suffice to indicate the progressive movement along carceral lines that has taken place in the civilized world during the last half century. That advancement has been remarkable, considering the long era of apathy preceding it. Punishment is now being administered upon broader principles, and the whole system of corrective justice, judicial and carceral, is in accord with this onward impulse. The reformatory idea is quickening the common pulse ; and the general prison theory once realized in substantial walls of stone and iron, the new method will be fully prepared for the second great progressive step in the treatment of the criminal incarcerate upon the reformatory theory, and in accord with the spirit of modern civilization and the gradual expansion of the altruistic sentiment of mankind.

II

The Reformatory Idea

This distinctively modern conception of the treatment of criminals in conjunction with combined industrial, educational, and religious appliances, opens a wide field for theoretic and experimental criminology. It at once elevates the whole subject upon another and higher plane of practical and scientific import and attainment, and summons to the task qualities and talents more adequate to the requirements of the case and the importance of the subject than was hitherto deemed necessary. The reformatory idea is the verdict of civilization upon past methods, and the substitution of moral agencies and the scientific spirit in place of brute force and coercive measures. It is becoming constantly more apparent to all students along these lines that simple punishment, as such, has in it little of the reformative principle. The theory that encounters force with force meets with but slight moral responsiveness in the subject, but serves rather to arouse the latent retaliatory and vindictive spirit that contain in them little of regenerative power. It is almost a prison maxim that the "worst prison sends out the worst prisoners." The most enlightened penologists and jurists confess to the entire inadequacy of punishment as either a preventive or repressive measure. It is a fallacy to suppose that it can in any sense prove a panacea for crime and wrongdoing. Punishment, however severe, does not reach the springs of human motive, or in any sense affect the sources of responsible conduct. It is a curious fact in the study of all repressive methods that inordinate severity, instead of proving a deterrent, more frequently operates as an incentive to the ills it would cure. Shocking punishment only lights anew the smouldering fires of resentment and stimulates the criminal mania. Montesquieu early noted this phase, and called attention to the fact that where robbers were broken on the rack, instead of decreasing, it only served to increase the tendencies to such crimes, and with his usual philosophic insight suggests that, " If we inquire into the causes of all human corruptions, we shall find that they proceed from the impunity of crimes, and not from the moderation of punishment." [1] Beccaria, animadverting against this same feature, adds, in confirmation of the views above advanced: " The countries and times most notorious for severity of punishment were always those in which the most bloody and inhuman actions and the most atrocious crimes were committed. In proportion as punishment became more cruel, the minds of men grew hardened and insensible." [2] The traditional belief that punishment is a cure for wrongdoing is based upon a fallacious generalization that has not the verification of experience back of it. The chief value of incarceration should lie in the *rational corrective measures that are possible under it*. Its force consists in the modifying and educative facilities, psychological and industrial, that may, under judicious adjustment of rewards and penalties reënforced by wise coercive measures, within limitations, become in time the germ of habits and substitutional tendencies that may eventually result in moral and social rehabilitation. The aggregate effects of punishment, in short, are negative and potential, and even thus considered, are oftentimes weakened by the many uncertainties, and the

[1] " Spirit of Laws," p. 107.
[2] " Essays on Crimes and Punishments," p. 94.

"law's delays," that render the matter of penalties a thing to be juggled with.

The modern movement, in its evolution from primitive forms to include this reformative concept, has been the outgrowth, not of a theory, but of necessity, forced upon the attention through moral persistency attested step by step. The ideal carceral system, in conjunction with this reformatory principle, is as yet in its formative stage. In the United States, it varies in its progressive march in proportion as it comes in contact with the different shadings of public sentiment and the varying degrees of civil and institutional growth that characterize state and local development. In most of the states, it is as yet crude and unscientific, the aim being principally confined to detention as the goal in prison attainment. In the aggregate, there are at present about 69 penitentiaries in the United States, 22 houses of correction, 12 workhouses, 2 houses of refuge, 3 military prisons, 3 convict farms, one asylum for insane convicts, a number of county prisons, and additional reformatories and industrial schools answering practically to the state prison, and about 3000 county jails for minor offenders and for those awaiting trial, etc. Where the Eastern and some of the New England states have made strides in these respects, which have been shared to some extent by the Middle, Western, and Northern states, the southerly and extreme westerly portions have been more slow to respond to the spirit of progress. The field of criticism, on the whole, is an inviting one. It is as suggestively rich in that which has been left undone as in what has been done.

As to the various systems of prison labor employed in the prisons of the United States, it may here be said, four leading methods for the employment of prisoners as the essence of the reformatory idea, have usually been adopted, which may be here briefly described as follows.

1. The contract system, under which the convict is employed by contractor at a specified price per day for his labor, under the immediate supervision of the employer.

2. The piece-price system, where the contractor furnishes the material and receives from the prison the completed article at a stated price, the supervision of the work being under prison authority.

3. The public account system, where the prison carries on the work under its own auspices, converting the raw material into the manufactured articles and disposing of them on their own account, like private corporations or individuals.

4. The lease system, where the convict is "hired out" to the contractor at specified rates for a fixed period, and upon terms contained in such lease in conformity to statutory provisions, which of course differ in different states, varying in degrees of responsibility, as where, in Nebraska, they are "leased to responsible parties" within the prison precincts; and in New Mexico, "hired out to the best advantage." The latter system is sometimes confined to labor upon public works, limited to the state, and at other times under the domination of the contractor who agrees to feed and clothe them. In 1890 there were 101 "camps" confined to the Southern States, and out of the aggregate of 2308 leased convicts,

2142, or 92.80 per cent, were males, and 166, or 7.20 per cent, were females. An analytical table of the work performed for successive periods illustrates their comparative values, as per United States Bulletin reports.

TABLE XLII

TABLE OF SUMMARY OF VALUE OF GOODS PRODUCED OR
WORK DONE, BY SYSTEMS

SYSTEMS OF WORK	VALUE	
	1885	1895
Public account system . .	$2,063,892.18	$4,888,563.36
Contract system	17,071,265.69	8,190,799.70
Piece-price system . . .	1,484,230.52	3,795,483.24
Lease system	3,651,690.00	2,167,626.03
Total	$24,271,078.39	$19,042,472.33

The above represents the value of the material on which the work has been done, plus the work itself.

It will be seen, the public account system increased in 1895 over 100 per cent above that of 1885. The contract system has decreased 40.6 per cent. The total wages paid by the contractors and lessees to states and counties for the labor of the convicts who produced these values was only $3,512,970, or $1 of convict-labor wages to $8.19 of finished product of convict labor.[1] The moral if not economic viciousness of the lease system hitherto so generally employed in the southerly states, is evident. The subject is being agitated by the people, and this relic of barbarism, as

[1] United States Convict Labor Bulletin, No. 5, July, 1896.

illustrating the worst features of the slavery period, is slowly giving way to the appliances of civilization. Its horrors in many instances are unspeakable, and reflect seriously (at least in the past) upon the civilization and humaneness of the fairest portion of the land. In Florida, public sales of convicts, mostly negroes, are common; and the laws of Mississippi provide for such lease of jail prisoners to the "highest bidder" under the supervision of the county officers. Leased convicts are divided into several classes, comprising those under immediate state supervision; in camps, or farms; under county and prison supervision; and directly under private bidders and sub-contractors, the latter presenting the most brutal features of the inhuman system. Under its methods male and female, old and young, may be, and usually are, indiscriminately herded together by day and by night, liable to punishment upon trifling infringements of rules, and subject in many instances to the unrestrained brutality of their taskmasters. The Howard Association reports that in one camp a mother was found with seven children, and in another, one with six. Mr. G. S. Griffith, President of the Maryland Society for the Protection of Children, found infants of eleven years of age in these camps and in one chain-gang he found 55 men, 3 women, and a boy of eleven years of age, and reported them all as "sleeping under a tent 70 by 24 feet." Women drove the carts, mingling with the men, white and black, indiscriminately.[1] The description given by Mr. J. W. Church, an

[1] "The Prison System of the South," G. S. Griffith, President Maryland Prisoner's Aid Association, Baltimore, Md., p. 6.

experienced newspaper man, and published in the *Atlanta Journal*, is appalling; men and women, white and black, and children scarce old enough to roam the streets alone, compose the degrading picture that would eclipse the worst days of pagan Rome. The mortality under such a system is, of course, terrible, reaching as high as 75 to 200 per 1000 annually, as against the 7.4 per 1000 mortality reported in the latest English Prison Report.[1] The lease system has decreased from 4879 in 1880 to 2308 in 1890, or over 47 per cent. It is to be hoped such a system will be speedily swept from the earth, no longer to disgrace the record of a boasted Christian civilization.

The indiscriminate method of herding together prisoners under the existing congregate plan is the bane of existing carceral method. No rational progressive prison system, in theory or in practice, is possible under it; as it brings the uncontaminated and comparatively sound portion into vital and indiscriminating contact with the more diseased and depraved of the criminal masses, which, of course, is ruinous to what is left of his moral wreckage and destructive of the whole character. The inevitable results have been already sufficiently sketched, and require no enlargement. Ninety per cent of the prisons of the United States are still conducted upon the congregate plan; labor, recreation, and cellular confinement by day and night being usually in company. No due regard can be systematically given to either age or condition, moral qualification or degree of criminal susceptibility,

[1] " Prison System of the South," pp. 11, 12, 13.

under such practice. The points of disadvantage require no elaboration. It is the chief incubus that curtails legitimate progressive penological effort, and stands in the path of reform. It successfully nullifies every effort put forth for the advancement of the prisoner and the proper management and supervision of the prison. The question of the segregation of prisoners, and the institutional facilities necessary thereto, is the organic basis of the whole theory and practice of enlightened criminal progression, institutional or otherwise, about which the perfected system must centre. The careful isolation and separate cellular confinement of prisoners by night, and their proper segregation in the daytime, according to their individual criminal susceptibilities and traits, are, it is easy to see, the chief ends to be attained in all intelligent institutional supervision, which, properly entered upon and wisely performed, make all other attainments and ideals possible. Wherever practised, and in whatever states adopted, in connection with proper reformatory appliances, crime has diminished, as witness the history of Prussia, England, and other countries where the same, in conjunction with the proper reformatory agencies, is fundamentally in force, and in all of which countries serious crime has uniformly decreased. Under its practice, not only the direct moral advantage to be gained by such a plan alone commends it, but the fact that a rational progressive system of marks and credits based upon actual merit and improvement in industrial and educational pursuits is practicable, and a progressional stage of prison advancement by successive steps upon self-attained merit is attainable. This progressive system is more or less in vogue in nearly all the foremost countries of Europe at all abreast with the onward movement. In both Germany and England, as well as in Belgium, Holland, Sweden, and Denmark, and in some parts of the Austro-Hungarian Empire, prisoners are divided into classes, with the right of promotion from a lower to a higher grade upon the basis of good conduct and industrial labor, regulated by a scientific credit system of marks for merit or demerit. The Probationary, or First-class Prisoners, are at first usually reduced to a minimum of privileges and conveniences, with little, if any, bedding, coarse food, etc. By dint of good behavior and industry, these restrictions are gradually removed, and better food and accommodations obtained throughout successive stages until the last is reached, where, in addition to a certain degree of freedom, they are permitted the privileges of communicating with friends, and an increasing pecuniary allowance granted for labor, from which, however, is deducted a reasonable charge for food and clothes, and also fines in case of misbehavior. The right of conditional release for the unexpired sentence is here also granted. These increasing privileges are thus earned by the prisoner, and are an inducement to good behavior and an incentive to diligence, the same having a natural tendency to ultimately crystallize into habit under the persistent holding of the attention and focussing the moral perceptivities upon the fact that right conduct brings its legitimate reward. This is the English Graded System, analogous with the Irish, or Crofton (named after Sir William Crofton) Progressive Classification, employed so successfully by Major Maconochei, at Norfolk Island. In Great Britain, the legal limit for such separate discipline is two years; in Holland and Germany, four years; in Belgium, ten years. It has been represented as being preferred by the better class of prisoners, and disliked by the worst. The system is practically carried out in the leading prisons of Belgium, Holland, Norway, Sweden, and Denmark, and in several of the foremost penitentiaries of the United States, at least so far as cellular isolation by night, gradation, promotion, conditional release, etc., are concerned.

The importance of trades industries, general education, and religious culture, in connection with criminal reform, has been so fully touched upon in preceding pages that further reference is unnecessary. Their value both as educatives and as aids toward a subsequent livelihood, besides acting as stimuli to honest living and moral quickening, is self-evident. A mere treadmill process of prison labor is purposeless, and consequently without moral force. The *best* trade in connection with the *best wages* is the most hopeful material counteractant of the criminal habit, and should be so inculcated independent of any questions of remuneration or expense to the State. As a late report of the Wardens' Association of the United States has well put it, "The higher the character of the daily pursuits, the greater the unlikelihood of falling into crime." Moderate wages are no mean inducement to conscientious toil in prison, and illustrate a principle in economics and reformation it would be well to heed. France, Italy, and Germany have adopted the plan with advantage.

The question as to whether prison trades and labor, together with their products, come into actual competition with free labor is only an incident, and should in no case be taken seriously when the regenerative and industrial features of the criminal problem are to be considered. The concrete features are of slight economic value, on the whole. In its purely economic aspect, the total output of all convict-made goods in the United States is not over $20,000,000; while the actual value of labor expended does not exceed $2,500,000. This amount of work, if rightly distributed toward supplying state and governmental requirements, and percolating naturally into the general bulk of labor, would find its level without perceptible disturbance. Moreover, it would contribute materially toward the support of the prison itself, and consequently lessen the burden of taxation to the general public, a feature to be considered quite as advantageous, on the whole, as when forced to respond to the demands of sumptuary legislation for the benefit of a class. The opposition of trades-unions and kindred organizations is based upon principles as fallacious as they are selfish, signally ignoring, as they do, the features above presented. New York, after many unsatisfactory efforts toward the solution of this vexed problem, on January 1, 1897, incorporated substantially the principles here advocated into the organic law of that state, by concentrating her convict labor upon supplying the demands of the state's institutions and its political divisions, thus practically withdrawing such labor from open competition and creating a special market for herself where she becomes a preferred buyer, thus lessening the expense of her prison institutions and aiding every taxpayer in the state, besides putting into the hands of the liberated prisoner the means to earn his own livelihood by an honorable and self-respecting trade thus acquired.   Foreign countries are more practical as well as more responsive to this political and economic necessity of prison labor and trade acquisition.   Germany receives 40 per cent of her prisoners without trades, but sends out none without one. The labor of convicts in English prisons, both local and convict, is performed in the greatest number of instances for and on behalf of the government, in the building and repairing of fortifications, tilling farms, in the manufacturing of supplies for the post-office department and for the army and navy, etc.   General Du Cane thinks that the argument against competing with free labor by manufacturing for the market is entirely fallacious, though some concession is usually made to allay labor agitation.   Industrial employment and trades are justly regarded as the sheet anchor of prison reform, whose salutary effects reach outside its walls and make themselves felt in giving permanent backbone to otherwise feeble recuperative efforts on the part of the financial and social bankrupt.

Indemnification by the prisoner to the injured party out of the proceeds of such labor, paid by the state at a reasonable valuation, should be part of a rational scheme in conjunction with a wise and scientific prison theory. Every breach upon property rights should be met with a bill of damages which the violator should be compelled to pay in services rendered the State during his term of imprisonment. The same should be sufficient in amount to make good the actual losses to his victim. There was a time when all punishment was pecuniary, and crime, we are told, was the inheritance of princes. While society is no longer interested in wrong-doing to this extent, nevertheless, since the function of punishment is to correct wrongs, the offender should be compelled to make good all losses for which he stands responsible, or give an equivalence in labor in lieu thereof at a given valuation. The State should be held surety for such compensatory damages to the victim of crime, recouping itself from the offender as above indicated. Crime is not only a private, but also a public wrong, the perpetration of which the State should be held responsible for, as a conservator of the public welfare. If the State is responsible in damages for civil negligence, why not in criminal cases, especially where she can recoup herself? The question has been repeatedly discussed at Prison Congresses, notably at the Fifth International Prison Congress, Paris, 1895, where the summary of conclusions appeared to favor the doctrine: "That the right to such damages existed. That the injured party should have a lien on the real estate, and a first lien upon the personal property of the guilty party. That in lieu of such lien and property, the State should indemnify, recouping itself out of the earnings of the prisoner, or out of the general fines, same to be assessed by the court."

The law, however, should work both ways if it would effect strict justice; hence it follows that those who have been wrongfully accused and convicted, especially when compelled unjustly to serve long and onerous sentences of imprisonment, should be fully reimbursed, not only in the nature of compensatory but also in exemplary damages, for the wrong imposed upon the innocent party in the name of justice. The force and reasonableness, as well as the inherent equitableness of such a conclusion is apparent, since it is plain that the most cruel and crushing wrong that can be inflicted upon an unfortunate human being is that of causing the weight of social reprobation to be unjustly fixed upon him. Such compensation for judicial errors was in vogue in France in the eighteenth century, and has been freely discussed from the time of Beccaria and Voltaire, and has been advocated by Necker, Bruso, Benham, Schwartz, Garofalo, and others, as well as debated in the Italian Parliament, and National Congress on Law, in 1891. Similar provisions exist in the penal codes of Hungary, Portugal, Sweden, Denmark, Mexico, and Switzerland. The legal principle involved is just and fair. It makes its appeal, in the name of traditional justice, to our highest sense of right and in the spirit of humanity and civilization.

Of course, all educational and religious appliances, such marked factors in criminal reformation and features in all intelligent and scientific prison management, so naturally fall into their proper places under such a system that it is unnecessary to go into detail in a work of this kind. They go side by side with other moral and industrial agencies in fortifying character and in laying deep and wide the foundations of mental and moral integrity and fidelity to high ideals. Where unfriendly critics can show what Christianity does *not* do for the criminal classes, its apologists can show what it is *able* to do upon its own terms, which is the reasonable test for the normal as well as for the abnormal man, in all matters vital to Christian dynamics in its last analysis.

It is plain, from above considerations, that there must of necessity be a distinction between the *crisis* period in the criminal activity of the first offender at the initial stage of his career, and in that of the experienced criminal habitué, whose psychological and anthropological equipment and characteristics are, as already portrayed, not only essentially different, but should, under any wise and discriminating carceral system, be equally subject to separate and distinctive modes of treatment, dependent, of course, upon his degree of mental and moral alienation and existing status, which must always be taken into consideration. The impromptu offence and the instinctive tendency stand at different angles of the criminal characterization, and, it is clear, in their personal representatives demand different handling. One requires punishment with moral suasion; the other, detention with scientific and therapeutic treatment. One meets reformatory methods with a certain measure of assent, if within wise and proper bound; the other faces it with the imperturbability of the unthinking ox and the instinctiveness of the tiger. One is amenable to moral suasion; the other chiefly to repressive measures. The degree of responsiveness above referred to, is in direct proportion to the moral susceptibility of the subject, plus the remedial agencies to be applied.

To subserve these ends, different classes of prisons should be inaugurated to meet these widely diverging exigencies, as exemplified in these differently constituted grades of offenders. For example, prisons should be set apart for first offenders, and others for habitual criminals — each class of institutions varying widely and radically both as to their nature and character, their construction, policy, and managerial requirements, and in the treatment and methods of handling the inmates. The prison for the former, while strictly within the purview of humanitarian methods, should not by any means be a place of ease and comfort, but of hard labor and coarse but healthy fare, with a correspondingly strict régime, without in any degree trenching upon the inmate's sense of self-respect and manhood. Strictness of discipline, hard labor, and physical inconvenience is one thing; unnecessary hardship and brutality, in the sense of self-degradation and physical pain, is quite another. For these reasons, all such senseless humiliations as "striped clothing," poll-shaving, or whatever other abominations tend to make a prisoner appear ridiculous, thereby correspondingly lowering his sense of self-respect, are as stupid as they are vicious, and betray an absolute ignorance of the root principles and springs of human nature, and should never be tolerated in any intelligent prison régime. The plea that they prevent escape and aid in identification is a reflection upon the prison police. The best prisons of the East are doing away with it in whole, or in part, as incentives to obedience, as in Michigan and Illinois. Deprivation of liberty is sufficient punishment to the average incarcerate, without the aid of studied affront. This love of liberty is a revelation to the uninitiated. The value in which it is held by the meanest is scarcely lessened by the long continuance of his detention. So intense is this desire for freedom, close observation and the testimony of the prison records convince me that nine-tenths of the prison mortality usually occurs within a brief period of the expiration of the term of sentence of the incarcerate, the knowledge of such event and the nervous strain imposed at the prospect of speedy release no doubt aiding in hastening demise. The place of detention for the first offender, therefore, should be an institution where the extremes of inconvenience and a proper degree of rational treatment are so wisely intermingled as to produce best results, and at the same time render the prison a place conscientiously to be avoided, which is in itself a desideratum.

The prison home of the recidivist and habitual criminal (who is as to the manor born) when associated with permanent life detention, should be cast upon a different plan. It should comprehend in itself a minimum of the punitive idea, with an average of humane supervisory care. If it be true that the congenital and habitual criminal is largely the product of causes and influences congenital and environmental, over which he had originally little control, it follows that he should be *detained*, not punished; sequestered, in short, much upon the theory of the defective who differs from the former chiefly in that one is a mental, and the other is a moral, defective. As the instinctive moral pervert slides low down in the scale of responsibility, that of society toward him correspondingly increases. If it be true, as shown, that the genuine criminal can be accounted for only upon the ground of bio-genetic law, we must also shelter him under the wings of a larger grace, for manifestly the same inexorable logic that discovers his moral inability must now also come to his temporal rescue. Accept the premises, and from the conclusion there is no escape.

The plea for his seclusion is one of social necessity. Society's claim is self-defensive. To eliminate what is dangerous sets the bounds. To *punish* is beyond her prerogative under given conditions. The born criminal is nature's protégé. Legal sequestration is the remedy. The theory of vigorous initiatives in this respect, pushed to extremes by the ultrafatalistic and positivist schools, to the extent of physical elimination — death, for all instinctive criminals — goes beyond the limits of a reasonable necessity. Assuming it to be true, as claimed, that the greater individual responsibility is diminished the more that of societies is increased, and the doctrine of physical elimination is a begging of the question, a confession of the inherent inability of society to cope with the same upon either scientific or humanitarian grounds. It is a recourse to the appliances of barbarism at the expense of civilization, and to that extent falls short of a scientific solution.

The death penalty as a moral element and deterrent

factor in criminal judicature, is perhaps open to discussion, and is as yet an unsolved problem. The brief tests thus far applied in the laws of the various states seem inconclusive as definitely determining the relative value of the death penalty as a deterrent factor in crime. In Michigan, prior to the abolition of capital punishment, there were thirty-seven murders in the thirteen years preceding the passage of the law abolishing it, and thirty-one in the thirteen years subsequent to its abandonment; and since the population in that state has increased 50 per cent, the actual decrease in murder was about 40 per cent. Rhode Island, likewise showed a similar decrease. In Wisconsin, it is said, murder has fallen off 3 per cent from 1871 to 1889. In Iowa, there was one murder for every 1,200,000 inhabitants while the penalty was not in force, as against one for every 800,000 while so in vogue. Foreign statistics also bear imperfectly upon the subject. In England, about 76 per cent of all the trials for crimes not punishable by the death penalty resulted in conviction, while only 33 per cent of the trials punishable by death resulted in convictions. In the United States, the trials for murder each year have averaged about from 100 to 150 convictions annually. In Prussia, from 1818 to 1854, 988 death sentences were passed, an average of 26.49 each year, and the total executions numbered 286.[1] In the German Empire, the aggregate number convicted of murder in 1882 was 151; in 1894, 110; in 1895, 113; in 1896, 108; a gradual decrease on the whole. In Austria, from 1870 to 1879, there were 806 death

1 "The Condition of Nations," Kolb, 1880, p. 235.

sentences, and only 16 executions. In Denmark, from 1870 to 1880, there were 94 sentenced to death, and one executed. In both Holland and Portugal, where the death penalty was abolished, there has been a decrease in capital offences. As to the comparison of the proportion of executions to the number of sentences, the following table may be gathered from the " Howard Association " publications of 1881, from which may be formulated the following tabulated comparison : —

TABLE XLIII

STATES	NUMBER OF DEATH SENTENCES	EXECUTIONS	PER CENT
Austria, 1870–79 . . .	806	16	1.98
France, 1870–79	198	93	6.96
Spain, 1868–77	291	126	43.29
Sweden, 1869–78 . . .	32	3	9.37
Denmark, 1868–77 . . .	94	1	1.06
Bavaria, 1870–79 . . .	249	7	2.81
Italy, 1867–76	392	34	8.67
Germany, 1869–78 . . .	404	1	0.20
England, 1860–79 . . .	665	372	55.94
Ireland, 1860–79 . . .	66	36	54.54
Scotland, 1860–79 . . .	40	15	37.50
Australia and New Zealand, 1870–79.	453	123	27.15
United States, about 2500 murders annually . .		about 100 and about 100 lynchings	4.

The death penalty has been abolished in Maine, Michigan, Rhode Island, Wisconsin, and Colorado. The states in which life imprisonment may be substituted for death are Alabama, Arizona, California, Illinois,

Indiana, Iowa, Massachusetts, Ohio, Kentucky, Nebraska, South Dakota, South Carolina, and Oklahoma. Those in which like discretion is given to the trial court are, North Dakota, Minnesota, Texas, and New Mexico.

Capital punishment in Europe is in vogue (with discretion, in many instances, in trial courts) in Great Britain, France, Germany, Austria, Denmark, Greece, Hawaii, Honduras, Japan, China, Columbia, Ecuador, Hayti, Corea, Liberia, Peru, Spain, Sweden, Turkey, Morocco, Persia, and Servia. It has been abolished in Argentine Republic, Belgium, Brazil, Chile, Costa Rica, Guatemala, Holland, Italy, Norway, Portugal, Russia, Roumania, and Switzerland (8 cantons), and in Venezuela.

The following data bear upon the subject in three different countries under different systems, Italy, where the death penalty has been abolished, England, where it is retained, and the United States, under a mixed system, respectively.

I. MURDER IN ITALY (No Death Penalty)

1876 . . 2,626   1872 . . 2,019   1874 . . 3,438   1887 . . 2,805

II. MURDER IN ENGLAND (Death Penalty) [1]

1860–69 . . Yearly average, 126   1880–89 . . Yearly average, 160
1870–79 . . Yearly average, 153

III. MURDER IN THE UNITED STATES (Mixed Penalties) [2]

1890 . . [3] 4,290   1892 . . 6,791   1894 . . 9,800
1891 . . 5,906   1893 . . 6,615   1895 . . 10,500

---

[1] *Nineteenth Century Review*, June, 1892.

[2] The Census (1890), gives 5,563 cases of murder.

[3] *The Arena*, April, 1899, from data collected by F. M. Archer and N. J. Barr.

W. F. Lord attributes the increase of crime in Italy to the abolition of capital punishment.[1]

On the whole, the question is a mixed one, the crucial point, of course, being as to the direct deterrent effect of capital punishment, as such. The criminal fears death. Commutation is to him a transformation. It means the natural love of life, hope, — the possibility of ultimate pardon. If an average prison statistic of the world could be summarized, it would undoubtedly be found that the capital offender has ample ground in indulging such anticipation, except in those countries where the law cuts off its possibility. In some prisons in the United States the average term of service of "life-timers," so-called, runs exceedingly low. Few but would choose life imprisonment to death. To this extent, the latter would seem, *a priori*, a deterrent. The real fact as touching the gist of the question would seem still to remain answered : Does the average homicide commit his offence with the fear of the law before his eyes? From a purely psychological standpoint, *does he stop to think of the consequence of his deed?* Manifestly not. A scientific criminologist is therefore as much at a loss to solve the enigma as the ordinarily acute observer with all the facts before him. It is a question of expediency, that requires the test of time and experience for its solution so far as effective deterrence is concerned, while, as to its purely mediæval feature, it might well be dispensed with in favor of the more civilized substitute of permanent detention.

The doctrine of asexualization, or the sterilization of

1 *Nineteenth Century*, March, 1892, p. 372.

criminals, is amenable to much the same criticism. Its consideration scarcely deserves passing notice, and is but the whim of the impractical theorist.

While life detention solves the problem for the instinctive and habitual criminal, short sentences should be the rule for first offenders. Imprisonment, up to a certain point, while beneficial to the latter class, careful observation and long personal study convinces me that there is a breaking point beyond which incarceration ceases to be either purely punitive or corrective, and reacts in a certain vindictiveness and retaliatory spirit that is hardly suggestive of correctional benefit to the subject. Foreign statistics show that leniency of sentence in the case of first offenders forms one of the conditions that is associated with decrease of crime. English authorities seem to regard it so. The average length of sentence in all convict and local prisons in Great Britain on March 31, 1896, was 7.01 years for males, and 7.56 years for females. On March 31, 1897, it was 6.86 years for males, and 7.58 years for females, a reduction of 1 per cent in one year.[1] The average length of sentences for penal offences from 1881 to 1895 fell from 5.86 per 100,000 population to 2.64, or over 3.22 per cent in four years; while lesser sentences for one year and upward fell from 4.73 to 2.51 per 100,000 during the same period.[2] The tendency of English sentences, tentatively speaking, seems to be toward greater leniency. In the United States, the

[1] Report of Commissioner of Prisons, and Directors of Convict Prisons, 1897.

[2] *Pall Mall Gazette*, 1898, p. 355.

summary shows, in combination for prisoners and juvenile offenders, term sentences out of a total of 65,479 sentenced, 18,950 were for fractions of one year, 7992 for one year, 9143 for two years, 6268 for three years, 3492 for four years, 7561 for five years, 4526 for from six to nine years, 5850 for from ten to nineteen years, and 1697 for twenty years and over. The average sentence for 1890 was 3.88 years (the least — 2.72 years — being for the North Atlantic division; and the highest rate, — 5.40 years, — for the South Central division), as against an average of 5.45 years in 1880, an increase of 1.57 per cent in length of sentences during the decade. The favorite sentence for both periods (1880 and 1890) was two years.[1]

It is not *length* of sentence, but promptness and certainty of trial and strict enforcement of sentence after conviction, that are the best aids toward a wholesome respect for law and a guarantee against relapse. This is emphatically true when accomplished without the intervention of dilatory pleas and petty technicalities, and the gantlet of interminable courts of intermediary jurisdiction, each of which lessens the chance of ultimate conviction, and by so much tends to weaken respect for the correctional machinery. A single court of appeal should be sufficient. The right of appeal should be summary, after which the penalty swift and sure. A prompt judiciary would do more to break the backbone of rampant crime than all other instrumentalities combined.

[1] Report on Crime, Pauperism, and Benevolence in the United States, at the Eleventh Census, 1890, pp. 89, 93.

It will be seen, from these observations, that the principles as applied to the recidivist and to the first offender, are essentially different: brevity of sentence in the former case may be justly regarded the chief cause of recidivation, and *vice versa;* length of sentence in the other case, as a serious aid to crime. These distinctions I believe to be well founded. It requires but a glance to show that the same conditions that are demoralizing and ruinous to the novice, do not materially affect the hardened habitué; hence it follows as a logical inference, that the controlling principles in punishment and prison control should be as materially different as the characters and dispositions of the subjects. It may be mentioned, that one of the most mischievous features of the prevailing custom of definite sentence for all classes of offenders alike, lies in the inequalities of sentences, not only for dissimilar, but oftentimes for similar, offences. It not unfrequently happens under these practices that youths and first offenders, for some petty malfeasance, are given five, ten, or fifteen years imprisonment; while the hardened criminal who has already served his fifth or sixth term, perhaps for the self-same offence as the above novices, is let off with one year, or a year and a half. Such glaring inconsistencies lead to much distrust, and serve as the just grounds of invidious comparisons, doing much toward embittering the novice, while it encourages and confirms the habitual in his evil doing.

The Indeterminate Sentence for the instinctive and the professional criminal, in conjunction with a wise and proper prison segregation, presents a radical cure for all these evils. It is the logical outgrowth of necessity coexistent with the rise of the reformatory principle. The indeterminate theory comprehends the rational conception of the true criminal as a standing menace to society, and so justly demands his legal elimination and practically permanent seclusion upon the plea of social necessity. Society is paramount. So long as the individual is its enemy, society has the unquestioned right to protect itself ; and its legitimate defensive measure is the sequestration of these dangerous classes under a just and humane system of detention, not as a retaliatory penalty for past offences so much as a protective measure against future aggression, thus depriving him of the opportunity to attack, and relieving society of the necessity of maintaining an expensive defensive machinery.

The true indeterminate sentence implies the *permanent detention of the habitual criminal without minimum or maximum limitation*, but the same to continue indefinitely, or until such time as shall be determined by a quasi-judicial board clothed with proper authority and inquisitorial power to suspend the sentence upon given conditions, such release to be upon reasonable evidence shown on the part of the prisoner both of his willingness and ability to respond to the claims of society as a proper, industrious, and law-abiding citizen. An indeterminate sentence must be without statutory limitation. The moment such maximum limitation is fixed it ceases to be an *Indeterminate*, and becomes a *Determinate* sentence. The state having such an anomaly upon its statute books, labors under the absurdity of entertaining a contradiction in terms, having a determinate law under an indeterminate name, as is actually the case in the states of New York, Colorado, Indiana, Ohio, and perhaps in other portions of the Union. With such statutory limitation, it is apparent that the offender may be no more fitted to return to liberty at the expiration of the maximum limit affixed than when admitted to the prison; and such indeterminate sentence would therefore manifestly be no more conducive to the end sought than the conventional one.

The distinction between the fixed and the indeterminate theory is a vital one, as will readily appear upon analysis. The determinate sentence is based presumptively upon the nature of the offence. It falls back upon the purely expiatory idea of incarceration. As such it requires a greater or lesser degree of punishment in accordance with the apparent gravity of the offence, based upon the individual judgment of the court at the moment of trial. This is without reference to the mental, moral, or physiological qualifications of the offender, thereby not infrequently inflicting a grosser injustice than is sought to be cured. The absurdity of such a system has been well express as "being just as irrational to send a lunatic to an insane asylum for the predetermined period of two years as it is to sentence a felon to two years' imprisonment, decreeing in advance that when the two years are up both shall go scot free." The superiority of the indeterminate over the arbitrary method is thus apparent. As a self-defensive measure its value responds to every requisite of the individual, of society, and of abstract justice. Indefinite seclusion upon the ground of incorrigibility has been called to the attention of the leading countries of the world, and bids fair to revolutionize the present criminal judicial theory. It exists in different countries, in some instances based upon the cumulative or progressive sentence, as partly in vogue in England where the term of servitude increases upon each successive imprisonment; in the penal code of India; as established in Japan by a decree fixing the perpetual term after the fourth sentence; also in France, where it became a law in 1891; and in several states of the Union, notably in New York (though here generally confined to reformatories), Ohio, Minnesota, Indiana, Massachusetts, Pennsylvania, Illinois, Colorado, Kansas, etc., though in instances unfortunately rendered abortive by the maximum limit above referred to. The third or fourth offence is usually deemed sufficient to fix the criminal temper and safely assign him to the rôle of incorrigibles and habitués.

The superiority of such judicial method is self-evident. It takes the whole subject, so far as practicable, out of the reach of prejudice or chance or the possibility of error, and gives it over into the hands of a competent tribunal with time and opportunity to study character, weigh facts, and enter into a wise and judicious investigation both of the personality and antecedents of the subject upon whom has fallen the weight of social and civil reprobation. This, with the view of applying the principles of those moral, mental, and reformatory therapeutics that alone can save him from himself, and possibly serve to restore him to society when, at the discretion of such competent tribunal, he may be deemed fit to so again take his place therein. Thus both the ends of justice, the claim of morality, and the demands of society may be met by this judicial substitute. The court could hardly hope to accomplish within the brief period of a few hours what a competent committee of judicious men can only determine after prolonged familiarity and impartial investigation with direct personal contact and knowledge of the particular case and of the individual.

The Indeterminate Sentence thus makes the recalcitrant the arbiter of his own fate, placing into his hands not only the motive but the initiatives to a better life, tentative measures that promise in the course of time to approach as nearly to permanent reconstructive instrumentalities as is possible for human agencies to devise. There is, in short, less likelihood of releasing a prisoner unreformed under the indeterminate method, than under any other system that can be devised by man, which, of course, is the test of effectiveness. Not only does it recommend itself on the ground of social and legal preventives, but also as a direct stimulus upon the prisoner himself; for, instead of operating as a depressing influence upon him as under existing method, its effects are the reverse, inasmuch as it ever holds out before him the possibility of eventual release upon the ground of good behavior and permanent reformation and restoration.

Of course, such a system is only feasible in conjunction with a proper system of prison segregation and progressive methods, as already outlined. As this must of necessity precede its effective working, so a judicious plan of conditional release should also supplement the above indeterminate system as the only rational and proper mode of prison exit. The arbitrary manner of conventional pardon upon the dictum and caprice of the individual will is a perversion of authority whose use or abuse is wholly a matter of personal predilection, and as such lays too great a strain upon the shoulders of a single person. No pardon should ever be granted except upon the thorough and conscientious investigation of a delegated body having quasi-judicial authority; and such pardon should only be granted provisionally, upon just cause shown. The system of conditional pardon (parole) approaches nearest the ideal, supplying as it does salient features wanting in the arbitrary method. It provides for the most important necessities in connection with the outgoing prisoner, the advantages of which may be briefly summarized as follows : —

1. The conditional system of pardon, or "the Parole," as it is commonly called, bases such conditional release upon good behavior, after giving reasonable evidence of not only willingness, but ability, to return to society as a law-abiding and industrious citizen.

2. It provides and guarantees employment, the most important requisite for a newly released prisoner.

3. He is morally protected under police surveillance thrown around him to restrain him from bad habits and associates, at the risk of a forfeiture of his parole and return to prison control.

4. Provision is made for his return in case of violation of his parole, at his own expense, from moneys deposited by him for that express purpose, thus saving the State the expense of a re-conviction.

The most important essentials for the outgoing prisoner are thus provided for; and in the hands of a wise parole board constitute the only rational theory of pardons.

Societies for the purpose of " aiding discharged convicts " and enabling them to tide over the most critical period of their career are almost universally provided by law with adequate state aid, in European countries and also in a number of the United States, notably Massachusetts, where they have done much effective work under state support. In Prussia 29 out of 59 districts possess them; and Switzerland has one in every canton. Denmark, Sweden and Norway, Belgium, the Netherlands, Italy, Russia, and Austria have them. England has 113 such societies, and in the work done by them, as reported in 1892, they had assisted 19,366 prisoners to permanent employment and aid. They are supported by private contributions subsidized by the government to the amount of $20,000 per annum conditionally. As the crowning test of the prevenient method consists not so much in his reformation *within* the prison as in his so staying reformed when out, it follows that this is an important adjunct in the reformatory machinery, and one to which the State would do well to give heed in the way of providing by law for well-equipped and properly organized State Aid Societies. It is well to add that such aid should be chiefly confined to placing proper tools and appliances into the hands of the newly discharged convict, and in finding suitable employment for him and holding him to it when found. Money is the bane of the ex-convict, and should rarely be given, as it usually goes for drink. Homes for Discharged Convicts are, as a rule, impracticable. They become the rendezvous for the lazy and the unworthy, who usually resort thither and remain as long as possible in order to maintain themselves in idleness or to perpetrate their schemes and vices. They are a premium upon laziness, and such generally break down of their own weight unless conducted under a wise and discriminating management.

Public sentiment must of necessity be behind all effective prison regeneration, as that must be the inspirational force that gives life to such reform. Reformation itself, it may be well to remember in this connection, is not a sentiment, but the reverse; and as such well deserves public attention, embodying as it does the chief curative agencies of these moral and social ills. Without such well-defined public sentiment, properly educated and trained, all attempted reform here, as elsewhere, is apt to fall dead born, or is at best but spasmodic and weak. This is expressly true in a democratic form of government where law is the expressed will of the people. That will, properly enlightened, upholds these great counter movements and gives them a political history and stability.

While public interest is necessary to permanency and success in penal systems, mischief results when such institutions are made the instruments of political machination and by-play. The prison, above all other civil and corporate institutions, should be above the reach of partisan machination, and should in no case be classified among the perquisites and spoils of victory in the game of politics. It is demoralizing alike to prisoners, to officers, and to the management. It takes the life out of the régime, and lays it open to favoritism and corruption. A sound and healthy application of principles necessary to the best results is under such circumstances impossible. Where there are no guarantees of permanency, there can be no superiority or excellency in civil service, in the best sense. Prison officers should be born and bred to their profession. They should be trained with care, with an eye to practical proficiency at least equally as thorough as that required in ordinary professions under average educative and collegiate training, their task being more delicate and exacting, in theory, in execution, and in practical results, than any of the ordinary professions. Officers should be selected with the view to permanency, as well as adaptation, their tenure dependent upon good behavior, as in England and in other European countries. The importance of this is taking strong hold in foreign prison administration, notably in Italy, France, England, Austro-Hungary, and Japan, where the best and most eligible classes, especially trained to the work, are called into requisition. The establishment in the United States (presided over by ex-Presidents and high functionaries) of Wardens' Associations and Annual Prison Conventions, where methods are extensively discussed and plans devised for better prison management, attest to the continually increasing interest and importance that is being attached to this branch of civic life. The establishment, in England, of Training Schools for Prison Officers was begun in 1896, for the perfection in penological duties, from 80 to 100 males passing through them annually, from whose ranks selections are made to fill vacancies and make promotions in the prison staffs as they occur.

III

Prevention

The place of prevention in criminal therapeutics is a complex one, and its analysis presents greater difficulties to the student of penology than the more direct application of the reformative principles to the criminal problem under the carceral method. While in the latter instance, with the causes and sources of crime usually exposed, remedies may be pointed out and cures applied with a degree of certainty; in the former, causes and effects are so vitally interblended with a complex social mechanism that a modification in the one implies a modification in the other, reaching at times to the very core and fountainhead of the social theory. Prevention relates to the cause; reformation chiefly to the method. Relief, in the former, lies in the environment; cure, in the latter, in the appliances. Change the environment and you inaugurate the process that will eventually render these conditions impossible and after-remedies unnecessary. While here, perhaps, as in the physical realm, it is true that prevention is better than cure; unlike its prototype, be it said, it is also much more difficult. The social factors as feeders to the criminal propension have not only a special bearing thereupon with reference to offences peculiarly socialistic in their origin, but also upon many of the graver forms of crime, like homicide, larceny, burglary, and those that may be called more distinctively crimes of civilization, as: forgery, embezzlement, etc., the former of which are largely committed by the more pronounced criminals; the latter, by offenders by a single act. While, therefore, it is clear that these derelictions are largely contributed to by abnormal social entities, especially when attributed to those periodical movements which are effected by particular social, political, and industrial changes, it follows that what affects these pre-conditions correspondingly affects the bulk of criminality. A transformation of the criminal activity must therefore be preceded by a change in social conditions that present themselves in the nature of apparent causes, whether near or remote, direct or indirect. I have already shown the effect of certain industrial and economic, as well as morbid, social phases upon the criminal status, such as, variations in the financial market, "hard times," the scantiness of the harvest, the increase of drunkenness incident upon "good times," etc., all of which point more or less to disturbed social conditions for their answer and solution. Organically, all crime has its rise in anthropological sources. In process of time these personal factors may become so assimilated with the social mass as to almost lose their strictly personal identity. Under such circumstances the social element predominating may be considered as fully the resourceful feeder of the criminal propensity as the more strictly personal propensities. The greatest proportion of the crimes of civilization are of this

nature. Thus the varied industrial and economic features with their fluctuations and many distressing phases
and hardships so constantly facing the average wage-
worker, not infrequently present conditions that not
only render crime possible, but are at times a direct
invitation thereto. Greed begets greed, and cupidity
is a mental disease peculiar to the rich. The spectacle of the well-to-do and prosperous employer grinding
down the wages of his dependants in order to bring up
dividends to a fixed standard, in periods of great financial depression, is not a pleasant one to contemplate. It
is certainly not suggestive of either a social or economic
millennium. The selfishness that will force a conflict
upon labor upon such sophistical grounds, or for purely
selfish purposes, at the expense of human happiness, is
fully as anti-social as any isolated act of overt lawlessness born in the throes of private necessity. The underlying motive is here surely not far removed from the
impulse that prompts the midnight foray or the day-
light robbery. One is in the nature of an attack of
the individual upon the solidarity, the other is the
attack of the solidarity upon the individual; organized
capital *versus* unorganized labor. The former comes
to the onset backed by capitalized monopolies in the
shape of "trusts" (the miscellaneous and larger combines footing up in the neighborhood of a billion and
a half dollars each, and aggregating the enormous sum
of nearly three billions of concentrated wealth) to over-
awe labor and pit money against men. Where wages
are forced below the living point, or are cut off altogether, there the danger line begins; and "strikes" and

"lockouts" become the drastic remedies with which to enforce the mandates of the financial baron on the one hand, and repress the claim of the industrial dependant on the other — a method that not only essays to meet force with force, but lights the fires of brutal lawlessness and exalts the weapons of rapine and murder. The history of such abortive measures is disastrous alike to the oppressor and to the oppressed. In the aggregate of such methods in the United States alone, for the past dozen years (1881–1894), 4,174,158 employees have been thrown out of work, at an actual loss in wages to the extent of $190,493,173, which, with the $13,448,704 contributed to the strikers by their sympathizers, and the additional loss to employers of $94,825,237 more, aggregate in round numbers the enormous sum of nearly $300,000,000 of financial waste. It is to be hoped that wise legislation and a judicious system based on the principle of industrial coöperation may do something to avert these evils and thus benefit labor and capital alike.

The principle of participation by the workman in the net profits of the concern in the form of bonuses in addition to the regular wages, after a fair return to the employer upon the capital invested and a proper reduction for operating expenses, presents a just and at least partial solution of the labor question. The successes attending such ventures demonstrate the practicability of the principle and the mutual benefit accruing therefrom to employer and employee. From the date of the initial venture (1870) to 1882, the bonuses paid to employees in the pioneer establishment, in addition to

wages, have averaged over 16 per cent. Other industrial societies, as those founded in Guise, have paid still
higher bonuses. All manner of business, manufactures,
agricultural pursuits, and even railway enterprises, are
embraced within the scope of the coöperative principle.
Under its patronage, moreover, admirable systems of
pensioning, and insurance for the aged and incapaci-
tated are carried on; and savings societies are organized
and made obligatory, as under the German working-
man's laws.

While, in the United States, these varied forms of
coöperation are as yet but little developed (doubtless due
to the eagerness for gain), agricultural interests along
these lines have made some progress in nearly every
state in the Union in the forms of "Granges," "Farmers'
Alliances," Coöperative Stores, etc., which have succeeded to mutual advantages both as purchasing agencies and distributing centres.

These great and effective industrial aids are not only
the natural antidotes to strikes and lockouts and to the
causes that render them possible, but have entered the
field to dispute the autocracy of unfair monopolies and
trusts, which are not only too often themselves the exemplification of legalized dishonesty, but the weight
about the neck of honest toil and the apologetic instrumentalities that set the example and pave the way for
the lesser criminal aggression. No social substitutes
can more effectively stem the tide of potential criminalism, since they have the inlets and outlets of material
prosperity so largely at command, and hence help to
shape the final tendency of those semi-submerged classes

from whose ranks so large a proportion of legal defal-
cators are recruited.

The bettering of these industrial conditions for the
working-classes, besides their direct influences in ameliorating the indubitable tendency to crime incident upon
adverse circumstances and industrial depression, has
also a perceptible bearing upon the problem of the
housing of the same, a no mean factor in shaping the
moral temper, including, as it does, sanitary, economic,
and ethical relations. It has been clearly demonstrated by actual facts that one of the worst incentives
to vice and crime is the tenement and single-room system so universally in vogue among the poor and the
laboring classes in crowded cities. So marked is this
among the lower strata, that the policy of breaking up
these families, or of concentrating them in municipal
lodgings under immediate police control, has been considered. However, increasing sanitary laws are forc-
ing them into lodging-house systems, where discipline
and regularity are having their effect in inculcating
better habits. Aside from any arbitrary distinctions
as between the upper, middle, and lower grades of
working-people, sufficient to say the same general principle applies to all: the enlargement of tenements, the
separation of the sexes, proper sanitary conditions accompanied by cheapness of rents consistent with a fair
return upon capital invested, are among the chief saving requirements of the imperilled poor. Great head-
way has been made in this respect both here and
abroad, which is undoubtedly having its beneficial effect
upon the moral phases of the problem. Nearly all

leading cities have their private and public enterprises to cheapen tenement dwellings, — "Coöperative and Mutual Building Societies," "Industrial Dwelling Companies," "Working-men's Building Societies," etc., — many of them renting as low as 37 cents a room per week, and from 42 to 90 cents; as, for instance, "The Boston Coöperative Building Company," which affords thus cheaply all the sanitary conditions, free reading rooms and libraries, concert halls, clubrooms, and playgrounds for children, and at the same time is able to yield 6 per cent to the owners upon the capital invested. The average rental of the Peabody Building is 52 cents per room per week.[1] The ethical value of these sanitations is amply attested, and have their marked bearing upon the subject matter under consideration.

Poor laws, for the relief of the indigent by reason of age or accident, have their origin in Christian sentiment. This expresses itself in systematized charitological effort and municipal institutional help, growing in scope and general effectiveness. Such measures are aids that reduce the criminal environment, and correspondingly the criminal army. On June 1, 1890, there were in the almshouses of the United States, 73,045 paupers (40,741 males and 32,304 females), of whom 27,648 were foreign born, and 2274 unknown. The ratio per one million has decreased in the last three decades as follows: in 1860, 2638; in 1870, 1990; in 1880, 1320; and in 1890, 1166. This attests to the salutary

[1] Eighth United States Special Report of Commission of Labor, 1895, "Houses of the Working-classes," pp. 228, 419, 420.

improvement of economic and social conditions; to the curtailment of undesirable foreign immigration (at least since 1860), and doubtless implies an increased ability on the part of the working-classes to better care for their dependants. Some of this decrease is undoubtedly due to the erection of new private homes for certain classes, and the closer sequestration of defectives to proper asylums. The effective operation of the English poor laws (originally arising in Church charity dispensations) has been assigned by some authorities as one of the causes for the decrease of crime in England.

Systematized charitology has of late received a strong impetus in this country through the legal organization into single large state and municipal bodies of the varied charitable elements, with supervisorial charge over all such work throughout a given area, or over the state at large. "Associated Charities," as they are termed, are regularly incorporated under legislative enactment, with paid officers and regularly appointed deliberative body, whose duty it is to gather up and systematize into one effective working corporation the numerous local charitable organizations. The Board of State Charities, composed of public-spirited citizens, are given advisory power to investigate all State institutions, and to examine the direct distribution of charitable aid provided by the local authorities. Constitution and by-laws prescribe the methods of procedure. They promise to revolutionize the principles of practical charity and to establish it upon a scientific basis.

Proper relaxation in the way of cheap amusements,

may be looked upon as a criminal palliative, directing relaxations into such non-criminal channels as are not destructive to health and morals. The establishment of cheap coffee-houses and the serving of harmless drinks have undoubtedly done much toward modifying the drink habit.

The decrease in the use of alcoholic drinks must ever remain the great aim of all anti-criminal legislation, as well as of moral and social reform. Intemperance is the chief source of crime, both directly and indirectly. It affects alike the social, the habitual, and the congenital criminal. The limitation of this gigantic evil as a socio-anthropological factor has been much discussed, especially in the United States, where perhaps more drastic measures as the result of repeated and continuous temperance agitation have prevailed than in the Continental countries. Discussion has its place in the list of efficient means, and the place of the temperance agitator has been that of an educator and has served the purpose of setting the issues fairly before the public. Much of the absurd ultraradicalism, as effective means to ends, has been lopped off in the friction; and the main issue now stands out clear of polemic discussion. The vital point and storm centre is the Saloon, the local distributing point and crux of the liquor problem. Its organic hold is politico-social. It is hedged about by legal protection, backed by self-interest. Its solution, therefore, must of necessity be semi-political, under cover of law, and sustained by the power of associated public opinion. That power, when organized, no doubt stands fully ready, properly harmonized, to successfully cope with the task of the proper legal limitation of this gigantic evil. Fortunately, the genius of our institutions is well adapted to handle the question through the fundamental theory of local self-government that lies at the basis of our political existence. In this fact lies the ultimate solution of the liquor problem, laying this, as it has other great problems of public welfare, finally at the door of municipal and local self-government to adjust. Each community thus carries its determinative power in its own hands to decide the fate of such social, moral, or corporate evils for itself.

The nearest approximate thus far reached to the legal ideal in the matter of the restriction of the liquor traffic as a political feature, is found in the organic laws of South Carolina, in the form of the new "Dispensary Law," passed March 6, 1896, which may well serve as the model for future legislation upon this subject. Briefly, its salient features are these: 1. The sale of pure liquor only under authorized chemical analysis by "dispensers," appointed and paid by the state, who are to dispense the same at stated price, direct to purchaser, under written permit, stating age, habits, residence, etc., of the purchaser, and for what use required. 2. All liquors must be sold in sealed packages of not less than one-half pint and not more than five gallons, the same not to be opened nor drunk upon the place. 3. Such sales to be made only by day, not on Sundays nor holidays, and only to persons not addicted to intoxication, not to minors, and not to those forbidden by friends or relatives. 4. Violation of the law, or adulteration, shall subject the sellers, or their sureties, to a fine. 5. All liquor clubs are prohibited; though hotels entertaining guests, may be exempt, under certain conditions. 6. One-fourth of the votes in a locality may petition for a Dispensary, when an election determines by majority. 7. The legislature selects the State Board, and the latter chooses the County Boards. A Dispensary may be closed by the State Board. Licenses may be granted by the State Board of Control to manufacturers or distillers of liquor, and licensed druggists are authorized to purchase from Dispensaries for medical purposes, as also manufacturing chemists.

This, in general scope and detail, is practically the same as the "Norwegian Plan," though differing essentially in the paramount fact that, whereas the latter commits the sale of liquors to public corporations upon moderate profit, the Carolina Dispensary System places the whole matter in the hands of the State, for the moral welfare of the community.

Aside from this ideal measure, the multitudinous state laws that have been enacted from time to time, the stand so universally being taken by the larger corporations and employers in exacting habits of strict temperance in the use of intoxicants on the part of their employees, all are having their effects in curtailing the consumption of intoxicants. Among Transportation Companies, in answer to inquiries upon this question issued from the United States Department of Labor (1898), 703 reported that inquiries were made of employees upon this subject; and but 24 reported that men were employed without regard to such habits. In trades, 471 reported that habits were considered; and 64, that they were not. In manufactories, 2940 reported some consideration; and 783, none. Of 6792 such different establishments, 3527 required that in certain occupations and under certain circumstances, the employees shall not use intoxicants.[1] Under these potent measures the drink bill of the United States has decreased since 1891, the official reports indicating a falling off of 13.3 per cent for 1894 over the previous year, and a small per cent of 1895 over 1894 and down to 1898. The abstract of the Bureau of Statistics of the United States similarly reported a material falling off, on the whole, in the "Home Production of Distilled and Malt Liquors and Domestic Wines," since 1893, at which period they reached their highest point since 1880. The imports of the same have increased but slightly in the same period.[2]

The proper care and education of the children of the dependent classes and the very poor, and the enactment of compulsory educational laws, free kindergartens, and industrial schools, with provision for temporary feeding and clothing, necessary schoolbooks for the indigent poor, taking away such children from their vicious surroundings and placing them under public control, or with families under legal guardianship or proper apprenticeship, would do much toward reaching the sources of incipient crime and effectively checking it in the bud. This (as already pointed out under the head of "The Juvenile Delinquent and the Reforma-

[1] Twelfth Annual Report of the Commission of Labor, 1897, pp. 71, 72.
[2] Ibid., 1897, pp. 17, 18.

tories ") is the only true and radical theory of incipient criminal prevention, and is better than attempted cure at the chronic or prison stage of the disease.

State Industrial and Employment Bureaus, under government subsidy and inspection, to aid the working-classes to obtain employment, and, when necessary, furnish tools and temporary assistance free of charge to them, are a great aid in the way of ameliorating the lot of the industrial classes, and well deserve liberal legislative support. One such (that of California) has assisted in one year over 5000 individuals to employment, representing actual wage-earnings of $150,422.50, and a total of wages, board, etc., of $240,122.50. Five of such free bureaus organized in the leading cities of Ohio, in the second year of their existence (1892), obtained work for 6967 males and 8628 females. This is a scientific solution of the employment bureau question, taking it out of the hands of dishonest employment agents, where it has hitherto been not infrequently used to fatten the thrifty at the expense of the hard-pressed and confiding laboring man. No more practical adjunct to the systematic reduction of want and enforced idleness can be devised; and as the above conditions are the precursors to crime, they indirectly affect the criminal as well as the economic problem. Money thus expended by the State for its industrial producers will flow back again into its resources, whereas in pauper support and almshouses it represents only dead capital and congested outlay in gratuitous, though laudable, charities.

Agricultural industrial pursuits, on the whole, may

be properly denominated the mainstay in the list of effective agencies for criminal prevention, through the substitution of habits of thrift and of healthful, self-respecting employment. It is a principle that applies as well to the chronic as to the incipient stage of the criminal malady. No form of labor is so conducive to both physical and moral health, and none affords better inducements to a sterling independence and manhood. All reformatory and prevenient methods should have this in consideration when studying the subject of industrial appliances as a remedial agency. Statistics prove that crime greatly diminishes in agricultural communities, as compared with metropolitan and even manufacturing centres; as for instance, crimes in general in England (as shown by Mr. Schooling) vary in the ratio of 663 in seaport towns; 413 in the metropolis; 358 in manufacturing towns; 233 in mining counties; as against 138-194 in agricultural communities. Crimes of violence are especially large in seaports, 20.1; and in metropolis, 9.8; and small in agricultural communities, 3.6-5.1. The same may be said with reference to drunkenness, that gives us 116 per 100,000 in agricultural districts, as against 1328 in seaports; 601 in metropolis; 457 in manufacturing communities; and 963 in mining counties. This shows that agricultural employment is a healthy, moral environment, and is especially conducive to criminal prevention, all the incentives thereto being reduced to a minimum. Industry has first place as crime's counteractant, in any event. The county of Cornwall, England, an industrial and mining county where all are employed, though among the first in illiteracy and much subject to periodical drunkenness, stands lowest in the list of crime in English counties, being at the rate of but 57 criminals to every 100,000 of her population, as against Monmouth (the worst), 369 per 100,000. Agricultural and farming appliances, the inauguration of agricultural colonies, vacant lot cultivation, and the establishment of the industrious poor upon small acreages with pecuniary aids and credits, not in the shape of gifts but as advances to be repaid in instalments when they reach self-support, — are all valuable aids in this direction, and may be rendered effective as solvents of the criminal problem from an industrial standpoint. Such enterprises might even receive the backing of the State, as in the case of the " Poor Colonies of Holland," where they have been subsidized to the extent of a million and a half of dollars, in 1895 furnishing permanent homes for nearly 2000 people, at the same time adding to the productiveness and wealth of the country.

Both legal and criminological authorities have written much upon the legal and judicial phases of the criminal subject, with special reference to punishment and prevention, and the consequent suppression of crime. Stress has been laid upon the modification of the jury system. Ferri, Garofalo, and others, have advocated the retention of the latter only in cases of flagrant wrongs against the government or against the person. Probationary laws, in the cases of juvenile and first offenders, have been strongly advocated, also " suspended sentence," with the alternative of prison only as a last resource; a more rational penal system; and con-

ditional release, together with the adoption of the indeterminate sentence as already sketched, in the case of
repeated offenders. Methods of intercomity between
the states in the way of greater unanimity as to sentences for given offences; the greater uniformity of
sentences for similar crimes within the same state;
harmony in legal proceedings, especially as they
relate to semi-political offences, with federal jurisdiction over such as relate to aliens, especially where
damages are claimed; bankrupt laws and extradition
proceedings (crimes begun in one state and completed
in another); divorce laws, etc., — all point to the necessity of uniformity as the certain prerequisite to proper
legal efficiency and may well deserve the attention of
legal and political effort as the precondition of future
permanent moral, civil, and judicial stability and proportion.

No attempt has been made in these pages to treat
the subject of special criminology discursively, or to dis-
cuss practical and prevenient methods exhaustively,
satisfying myself largely in this respect by presenting
the same as a case stated. The time is not ripe when
the literature upon the subject will admit of more pre-
tentious treatment to satisfy the demands of a reading
public, whose interest is as yet confined in the main to
mental absorption of isolated morbid phases of the
criminal phenomenon through the media of the public
newspaper and the sensational novel, rather than any
philosophical insight or clear apprehension as to the
sociological and anthropological features of the criminal
problem with a view to ultimate solution and approxi-

mate cure. When such investigation shall have reached a higher stage, and at such time, and not before, as when the study itself shall have attained the dignity of a science, it will doubtless receive the attention it deserves.

ALPHABETICAL LIST OF WORKS UPON CRIMINOLOGY, IN THE ENGLISH LANGUAGE, WITH AUTHORS, ETC.

Abnormal Man. Dr. Arthur MacDonald. Bureau of Education. Washington. With Extensive Bibliography. 445 pp.

Anatomical Studies upon Brains of Criminals. N.Y., 1881. 185 pp.

Annual Reports of the National Conference of Charities and Correction.

Bertillon System for the Identification of Criminals. Results in Paris and Chicago. *Phila. Times*, July 24, 1892. 2500 words.

Bulletin No. 5, U. S. July, 1896. "Convict Labor." Washington.

Crime and Automatism. W. Holmes. *Atlantic*, May, 35, p. 466.

Crime, and Causes of its Increase. Pamph. 15, p. 27; 29, p. 307; *Blackw.*, 3, p. 176; 55, p. 583; 56, p. 1.

Crime and its Causes. D. W. Morrison. London, 1891.

Crime and its Treatment. *Can. Mo.*, 11, p. 166; Editorial in *London Sat. Rev.*, Oct. 29, 1892. 1200 words.

Crime and Science. *All the Year*, 44, pp. 347, 372; *Appleton*, 23, p. 458.

Crime, a Social Study. Joly. Appleton & Co., July, 1898.

Crime, Causes and Cure of. E. C. Wines. *Princ. Rev.*, 1, p. 784.

Crime, Causes and Prevention of. *Educ. Rev.*, 48, p. 411.

Crime, Hereditary Nature of. Thompson. *Jour. of Ment. Sci.*, 1870.

Crime, Increase and Causes of. *Ecl. Rev.*, 55, p. 314.

Crime Increasing. Why? J. L. Packard. *North Amer. Rev.*, 140, p. 456.

Crime, its Causes and Remedy. L. G. Ryland. London, 1889. 264 pp.

Crime. Its Nature, Causes, Treatment, and Prevention. Sanford M. Green. Philadelphia, 1889. 346 pp.

Crime, Origin of. *Educ. Rev.* 35, p. 342.

Crime, Origin of, in Society. R. L. Dugdale. 48, pp. 452, 735; 49, p. 243.

Crime, Prevention of. *North Amer. Rev.*, 9, p. 288.

Crime, Punishment and Prevention of. *Cornhill*, 7, p. 189.

Crime, Punishment and Prevention of. Sir Edward Du Cane. English Citizen Series. London and New York, 1885. 255 pp.

Crime, Suppression of. Syd. Smith. *Educ. Rev.*, 13, p. 333.

Crimes and Criminals. A. Shuman. *Lakeside*, 6, p. 316.

Crimes and Punishments, Essay on. Beccaria. London, 1770.

Crimes, Causes of, Relation of Economic Conditions to. *Ann. Amer. Acad. Soc. Sci.*, May, 1893.

Crimes, Increase of, against Life. H. Dalton. *New Eng.*, 2, p. 346.

Criminal and the State. Brockway. *Forum*, 2, p. 262.

Criminal Anthropology. H. D. Wey. Elmira, N. Y., 1890.

Criminal Anthropology. I. W. Rolleston. *Acad.*, 38.

Criminal Anthropology. J. Fletcher. Washington, 1891.

Criminal Anthropology. Thomas Wilson. Smithsonian Reports for 1890.

Criminal Anthropology, The New School of. Robert Fletcher. Washington, D. C., 1891.

Criminal Identification and Type. Rev. A. Drähms. *The Summary*, Elmira, N. Y., 1898.

Criminal Law of the Future. *Jour. of Sci.*, 16, p. 591.

Criminal Law, Stephen's History of. *Blackw.* 133, p. 731 ; *Educ. Rev.*, 159, p. 297.

Criminal Law, Stephen's View of. *St. James*, 11, p. 500.

Criminal Life, Phenomena of. *Leis. Hour*, 6, pp. 377, 639.

Criminal Neurosis. Editorial. *N. Y. Medical Times*, July, 1892. 1000 words.

Criminals, Heads of. James Berry. *Boston Herald*, May 22, 1892. 2000 words.

Criminal Sociology. E. Ferri. D. Appleton & Co., N. Y. 284 pp.

Criminals, Pleas for. Carpenter.

Criminals, Professional, in America. Byrnes. With Photos. N. Y., 1889.

Criminal, The. Havelock Ellis.

Criminals, The Study of. Ellis. *Jour. of Ment. Sci.*, 1890.

Criminological Studies. U. S. Education Report. Dr. MacDonald. Washington, 1893–1894.

Criminology. Arthur MacDonald. " How Convicts often Resemble the Insane." Book Review, *Boston Globe*, Jan. 22, 1893. 1400 words.

Criminology. Dr. MacDonald. "A Study of Punishment." Book
Review, *N. Y. Press*, Jan. 15, 1893. 2500 words.

Criminology. MacDonald. Book Review, *N. Y. Times*, Jan. 23,
1893; 1600 words. *N. Y. Sun*, March 26, 1893; 4000 words.
St. Louis Globe-Democrat, Feb. 12, 1893; 2000 words. *Hart-
ford Courant*, March 25, 1893; 1500 words. *Daily Chronicle*,
London, March 30, 1893; 1800 words. *N. Y. Herald*, Jan. 22,
1893; 1000 words. *The Leader*, Cleveland, Jan. 22, 1893;
3000 words. Book Review, by Dr. A. Corre, *Revue Inter-
nationale et Bibliographie Medicale*, 10 Mai, 1893. *The Arena*,
June, 1893.

**Dangerous Classes of New York. Twenty Years' Work among
Them.** Charles Loring Brace. 3d Ed. N. Y., 1880. 446 pp.

Discharged Convict, The. W. Gilbert. *Good Words*, 6, p. 468.

Female Offender, The. Lombroso and Ferreri. Appleton & Co.,
1896.

Heredity. M. Ribot.

International Prison Congress Reports.

Japanese Prisons. W. E. Griffith. *Overland*, 15, p. 289.

Jukes, The. Dugdale. N. Y., 1888.

Juvenile Criminals, Correction of. *Educ. Rev.*, 101, p. 383.

Juvenile Criminals, Treatment of. *Ecl. M.*, 2, p. 350.

Juvenile Delinquency. M. Carpenter. London, 1853.

Juvenile Delinquency. *North Amer. Rev.*, 79, p. 206.

Juvenile Delinquency. W. C. Taylor. Butley, 7, p. 470.

Juvenile Delinquents, Treatment of. A Symposium by I. C. Jones,
E. I. Gerry, C. L. Brace.

Juvenile Depravity, Remedies of. Hogg, 4, p. 300.

Juvenile Offenders, Our. W. D. Morrison. Appleton & Co., 1896.

Maffia. *Medico-Legal Jour.*, June, 1891; *Evening Gazette*, Worces-
ter, Mass., 1891.

Papers in Penology. *The Summary*. Elmira, N. Y.

Pathology of Mind, The. H. Maudsley. Being the 3d Ed. of the
Second Part of the "Physiology and Pathology of the Mind,"
Recast, Enlarged, and Rewritten 8°. N. Y., 1880.

Penological and Preventive Principles. William Tallack. London,
1889. 414 pp.

Penological Progress, Two Decades of. F. C. Hare. *Christian
Union*, Jan. 14, 1893.

Physical Training of Youthful Criminals. H. D. Wey. Boston,
1888. 14 pp.

Prevention of Crime by the State. W. Crofton. *Good Words*, 16, p. 204.

Prison Discipline in the United States. F. B. Sanborn. *O. and N.*, 2, p. 239.

Prison Discipline, Reform in. *Educ. Rev.*, 68, p. 568.

Prison Labor. E. Smith. *Princ. N. S.*, 5, p. 225.

Prison Reform. A. Woodbury. *O. and N.*, 3, p. 755.

Prison Reform, etc. F. H. Wines. 1877.

Prison Reform, International. E. C. Wines. *Int. Rev.*, 3, p. 368.

Prison Reform in United States. E. C. Wines. *Hours at Home*, 8, p. 539.

Prisons and Reformatories at Home and Abroad. Being the Transactions of the International Penitentiary Congress, held in London. E. Pease. July 3–13, 1872. Londres, 1872. In 8°.

Psychological, Criminological, and Demographical Congresses in Europe. Dr. A. MacDonald. *Educ. Rep.*, 1893–1894.

Punishment and Reformation. F. H. Wines. 1897.

Reformatories, Agricultural Labor in. *Amer. Jour. Educ.*, 1, p. 609.

Reformatories, English and Industrial Schools. W. G. Todd. *Month.*, 13, p. 319.

Reformatory Movement in California. Rev. A. Drähms. *Overland*, October, 1892.

Reforms in Prison Discipline. F. B. Sanborn. *North Amer. Rev.*, 102, p. 210.

Reparation to Innocent Convicts. H. Jacques. *Pop. Sci. Mo.*, 25, p. 508.

Reports of the Inspectors appointed to visit the Different Reformatory Schools of Great Britain. London, 1858–1859.

Reports of the National Prison Associations of the United States.

Responsibility in Mental Disease. Maudsley. Appleton & Co., 1897.

Sources of Crime. E. C. Wines. *Amer. Presby. Rev.*, 12, p. 558.

State of Prisons and Child-saving Institutions in the Civilized World. Cambridge, 1880. 719 pp.

Study of Crime, The. W. D. Morrison. *Mind*, October, 1892.

Supervision of Habitual Criminals. W. Crofton. *Good Words*, 16, p. 432.

Surgery for Criminals. Defective Brains and their Relation to Criminal Careers. *N. Y. Sun*, March 27, 1892. 4000 words.

INDEX

Talent, transmission of, 129, 132, 133.
Taste, criminal's, the, 78.
Tattooing among criminals, 115.
Teeth of criminals, 110.
Temperance. *See* Intemperance.
Tenement, the, and crime, 287, 378, 379.
Theft, 157–159; transmission of the habit, 138, 139.
Tobacco, use of, among criminals, 120; females, 120; juveniles, 120.
Touch of criminals, 78.
Trades. *See* Industrial Training.
Transverse inheritance, law of, 130.
Tribal laws and crime, 10, 11.
Type: analysis and definition of, 27–40; criminal, 24–40; criminal identification, 20–40; criminal, of Positivist's (Lombroso's) school, 25; (Garofalo's), 26; ethnic, 34, 35; special, 26, 27; transmissible, 38.

U

Unicellular theory of reproduction, 26.
Uniformity, law of, the, 126, 128.
Unilateral law of, in transmission, 130.
Untruthfulness of criminals, 71.
Uterine influences upon child, 139, 140.

V

Vanity of criminals, 71, 72.
Vertical index, 97, 98.
Vision, 78.
Vital statistics of prisoners, 117.

W

War, a crime, 13, 19.
Weather, the, and the criminals, 70.
Weight of criminals, 116.
Wesley, brothers, the, 141.
Will, freedom of the, *see* Freedom; hypnotism and, 317.
Wrinkles in criminals, 114, 115.

Z

Zygomatic process in criminals, 108.
Zygomatic wrinkle, the, in criminals, 114.